Process Groups:
A Practice Guide

Process Groups: A Practice Guide

ISBN: 978-1-62825-783-0

Published by:
    Project Management Institute, Inc.
    14 Campus Boulevard
    Newtown Square, Pennsylvania 19073-3299 USA
    Phone: +1 610 356 4600
    Email: customercare@pmi.org
    Internet: www.PMI.org

To place an order or for pricing information, please contact Independent Publishers Group:
    Independent Publishers Group
    Order Department
    814 North Franklin Street
    Chicago, IL 60610 USA
    Phone: 800 888 4741
    Fax: +1 312 337 5985
    Email: orders@ipgbook.com (For orders only)

10 9 8 7 6 5 4 3 2 1

Notice

The Project Management Institute, Inc. (PMI) standards and guideline publications, of which the document contained herein is one, are developed through a voluntary consensus standards development process. This process brings together volunteers and/or seeks out the views of persons who have an interest in the topic covered by this publication. While PMI administers the process and establishes rules to promote fairness in the development of consensus, it does not write the document and it does not independently test, evaluate, or verify the accuracy or completeness of any information or the soundness of any judgments contained in its standards and guideline publications.

PMI disclaims liability for any personal injury, property or other damages of any nature whatsoever, whether special, indirect, consequential or compensatory, directly or indirectly resulting from the publication, use of application, or reliance on this document. PMI disclaims and makes no guaranty or warranty, expressed or implied, as to the accuracy or completeness of any information published herein, and disclaims and makes no warranty that the information in this document will fulfill any of your particular purposes or needs. PMI does not undertake to guarantee the performance of any individual manufacturer or seller's products or services by virtue of this standard or guide.

In publishing and making this document available, PMI is not undertaking to render professional or other services for or on behalf of any person or entity, nor is PMI undertaking to perform any duty owed by any person or entity to someone else. Anyone using this document should rely on his or her own independent judgment or, as appropriate, seek the advice of a competent professional in determining the exercise of reasonable care in any given circumstances. Information and other standards on the topic covered by this publication may be available from other sources, which the user may wish to consult for additional views or information not covered by this publication.

PMI has no power, nor does it undertake to police or enforce compliance with the contents of this document. PMI does not certify, test, or inspect products, designs, or installations for safety or health purposes. Any certification or other statement of compliance with any health or safety-related information in this document shall not be attributable to PMI and is solely the responsibility of the certifier or maker of the statement.

Preface

This practice guide provides supplementary information to the principles-based *A Guide to the Project Management Body of Knowledge (PMBOK® Guide)* – Seventh Edition [1].[1] Usage depends on the individual project professional, the organization, the model selected, and how it is tailored to best meet the project's desired outcomes.

In this practice guide, project management processes are organized into Process Groups and the inputs, tools and techniques, and outputs that are tailored to meet the needs of the organization, stakeholders, and the project. Process Groups interact with each phase of a project life cycle. The number of iterations and interactions between processes varies based on the needs of the project.

For organizations and project management practitioners who wish to adopt a process-based approach, this practice guide will explain the basic framework based on the following five Project Management Process Groups:

- ▶ **Initiating.** Those processes performed to define a new project or a new phase of an existing project by obtaining authorization to start the project or phase.

- ▶ **Planning.** Those processes required to establish the scope of the project, refine the objectives, and define the course of action required to attain the objectives that the project was undertaken to achieve.

- ▶ **Executing.** Those processes performed to complete the work defined in the project management plan to satisfy the project requirements.

- ▶ **Monitoring and Controlling.** Those processes required to track, review, and regulate the progress and performance of the project; identify any areas in which changes to the plan are required; and initiate the corresponding changes.

- ▶ **Closing.** Those processes performed to formally complete or close the project, phase, or contract.

---

[1] The numbers in brackets refer to the list of references at the end of this practice guide.

Table of Contents

List of Figures and Tables

Introduction

This practice guide describes a process-based approach to project management. The framework for this approach is based on the five Project Management Process Groups:

- **Initiating.** Those processes performed to define a new project or a new phase of an existing project by obtaining authorization to start the project or phase.

- **Planning.** Those processes required to establish the scope of the project, refine the objectives, and define the course of action required to attain the objectives that the project was undertaken to achieve.

- **Executing.** Those processes performed to complete the work defined in the project management plan to satisfy the project requirements.

- **Monitoring and Controlling.** Those processes required to track, review, and regulate the progress and performance of the project; identify any areas in which changes to the plan are required; and initiate the corresponding changes.

- **Closing.** Those processes performed to formally complete or close the project, phase, or contract.

The Process Groups are independent of the development approach (i.e., predictive, adaptive, agile, or hybrid), application area (e.g., marketing, information services, accounting, etc.), and industry (e.g., construction, aerospace, telecommunications, pharmaceuticals, etc.) but are intended for practitioners who primarily follow a predictive or waterfall approach. This practice guide describes the 49 processes within these five Process Groups along with the inputs, tools and techniques, and outputs associated with those processes.

This practice guide identifies the processes that are considered good practices on most projects, most of the time. Project management should be tailored to fit the needs of the project. *There is no requirement that any particular process or practice be performed.* The processes should be tailored for the specific project and/or organization. Specific methodology recommendations are outside the scope of this practice guide.

1.1 PROJECT MANAGEMENT

Project management is the application of knowledge, skills, tools, and techniques to project activities to meet project requirements. Project management is accomplished through the appropriate application and integration of the project management processes identified for the project.

Managing a project typically includes but is not limited to the following activities:

▶ Identify project requirements.

▶ Address the various needs, concerns, and expectations of stakeholders.

▶ Establish and maintain active communication with stakeholders.

▶ Execute the work required to deliver the project outcomes.

▶ Manage resources.

▶ Balance the competing project constraints, which include but are not limited to scope, schedule, cost, quality, resources, and risk.

Project circumstances will influence how each project management process is implemented and how the project constraints are prioritized.

1.1.1 IMPORTANCE OF PROJECT MANAGEMENT

Project management enables organizations to execute projects effectively and efficiently. *Effective project management* helps individuals, groups, and public and private organizations to:

▶ Meet business objectives.

▶ Satisfy stakeholder expectations.

▶ Be more predictable.

▶ Increase chances of success.

▶ Deliver the right products at the right time.

- Resolve problems and issues.
- Respond to risks in a timely manner.
- Optimize the use of organizational resources.
- Identify, recover, or terminate failing projects.
- Manage constraints (e.g., scope, quality, schedule, costs, resources).
- Balance the influence of constraints on the project (e.g., increased scope may increase cost or schedule).
- Respond to rapidly evolving markets.
- Manage change using a controlled process.

Poorly managed projects or the absence of project management may result in:

- Missed requirements,
- Missed deadlines,
- Cost overruns,
- Poor quality,
- Rework,
- Waste,
- Uncontrolled expansion of the project,
- Loss of reputation for the organization,
- Unsatisfied stakeholders, and/or
- Failure in achieving the objectives for which the project was undertaken.

1.1.2 FOUNDATIONAL ELEMENTS

The foundational elements that are essential for working in and understanding the discipline of project management are:

▶ **Project.** A temporary endeavor undertaken to create a unique product, service, or result. (See Section 1.2 for additional information.)

▶ **Program.** Related projects, subsidiary programs, and program activities that are managed in a coordinated manner to obtain benefits not available from managing them individually. (See Section 1.3 for additional information.)

▶ **Program management.** The application of knowledge, skills, and principles to a program to achieve the program objectives and obtain benefits and control not available by managing program components individually. (See Section 1.3 for additional information.)

▶ **Portfolio.** Projects, programs, subsidiary portfolios, and operations managed as a group to achieve strategic objectives. (See Section 1.4 for additional information.)

▶ **Portfolio management.** The centralized management of one or more portfolios to achieve strategic objectives. (See Section 1.4 for additional information.)

▶ **Relationship of project, program, portfolio, and operations management.** Projects may be managed in three separate scenarios: as a stand-alone project that is outside of a program or portfolio, within a program, or within a portfolio. (See Section 1.5 for additional information.)

▶ **Operations management.** The ongoing production of goods and/or services. It ensures that business operations continue efficiently by using the optimal resources needed to meet customer demands. It is concerned with managing processes that transform inputs (e.g., materials, components, energy, and labor) into outputs (e.g., products, goods, and/or services).

Operations management is an area that is outside the scope of formal project management as described in this practice guide.

▶ **Operations and project management.** Ongoing operations are outside of the scope of a project; however, there are intersecting points where the two areas cross. (See Section 1.6 for additional information.)

▶ **Organizational project management (OPM).** A framework in which portfolio, program, and project management are integrated with organizational enablers in order to achieve strategic objectives. (See Section 1.6 for additional information.)

1.2 PROJECTS

A *project* is a temporary endeavor undertaken to create a unique product, service, or result. Projects are undertaken to fulfill objectives by producing deliverables that result in the desired outcomes. An *objective* is defined as an outcome toward which work is to be directed, a strategic position to be attained, a purpose to be achieved, a result to be obtained, a product to be produced, or a service to be performed. A *deliverable* is defined as any unique and verifiable product, result, or capability to perform a service that is required to be produced to complete a process, phase, or project. Deliverables may be tangible or intangible.

The temporary nature of projects indicates that a project has a definite beginning and end. Temporary does not necessarily mean a project has a short duration. The end of the project is reached when one or more of the following is true:

▶ The project's objectives have been achieved.

▶ The objectives will not or cannot be met.

▶ Funding is exhausted or no longer available for allocation to the project.

▶ The need for the project no longer exists (e.g., the customer no longer wants the project completed, a change in strategy or priority ends the project, the organizational management provides direction to end the project).

▶ The human or physical resources are no longer available.

▶ The project is terminated for legal cause or convenience.

1.2.1 PROJECTS DRIVE CHANGE

Projects drive change in organizations. From a business perspective, a project is aimed at moving an organization from one state to another state in order to achieve a specific objective (see Figure 1-1). Before the project begins, the organization is commonly referred to as being in the current state. The desired result of the change driven by the project is described as the future state.

The successful completion of a project results in the organization moving to the future state and achieving the specific objective.

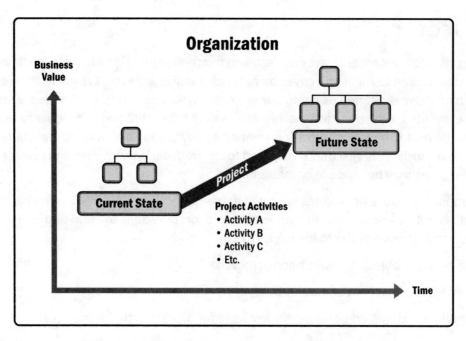

Figure 1-1. Organizational State Transition via a Project

1.2.2 PROJECTS ENABLE BUSINESS VALUE CREATION

PMI defines business value as the net quantifiable benefit derived from a business endeavor. The benefit may be tangible, intangible, or both. In business analysis, business value is considered the return, in the form of elements such as time, money, goods, or intangibles in return for something. Business value in projects refers to the benefit that the results of a specific project provide to its stakeholders. The benefit from projects may be tangible, intangible, or both.

Social and Environmental Impacts

It is becoming more common for initial planning to consider social and environmental impacts in addition to the financial impacts (sometimes referred to as the triple bottom line). This may take the form of a product life cycle assessment which evaluates the potential environmental impacts of a product, process, or system. The product life cycle considers the impacts of materials and processes with regard to sustainability, toxicity, and the environment.

1.2.3 CONTEXTS FOR PROJECT INITIATION

Organizational leaders initiate projects in response to factors acting upon their organizations. Projects provide the means for organizations to successfully make the changes necessary to deal with these factors. There are four fundamental categories for these factors, which illustrate the context of a project:

▶ Meet regulatory, legal, or social requirements;

▶ Satisfy stakeholder requests or needs;

▶ Create, improve, or fix products, processes, or services; and

▶ Implement or change business or technological strategies.

These categories should map directly to the strategic objectives of the organization and projects will fulfill the objectives and, ultimately, deliver business value. Examples of factors that lead to the creation of a project are shown in Table 1-1.

Table 1-1. Factors that Lead to the Creation of a Project

Specific Factor	Examples of Specific Factors	Meet Regulatory, Legal, or Social Requirements	Satisfy Stakeholder Requests or Needs	Create, Improve, or Fix Products, Processes, or Services	Implement or Change Business or Technological Strategies
New technology	An electronics firm authorizes a new project to develop a faster, cheaper, and smaller laptop based on advances in computer memory and electronics technology			X	X
Competitive forces	Lower pricing on products by a competitor results in the need to lower production costs to remain competitive				X
Material issues	A municipal bridge developed cracks in some support members resulting in a project to fix the problems	X		X	
Political changes	A newly elected official instigating project funding changes to a current project				X
Market demand	A car company authorizes a project to build more fuel-efficient cars in response to gasoline shortages		X	X	X
Economic changes	An economic downturn results in a change in the priorities for a current project				X
Customer request	An electric utility authorizes a project to build a substation to serve a new industrial park		X	X	
Stakeholder demands	A stakeholder requires that a new output be produced by the organization		X		
Legal requirement	A chemical manufacturer authorizes a project to establish guidelines for the proper handling of a new toxic material	X			
Business process improvements	An organization implements a project resulting from a Lean Six Sigma value stream mapping exercise			X	
Strategic opportunity or business need	A training company authorizes a project to create a new course to increase its revenues			X	X
Social need	A nongovernmental organization in a developing country authorizes a project to provide potable water systems, latrines, and sanitation education to communities suffering from high rates of infectious diseases		X		
Environmental considerations	A public company authorizes a project to create a new service for electric car sharing to reduce pollution			X	X

1.3 PROGRAMS AND PROGRAM MANAGEMENT

A program is defined as related projects, subsidiary programs, and program activities managed in a coordinated manner to obtain benefits not available from managing them individually. Programs include program-related work outside the scope of the discrete projects in the program. Program management is the application of knowledge, skills, and principles to a program to achieve the program objectives and obtain benefits and control not available by managing related program components individually. Programs may also include work that is operational in nature.

Program management supports organizational strategies by authorizing, changing, or terminating projects and managing their interdependencies.

1.4 PORTFOLIOS AND PORTFOLIO MANAGEMENT

A portfolio is defined as projects, programs, subsidiary portfolios, and operations managed in a coordinated manner to achieve strategic objectives. Portfolio management is the centralized management of one or more portfolios to achieve strategic objectives. Portfolio management focuses on ensuring the portfolio is performing consistent with the organization's objectives and evaluating portfolio components to optimize resource allocation. Portfolios may include work that is operational in nature.

1.5 RELATIONSHIP AMONG PORTFOLIOS, PROGRAMS, AND PROJECTS

A project may be managed in three separate scenarios: as a stand-alone project (outside a portfolio or program); within a program; or within a portfolio. Project management has interactions with portfolio and program management when a project is within a portfolio or program. Figure 1-2 shows the relationships between portfolios and programs, between portfolios and projects, and between programs and individual projects. These relationships are not always hierarchical.

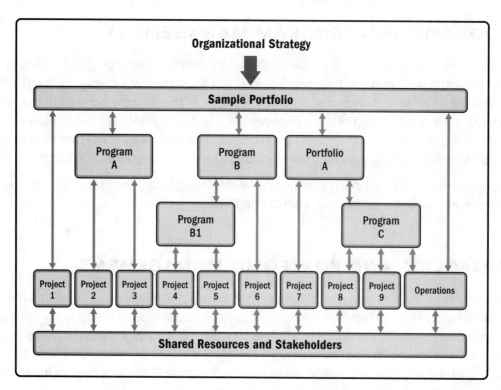

Figure 1-2. Example of Portfolio, Program, and Project Management Interfaces

Table 1-2 gives a comparative overview of portfolios, programs, and projects.

Table 1-2. Comparative Overview of Portfolios, Programs, and Projects

Organizational Project Management			
	Projects	**Programs**	**Portfolios**
Definition	A project is a temporary endeavor undertaken to create a unique product, service, or result.	A program is a group of related projects, subsidiary programs, and program activities that are managed in a coordinated manner to obtain benefits not available from managing them individually.	A portfolio is a collection of projects, programs, subsidiary portfolios, and operations managed as a group to achieve strategic objectives.
Scope	Projects have defined objectives. Scope is progressively elaborated throughout the project life cycle.	Programs have a scope that encompasses the scopes of its program components. Programs produce benefits to an organization by ensuring that the outputs and outcomes of program components are delivered in a coordinated and complementary manner.	Portfolios have an organizational scope that changes with the strategic objectives of the organization.
Change	Project managers expect change and implement processes to keep change managed and controlled.	Programs are managed in a manner that accepts and adapts to change as necessary to optimize the delivery of benefits as the program's components deliver outcomes and/or outputs.	Portfolio managers continuously monitor changes in the broader internal and external environments.
Planning	Project managers progressively elaborate high-level information into detailed plans throughout the project life cycle.	Programs are managed using high-level plans that track the interdependencies and progress of program components. Program plans are also used to guide planning at the component level.	Portfolio managers create and maintain necessary processes and communication relative to the aggregate portfolio.
Management	Project managers manage the project team to meet the project objectives.	Programs are managed by program managers who ensure that program benefits are delivered as expected, by coordinating the activities of a program's components.	Portfolio managers may manage or coordinate portfolio management staff, or program and project staff that may have reporting responsibilities into the aggregate portfolio.
Monitoring	Project managers monitor and control the work of producing the products, services, or results that the project was undertaken to produce.	Program managers monitor the progress of program components to ensure the overall goals, schedules, budget, and benefits of the program will be met.	Portfolio managers monitor strategic changes and aggregate resource allocation, performance results, and risk of the portfolio.
Success	Success is measured by product and project quality, timeliness, budget compliance, and degree of customer satisfaction.	A program's success is measured by the program's ability to deliver its intended benefits to an organization, and by the program's efficiency and effectiveness in delivering those benefits.	Success is measured in terms of the aggregate investment performance and benefit realization of the portfolio.

1.6 ORGANIZATIONAL PROJECT MANAGEMENT (OPM)

Organizational project management (OPM) is a strategy execution framework utilizing portfolio, program, and project management. It provides a framework that enables organizations to consistently and predictably deliver on organizational strategy, producing better performance; better results; and a sustainable, competitive advantage.

Figure 1-3 shows the organizational environment where strategy, a portfolio, programs and projects, and operations interact.

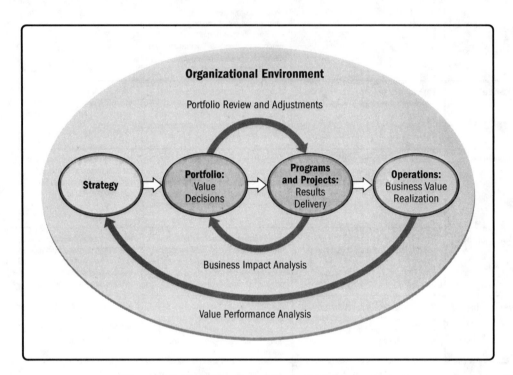

Figure 1-3. Organizational Project Management

For more information on OPM, refer to *The Standard for Organizational Project Management* [2].

1.7 PROJECT COMPONENTS AND CONSIDERATIONS

Projects comprise several key components that, when effectively managed, result in their successful completion. This section of the practice guide identifies and explains these components. The various components interrelate to one another during the management of a project.

The key components are described briefly in Table 1-3. These components are more fully explained in Sections 1.7.1 through 1.7.5.

Table 1-3. Description of Key Components

PMBOK® Guide Key Component	Brief Description
Project life cycle (Section 1.7.1)	The series of phases that a project passes through from its start to its completion.
Project phase (Section 1.7.2)	A collection of logically related project activities that culminates in the completion of one or more deliverables.
Phase gate (Section 1.7.3)	A review at the end of a phase in which a decision is made to continue to the next phase, to continue with modification, or to end a program or project.
Project management processes (Section 1.7.4)	A systematic series of activities directed toward causing an end result where one or more inputs will be acted upon to create one or more outputs.
Project Management Process Group (Section 1.7.5)	A logical grouping of project management inputs, tools and techniques, and outputs. The Project Management Process Groups include Initiating, Planning, Executing, Monitoring and Controlling, and Closing. Project Management Process Groups are not project phases.

1.7.1 PROJECT AND DEVELOPMENT LIFE CYCLES

A project life cycle is the series of phases that a project passes through from its start to its completion. It provides the basic framework for managing the project. This basic framework applies regardless of the specific project work involved. The phases may be sequential, iterative, or overlapping. All projects can be mapped to the generic life cycle shown in Figure 1-4.

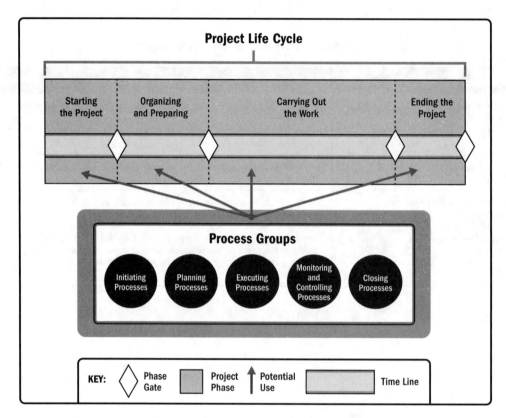

Figure 1-4. Interrelationship of Key Components in Projects

Project life cycles can be predictive or adaptive. Within a project life cycle, there are generally one or more phases that are associated with the development of the product, service, or result. These are called development life cycles, which can be predictive, adaptive, iterative, incremental, or a hybrid model:

- *In a predictive life cycle,* the project scope, time, and cost are determined in the early phases of the life cycle. Any changes to the scope are carefully managed. Predictive life cycles may also be referred to as waterfall life cycles.

- *Adaptive life cycles* can be iterative, or incremental. The scope is outlined and agreed before the start of an iteration. Adaptive life cycles are also referred to as agile or change-driven life cycles.

  - ▷ *In an iterative life cycle,* the project scope is generally determined early in the project life cycle, but time and cost estimates are routinely modified as the project team's understanding of the product increases. Iterations develop the product through a series of repeated cycles, while increments successively add to the functionality of the product.

  - ▷ *In an incremental life cycle,* the deliverable is produced through a series of iterations that successively add functionality within a predetermined time frame. The deliverable contains the necessary and sufficient capability to be considered complete only after the final iteration.

- *A hybrid life cycle* is a combination of a predictive and an adaptive life cycle. Those elements of the project that are well known or have fixed requirements follow a predictive development life cycle, and those elements that are still evolving follow an adaptive development life cycle.

It is up to the project management team to determine the best life cycle for each project, based on the project's inherent characteristics. The project life cycle needs to be flexible enough to deal with the variety of factors included in the project.

Project life cycles are independent of product life cycles, which may be produced by a project. A product life cycle is the series of phases that represent the evolution of a product, from concept through delivery, growth, maturity, and to retirement.

Planning is Always There

A key thing to remember about life cycles is that each life cycle shares the element of planning. What differentiates a life cycle is not whether planning is done, but rather how much planning is done, when, and by whom. Agile approaches engage the team more in planning while predictive approaches are driven by the project manager.

For *predictive approaches*, the plan drives the work. More planning is performed up front and requirements are identified in more detail when compared to adaptive approaches. The team estimates when they can deliver which deliverables and performs comprehensive procurement activities.

In *iterative approaches*, prototypes and proofs are also planned, but the outputs are intended to modify the plans created in the beginning. Meanwhile, *incremental initiatives* plan to deliver successive subsets of the overall project. Teams may plan several successive deliveries in advance or only one at a time. The deliveries inform the future project work.

Agile projects also plan. The key difference is that the team plans and replans as more information becomes available from review of frequent deliveries. Regardless of the project life cycle, the project requires planning.

1.7.2 PROJECT PHASE

A project phase is a collection of logically related project activities that culminates in the completion of one or more deliverables. The phases in a life cycle can be described by a variety of attributes. Attributes may be measurable and unique to a specific phase. Attributes may include but are not limited to:

▶ Name (e.g., Phase A, Phase B, Phase 1, Phase 2, proposal phase),

▶ Number (e.g., three phases in the project, five phases in the project),

▶ Duration (e.g., 1 week, 1 month, 1 quarter),

- ▶ Resource requirements (e.g., people, buildings, equipment),

- ▶ Entrance criteria for a project to move into that phase (e.g., specified approvals documented, specified documents completed), and

- ▶ Exit criteria for a project to complete a phase (e.g., documented approvals, completed documents, completed deliverables).

Projects may be separated into distinct phases or subcomponents. These phases or subcomponents are generally given names that indicate the type of work done in that phase. Examples of phase names include but are not limited to:

- ▶ Concept development,

- ▶ Feasibility study,

- ▶ Customer requirements,

- ▶ Solution development,

- ▶ Design,

- ▶ Prototype,

- ▶ Build,

- ▶ Test,

- ▶ Transition,

- ▶ Commissioning,

- ▶ Milestone review, and

- ▶ Lessons learned.

Establishing Project Phases

The project phases may be established based on various factors including but not limited to:

- ▶ Management needs;

- ▶ Nature of the project;

- ▶ Unique characteristics of the organization, industry, or technology;

- ▶ Project elements including, but not limited to, technology, engineering, business, process, or legal; and

- ▶ Decision points (e.g., funding, project go/no-go, and milestone review).

Using multiple phases may provide better insight to managing the project. It also provides an opportunity to assess the project performance and take necessary corrective or preventive actions in subsequent phases. A key component used with project phases is the phase gate or review (see Section 1.7.3).

1.7.3 PHASE GATE

A phase gate (or review) is held at the end of a phase. The project's performance and progress are compared to project and business documents including but not limited to:

- ▶ Project business case,

- ▶ Project charter,

- ▶ Project management plan, and

- ▶ Benefits management plan.

A decision (e.g., go/no-go decision) is made as a result of this comparison to:

▶ Continue to the next phase,

▶ Continue to the next phase with modification,

▶ End the project,

▶ Remain in the phase, or

▶ Repeat the phase or elements of it.

Depending on the organization, industry, or type of work, phase gates may be referred to by other terms, such as phase review, stage gate, kill point, and phase entrance or phase exit. Organizations may use these reviews to examine other pertinent items which are beyond the scope of this guide, such as product-related documents or models.

1.7.4 PROJECT MANAGEMENT PROCESSES

The project life cycle is managed by executing a series of project management activities known as project management processes. There are a total of 49 processes; however, the selection of processes used for any given project depends on the organization and the project—more than likely, all processes will not be used. The outputs can be deliverables or outcomes. Outcomes are the end result of a process. Project management processes apply globally across industries.

Project management processes are logically linked by the outputs they produce. Processes may contain overlapping activities that occur throughout the project. The output of one process generally results in either:

▶ An input to another process, or

▶ A deliverable of the project or project phase.

Figure 1-5 shows an example of how inputs, tools and techniques, and outputs relate to each other within a process, and with other processes.

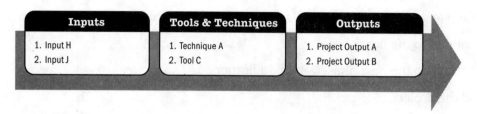

Figure 1-5. Example Process: Inputs, Tools & Techniques, and Outputs

The number of process iterations and interactions between processes varies based on the needs of the project. Processes generally fall into one of three categories:

▶ **Processes used once or at predefined points in the project.** The processes *Develop Project Charter* and *Close Project or Phase* are examples.

▶ **Processes that are performed periodically as needed.** The process *Acquire Resources* is performed as resources are needed. The process *Conduct Procurements* is performed prior to needing the procured item.

▶ **Processes that are performed continuously throughout the project.** The process *Define Activities* may occur throughout the project life cycle, especially if the project uses rolling wave planning or an adaptive development approach. Many of the Monitoring and Controlling processes are ongoing from the start of the project, until it is closed out.

Project management is accomplished through the appropriate application and integration of logically grouped project management processes. While there are different ways of grouping processes, PMI groups processes into five categories called Process Groups (see Section 1.7.5).

1.7.5 PROJECT MANAGEMENT PROCESS GROUPS

A Project Management Process Group is a logical grouping of project management processes to achieve specific project objectives. Process Groups are independent of project phases. Project management processes are grouped into the following five Project Management Process Groups:

▶ **Initiating Process Group.** Those processes performed to define a new project or a new phase of an existing project by obtaining authorization to start the project or phase.

▶ **Planning Process Group.** Those processes required to establish the scope of the project, refine the objectives, and define the course of action required to attain the objectives that the project was undertaken to achieve.

▶ **Executing Process Group.** Those processes performed to complete the work defined in the project management plan to satisfy the project requirements.

▶ **Monitoring and Controlling Process Group.** Those processes required to track, review, and regulate the progress and performance of the project; identify any areas in which changes to the plan are required; and initiate the corresponding changes.

▶ **Closing Process Group.** Those processes performed to formally complete or close the project, phase, or contract.

Process flow diagrams are used throughout this practice guide. The project management processes are linked by specific inputs and outputs where the result or outcome of one process may become the input to another process that is not necessarily in the same Process Group. Note that Process Groups are not the same as project phases.

Table 1-4 provides a list of the 49 processes mapped to their respective Process Groups. The numbers refer to the section numbers in this practice guide.

Table 1-4. Process Groups and Project Management Processes

Project Management Process Groups				
Initiating Process Group	**Planning Process Group**	**Executing Process Group**	**Monitoring and Controlling Process Group**	**Closing Process Group**
4.1 Develop Project Charter 4.2 Identify Stakeholders	5.1 Develop Project Management Plan 5.2 Plan Scope Management 5.3 Collect Requirements 5.4 Define Scope 5.5 Create WBS 5.6 Plan Schedule Management 5.7 Define Activities 5.8 Sequence Activities 5.9 Estimate Activity Durations 5.10 Develop Schedule 5.11 Plan Cost Management 5.12 Estimate Costs 5.13 Determine Budget 5.14 Plan Quality Management 5.15 Plan Resource Management 5.16 Estimate Activity Resources 5.17 Plan Communications Management 5.18 Plan Risk Management 5.19 Identify Risks 5.20 Perform Qualitative Risk Analysis 5.21 Perform Quantitative Risk Analysis 5.22 Plan Risk Responses 5.23 Plan Procurement Management 5.24 Plan Stakeholder Engagement	6.1 Direct and Manage Project Work 6.2 Manage Project Knowledge 6.3 Manage Quality 6.4 Acquire Resources 6.5 Develop Team 6.6 Manage Team 6.7 Manage Communications 6.8 Implement Risk Responses 6.9 Conduct Procurements 6.10 Manage Stakeholder Engagement	7.1 Monitor and Control Project Work 7.2 Perform Integrated Change Control 7.3 Validate Scope 7.4 Control Scope 7.5 Control Schedule 7.6 Control Costs 7.7 Control Quality 7.8 Control Resources 7.9 Monitor Communications 7.10 Monitor Risks 7.11 Control Procurements 7.12 Monitor Stakeholder Engagement	8.1 Close Project or Phase

1.8 PROJECT MANAGEMENT DATA AND INFORMATION

Throughout the life cycle of a project, a significant amount of data is collected, analyzed, and transformed. Project data are collected as a result of various processes and are shared within the project team. The collected data are analyzed in context, aggregated, and transformed to become project information during various processes. Information is communicated verbally or stored and distributed in various formats as reports.

Key Terminology Regarding Project Data and Information

Project data are regularly collected and analyzed throughout the project life cycle. The following definitions identify key terminology regarding project data and information:

▶ **Work performance data.** The raw observations and measurements identified during activities performed to carry out the project work. Examples include reported percentage of work physically completed, quality and technical performance measures, start and finish dates of schedule activities, number of change requests, number of defects, actual costs, actual durations, etc. Project data are usually recorded in a project management information system (PMIS) and in project documents.

▶ **Work performance information.** The performance data collected from various controlling processes, analyzed in context and integrated based on relationships across areas. Examples of performance information are status of deliverables, implementation status for change requests, and forecast estimates to complete.

▶ **Work performance reports.** The physical or electronic representation of work performance information compiled in project documents, which is intended to generate decisions or raise issues, actions, or awareness. Examples include status reports, memos, justifications, information notes, electronic dashboards, recommendations, and updates.

Figure 1-6 shows the flow of project information across the various processes used in managing a project.

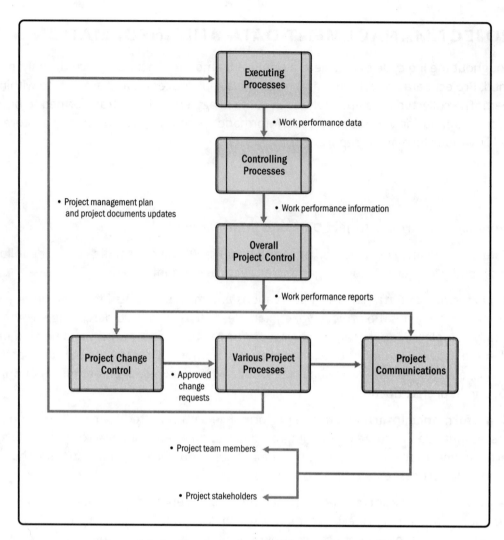

Figure 1-6. Project Data, Information, and Report Flow

1.9 TAILORING

Usually, project managers apply a project management methodology to their work. A methodology is a system of practices, techniques, procedures, and rules used by those who work in a discipline. *Specific methodology recommendations are outside the scope of this practice guide.*

Project management methodologies may be:

▶ Developed by experts within the organization,

▶ Purchased from vendors,

▶ Obtained from professional associations, or

▶ Acquired from government agencies.

Tailoring is the deliberate adaptation of approach, governance, and processes to make them more suitable for the given environment and the task(s) at hand.

In a project environment, tailoring includes considering the approaches, processes, interim deliverables, and choice of people to engage with. The tailoring process is driven by a mindset and set of values that influence the tailoring decisions. The project manager collaborates with the project team, sponsor, organizational management, or combination thereof, in the tailoring. In some cases, an organization may require that specific project management methodologies be used.

Tailoring is necessary because each project is unique. Not every process, tool, technique, input, or output identified in this practice guide is required on every project. Tailoring should address the competing constraints of scope, schedule, cost, resources, quality, and risk. The *importance* of each constraint is different for each project, and the project manager tailors the approach to manage these constraints based on the project environment, organizational culture, stakeholder needs, and other variables.

Sound project management methodologies take into account the unique nature of projects and allow tailoring, to some extent, by the project manager.

Tailoring produces direct and indirect benefits to organizations. These include, but are not limited to:

▶ More commitment from project team members who helped to tailor the approach,

▶ Customer-oriented focus, as the needs of the customer are an important influencing factor in its development, and

▶ More efficient use of project resources.

In tailoring project management, the project manager should also consider the varying levels of governance that may be required and within which the project will operate, as well as considering the culture of the organization (see Section 2.3). In addition, consideration of whether the customer of the project is internal or external to the organization may affect project management tailoring decisions.

The *PMBOK Guide®* – Seventh Edition outlines a four-step tailoring process:

▶ **Step 1: Select Initial Development Approach**—This step determines the development approach that will be used for the project. Project teams apply their knowledge of the product, delivery cadence, and awareness of the available options to select the most appropriate development approach for the situation.

▶ **Step 2: Tailor for the Organization**—While project teams own and improve their processes, organizations often require some level of approval and oversight. Many organizations have a project methodology, general management approach, or general development approach that is used as a starting point for their projects. Organizations that have established process governance need to ensure tailoring is aligned to policy. To demonstrate that the project team's tailoring decisions do not threaten the organization's larger strategic or stewardship goals, project teams may need to justify using a tailored approach.

▶ **Step 3: Tailor for the Project**—Many attributes influence tailoring for the project. These include, but are not limited to, product/deliverable, project team, and culture. The project team should ask questions about each attribute to help guide them in the tailoring process. Answers to these questions can help identify the need to tailor processes, delivery approach, life cycle, tools, methods, and artifacts.

▶ **Step 4: Implement Ongoing Improvement**—The process of tailoring is not a single, one-time exercise. During progressive elaboration, issues with how the project team is working, how the product or deliverable is evolving, and other learnings will indicate where further tailoring could bring improvements. Review points, phase gates, and retrospectives all provide opportunities to inspect and adapt the process, development approach, and delivery frequency as necessary.

1.10 BENEFITS MANAGEMENT AND BUSINESS DOCUMENTS

Projects are initiated to realize opportunities that are aligned with an organization's strategic goals. Prior to initiating a project, a business case is often developed to outline the project objectives, the required investment, and financial and qualitative criteria for project success. The business case provides the basis to measure success and progress throughout the project life cycle by comparing the results with the objectives and the identified success criteria. The business case may be used before project initiation and may result in a go/no-go decision for the project.

A needs assessment often precedes the business case. The needs assessment involves understanding business goals and objectives, issues, and opportunities and recommending proposals to address them. The results of the needs assessment may be summarized in the business case document.

Projects are typically initiated as a result of one or more of the following strategic considerations:

- ▶ Market demand,
- ▶ Strategic opportunity/business need,
- ▶ Social need,
- ▶ Environmental consideration,
- ▶ Customer request,
- ▶ Technological advancement,
- ▶ Legal or regulatory requirement, and
- ▶ Existing or forecasted problem.

A benefits management plan describes how and when the benefits of the project will be delivered and how they will be measured. The benefits management plan may include the following:

- ▶ **Target benefits.** The expected tangible and intangible business value to be gained by the implementation of the product, service, or result.

- ▶ **Strategic alignment.** How the project benefits support and align with the business strategies of the organization.

- ▶ **Time frame for realizing benefits.** Benefits by phase: short term, long term, and ongoing.

- ▶ **Benefits owner.** The accountable person or group that monitors, records, and reports realized benefits throughout the time frame established in the plan.

- ▶ **Metrics.** The direct and indirect measurements used to show the benefits realized.

- ▶ **Risks.** Risks associated with achieving target benefits.

The success of the project is measured against the project objectives and success criteria. In many cases, the success of the product, service, or result is not known until sometime after the project is complete. For example, an increase in market share, a decrease in operating expenses, or the success of a new product may not be known when the project is transitioned to operations. In these circumstances, the project management office (PMO), portfolio steering committee, or some other business function within the organization should evaluate the success at a later date to determine if the outcomes met the business objectives.

Development and maintenance of the project benefits management plan is an iterative activity. This document complements the business case, project charter, and project management plan. The project manager works with the sponsor to ensure that the project charter, project management plan, and the benefits management plan remain in alignment throughout the life cycle of the project. See *Business Analysis for Practitioners: A Practice Guide* [3], *The Standard for Program Management* [4], and *The Standard for Portfolio Management* [5].

A project manager needs to ensure that the project management approach captures the intent of business documents. These documents are defined in Table 1-5. These two documents are interdependent and iteratively developed and maintained throughout the life cycle of the project.

The project sponsor is generally accountable for the development and maintenance of the project business case document. The project manager is responsible for providing recommendations and oversight to keep the project business case, project management plan, project charter, and project benefits management plan success measures in alignment with one another and with the goals and objectives of the organization.

Both the business case and the benefits management plan are developed prior to the project being initiated. Additionally, both documents are referenced after the project has been completed. Therefore, they are considered business documents rather than project documents or components of the project management plan. As appropriate, these business documents may be inputs to some of the processes involved in managing the project, such as developing the project charter.

Table 1-5. Project Business Documents

Project Business Documents	Definition
Project business case	A documented economic feasibility study used to establish the validity of the benefits of a selected component lacking sufficient definition and that is used as a basis for the authorization of further project management activities.
Project benefits management plan	The documented explanation defining the processes for creating, maximizing, and sustaining the benefits provided by a project.

Project managers tailor the noted project management documents for their projects. In some organizations, the business case and benefits management plan are maintained at the program level. Project managers then work with the appropriate program managers to ensure the project management documents are aligned with the program documents. Figure 1-7 illustrates the interrelationship of these critical project management business documents and the needs assessment. Figure 1-7 shows an approximation of the life cycle of these various documents against the project life cycle.

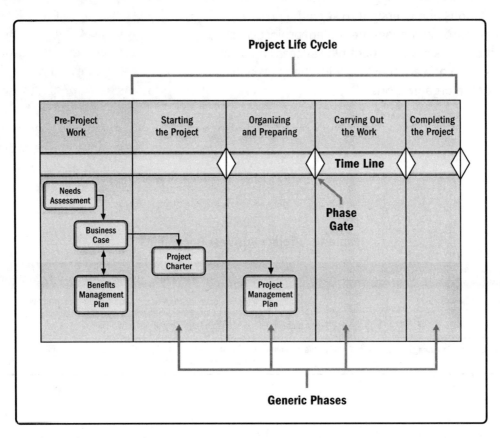

Figure 1-7. Interrelationship of Needs Assessment and Critical Business/Project Documents

1.11 PROJECT CHARTER, PROJECT MANAGEMENT PLAN, AND PROJECT DOCUMENTS

The project charter is defined as a document issued by the project sponsor that formally authorizes the existence of a project and provides the project manager with the authority to apply organizational resources to project activities.

The project management plan is defined as the document that describes how the project will be executed, monitored, and controlled. It integrates and consolidates all of the subsidiary management plans and baselines, and other information that is essential for managing the project. The individual aspects of the project determine which components of the project management plan are needed.

Project management plan components include but are not limited to:

▶ **Subsidiary management plans:**

▷ *Scope management plan.* Establishes how the scope will be defined, developed, monitored, controlled, and validated.

▷ *Requirements management plan.* Establishes how the requirements will be analyzed, documented, and managed.

▷ *Schedule management plan.* Establishes the criteria and the activities for developing, monitoring, and controlling the schedule.

▷ *Cost management plan.* Establishes how the costs will be planned, structured, and controlled.

▷ *Quality management plan.* Establishes how an organization´s quality policies, methodologies, and standards will be implemented in the project.

▷ *Resource management plan.* Provides guidance on how project resources should be categorized, allocated, managed, and released.

▷ *Communications management plan.* Establishes how, when, and by whom information about the project will be administered and disseminated.

▷ *Risk management plan.* Establishes how the risk activities will be structured and performed.

▷ *Procurement management plan.* Establishes how the project team will acquire goods and services from outside of the performing organization.

▷ *Stakeholder engagement plan.* Establishes how stakeholders will be engaged in project decisions and execution, according to their needs, interests, and impact.

▶ **Baselines:**

▷ *Scope baseline.* The approved version of a scope statement, work breakdown structure (WBS), and its associated WBS dictionary, which can be changed using formal change control procedures and is used as a basis for comparison.

▷ *Schedule baseline.* The approved version of a schedule model that can be changed using formal change control procedures and is used as a basis for comparison to the actual results.

▷ *Cost baseline.* The approved version of the time-phased project budget, excluding any management reserves, which can be changed using formal change control procedures and is used as a basis for comparison to the actual results.

▶ **Additional components.** Most components of the project management plan are produced as outputs from other processes, though some are produced during this process. Those components developed as part of this process will be dependent on the project; however, they often include but are not limited to:

▷ *Change management plan.* Describes how the change requests throughout the project will be formally authorized and incorporated.

▷ *Configuration management plan.* Describes how the information about the items of the project (and which items) will be recorded and updated so that the product, service, or result of the project remains consistent and/or operative.

▷ *Performance measurement baseline.* An integrated scope-schedule-cost plan for the project work against which project execution is compared to measure and manage performance.

▷ *Project life cycle.* Describes the series of phases that a project passes through from its initiation to its closure.

▷ *Development approach.* Describes the product, service, or result development approach, such as predictive, iterative, agile, or a hybrid model.

▷ *Management reviews.* Identifies the points in the project when the project manager and relevant stakeholders will review the project progress to determine if performance is as expected, or if preventive or corrective actions are necessary.

While the project management plan is one of the primary documents used to manage the project, other project documents are also used. These other documents are not part of the project management plan; however, they are necessary to manage the project effectively. Table 1-6 is a representative list of the project management plan components and project documents.

Table 1-6. Project Management Plan and Project Documents

Project Management Plan	Project Documents	
1. Scope management plan	1. Activity attributes	19. Quality control measurements
2. Requirements management plan	2. Activity list	20. Quality metrics
3. Schedule management plan	3. Assumption log	21. Quality report
4. Cost management plan	4. Basis of estimates	22. Requirements documentation
5. Quality management plan	5. Change log	23. Requirements traceability matrix
6. Resource management plan	6. Cost estimates	24. Resource breakdown structure
7. Communications management plan	7. Cost forecasts	25. Resource calendars
8. Risk management plan	8. Duration estimates	26. Resource requirements
9. Procurement management plan	9. Issue log	27. Risk register
10. Stakeholder engagement plan	10. Lessons learned register	28. Risk report
11. Change management plan	11. Milestone list	29. Schedule data
12. Configuration management plan	12. Physical resource assignments	30. Schedule forecasts
13. Scope baseline	13. Project calendars	31. Stakeholder register
14. Schedule baseline	14. Project communications	32. Team charter
15. Cost baseline	15. Project schedule	33. Test and evaluation documents
16. Performance measurement baseline	16. Project schedule network diagram	
17. Project life cycle description	17. Project scope statement	
18. Development approach	18. Project team assignments	

1.12 PROJECT SUCCESS MEASURES

One of the most common challenges in project management is determining whether or not a project is successful.

Traditionally, the project management metrics of time, cost, scope, and quality have been the most important factors in defining the success of a project. More recently, practitioners and scholars have determined that project success should also be measured with consideration toward achievement of the project objectives.

Project stakeholders may have different ideas as to what the successful completion of a project will look like and which factors are the most important. It is critical to clearly document the project objectives and to select objectives that are measurable. Three questions that the key stakeholders and the project manager should answer are:

▶ What does success look like for this project?

▶ How will success be measured?

▶ What factors may impact success?

The answer to these questions should be documented and agreed upon by the key stakeholders and the project manager.

Project success may include additional criteria linked to the organizational strategy and to the delivery of business results. These project objectives may include but are not limited to:

▶ Completing the project benefits management plan;

▶ Meeting the agreed-upon financial measures documented in the business case. These financial measures may include but are not limited to:

▷ Net present value (NPV),

▷ Return on investment (ROI),

▷ Internal rate of return (IRR),

▷ Payback period (PBP), and

▷ Benefit-cost ratio (BCR).

- ▶ Meeting business case nonfinancial objectives;

- ▶ Completing movement of an organization from its current state to the desired future state;

- ▶ Fulfilling contract terms and conditions;

- ▶ Meeting organizational strategy, goals, and objectives;

- ▶ Achieving stakeholder satisfaction;

- ▶ Acceptable customer/end-user adoption;

- ▶ Integration of deliverables into the organization's operating environment;

- ▶ Achieving agreed-upon quality of delivery;

- ▶ Meeting governance criteria; and

- ▶ Achieving other agreed-upon success measures or criteria (e.g., process throughput).

The project team needs to be able to assess the project situation, balance the demands, and maintain proactive communication with stakeholders in order to deliver a successful project.

When the business alignment for a project is constant, the chance for project success greatly increases because the project remains aligned with the strategic direction of the organization.

It is possible for a project to be successful from a scope/schedule/budget viewpoint, and to be unsuccessful from a business viewpoint. This can occur when there is a change in the business needs or the market environment before the project is completed.

The Project Environment

Projects exist and operate in environments that may have an influence on them. These influences can have a favorable or unfavorable impact on the project. Two major categories of influences are enterprise environmental factors (EEFs) and organizational process assets (OPAs).

EEFs originate from the environment outside of the project, and often outside of the enterprise. EEFs may have an impact at the organizational, portfolio, program, or project level.

OPAs are internal to the organization. These may arise from the organization itself, a portfolio, a program, another project, or a combination of these. Figure 2-1 shows the breakdown of project influences into EEFs and OPAs.

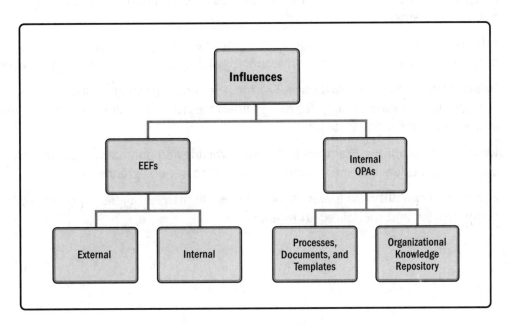

Figure 2-1. Project Influences

In addition to EEFs and OPAs, governance plays a significant role in the life cycle of the project (see Section 2.3).

2.1 ENTERPRISE ENVIRONMENTAL FACTORS

Enterprise environmental factors (EEFs) refer to conditions, not under the control of the project team, that influence, constrain, or direct the project. These conditions can be internal and/or external to the organization. EEFs are considered as inputs to many project management processes, specifically for most planning processes. These factors may enhance or constrain project management options. In addition, these factors may have a positive or negative influence on the outcome.

EEFs vary widely in type or nature. These factors need to be considered if the project is to be effective. EEFs include but are not limited to the factors described in Sections 2.1.1 and 2.1.2.

2.1.1 EEFS INTERNAL TO THE ORGANIZATION

The following are examples of EEFs that are internal to the organization:

▶ **Organizational culture, structure, and governance.** Examples include vision, mission, values, beliefs, cultural norms, leadership style, hierarchy and authority relationships, organizational style, ethics, code of conduct, policies, and procedures.

▶ **Geographic distribution of facilities and resources.** Examples include factory locations and virtual teams.

▶ **Infrastructure.** Examples include existing facilities, equipment, organizational telecommunications channels, information technology hardware, availability, and capacity.

▶ **Information technology software.** Examples include scheduling software tools, configuration management systems, web interfaces to other online automated systems, and work authorization systems.

▶ **Resource availability.** Examples include contracting and purchasing constraints, approved providers and subcontractors, and collaboration agreements.

▶ **Employee capability.** Examples include existing human resources expertise, skills, competencies, and specialized knowledge.

2.1.2 EEFS EXTERNAL TO THE ORGANIZATION

The following are examples of EEFs that are external to the organization:

▶ **Marketplace conditions.** Examples include competitors, market share brand recognition, and trademarks.

▶ **Social and cultural influences and issues.** Examples include political climate, codes of conduct, ethics, and perceptions.

▶ **Legal restrictions.** Examples include country or local laws and regulations related to security, data protection, business conduct, employment, and procurement.

▶ **Commercial databases.** Examples include benchmarking results, standardized cost estimating data, industry risk study information, and risk databases.

▶ **Academic research.** Examples include industry studies, publications, and benchmarking results.

▶ **Government or industry standards.** Examples include regulatory agency regulations and standards related to products, production, environment, quality, and workmanship.

▶ **Financial considerations.** Examples include currency exchange rates, interest rates, inflation rates, tariffs, and geographic location.

▶ **Physical environmental elements.** Examples include working conditions, weather, and constraints.

2.2 ORGANIZATIONAL PROCESS ASSETS

Organizational process assets (OPAs) are the plans, processes, documents, templates, and knowledge repositories specific to and used by the performing organization. These assets influence the management of the project.

OPAs include any artifact, practice, or knowledge from any or all of the performing organizations involved in the project, which can be used to execute or govern the project. The OPAs also include the organization's lessons learned from previous projects and historical information. OPAs may include completed schedules, risk data, and earned value data. OPAs are inputs to many project management processes. Since OPAs are internal to the organization, the project team members may be able to update and add to the organizational process assets as necessary throughout the project. They may be grouped into two categories:

- **Plans, processes, and documents.** Generally, these assets are not updated as part of the project work and are usually established by the project management office (PMO) or another function outside of the project. These assets can be updated only by following the appropriate organizational policies. Some organizations encourage the team to tailor templates, life cycles, and checklists for the project. In these cases, the project team should tailor those assets according to the needs of the project.

- **Organizational knowledge repositories.** These assets are updated throughout the project with project information. For example, information on financial performance, lessons learned, performance metrics and issues, and defects are continually updated throughout the project.

2.2.1 PLANS, PROCESSES, AND DOCUMENTS

The organization's plans, processes, and documents for conducting project work include but are not limited to:

- **Initiating and Planning:**
  - ▷ Guidelines and criteria for tailoring the organization's set of standard processes and procedures to satisfy the specific needs of the project;
  - ▷ Product and project life cycles, and methods and procedures (e.g., project management methods, estimation metrics, process audits, improvement targets, checklists, and standardized process definitions for use in the organization);

- ▷ Templates (e.g., project management plans, project documents, project registers, report formats, contract templates, risk categories, risk statement templates, probability and impact definitions, probability and impact matrices, and stakeholder register templates); and

- ▷ Preapproved supplier lists and various types of contractual agreements (e.g., fixed-price, cost-reimbursable, and time and materials [T&M] contracts).

▶ **Executing, Monitoring, and Controlling:**

- ▷ Change control procedures, including the steps by which performing organization standards, plans, or any project documents will be modified and how any changes will be approved and validated;

- ▷ Traceability matrices;

- ▷ Issue and defect management processes (e.g., defining issue and defect controls, identifying and resolving issues and defects, and tracking action items);

- ▷ Resource availability control and assignment management;

- ▷ Organizational communication requirements (e.g., specific communication technology available, authorized communication media, record retention policies, videoconferencing, collaborative tools, and security requirements);

- ▷ Processes for prioritizing, approving, and issuing work authorizations;

- ▷ Templates (e.g., risk register, issue log, and change log);

- ▷ Standardized guidelines, work instructions, proposal evaluation criteria, and performance measurement criteria; and

- ▷ Product, service, or result verification and validation processes.

▶ **Closing.** Project closure guidelines or requirements (e.g., final project audits, project evaluations, deliverable acceptance, contract closure, resource reassignment knowledge transfer to production and/or operations, and lessons learned).

2.2.2 ORGANIZATIONAL KNOWLEDGE REPOSITORIES

The organizational knowledge repositories for storing and retrieving information include but are not limited to:

▶ Configuration management knowledge repositories containing the versions of software and hardware components and baselines of all performing organization standards, policies, procedures, and any project documents;

▶ Financial data repositories containing information such as labor hours, incurred costs, budgets, and any project cost overruns;

▶ Historical information and lessons learned knowledge repositories (e.g., project records and documents, all project closure information and documentation, information regarding both the results of previous project selection decisions and previous project performance information, and information from risk activities);

▶ Issue and defect management data repositories containing issue and defect status, control information, issue and defect resolution, and action item results;

▶ Data repositories for metrics used to collect and make available measurement data on processes and products; and

▶ Project files from previous projects (e.g., scope, cost, schedule, and performance measurement baselines, project calendars, project schedule network diagrams, risk registers, risk reports, and stakeholder registers).

2.3 GOVERNANCE

Projects operate within the constraints imposed by the organization through their structure and governance framework. There are various types of governance including organizational governance; organizational project management (OPM) governance; and portfolio, program, and project governance.

2.3.1 ORGANIZATIONAL GOVERNANCE

Organizational governance is a structured way to provide direction and control through policies and procedures to meet strategic and operational goals. Organizational governance is typically conducted by a board of directors to ensure accountability, fairness, and transparency to its stakeholders. Organizational governance principles, decisions, and procedures may influence and impact the governance of portfolios, programs, and projects in the following ways:

▶ Enforces legal, regulatory, standards, and compliance requirements;

▶ Defines ethical, social, and environmental responsibilities; and

▶ Specifies operational, legal, and risk policies.

2.3.2 PROJECT GOVERNANCE

Project governance is the framework, functions, and procedures that guide project management activities in order to create a unique product, service, or result to meet organizational, strategic, and operational goals. Governance at the project level includes:

▶ Guiding and overseeing the management of project work;

▶ Ensuring adherence to policies, standards, and guidelines;

▶ Establishing governance roles, responsibilities, and authorities;

▶ Decision making regarding risk escalations, changes, and resources (e.g., team, financial, physical, facilities);

▶ Ensuring appropriate stakeholder engagement; and

▶ Monitoring performance.

A project governance framework provides project stakeholders with structure, procedures, roles, responsibilities, accountabilities, and decision-making models for managing the project. Elements of a project governance framework include but are not limited to principles or procedures for:

- ▶ Stage gate or phase reviews;
- ▶ Identifying, escalating, and resolving risks and issues;
- ▶ Defining roles, responsibilities, and authorities;
- ▶ Process for project knowledge management and capturing lessons learned;
- ▶ Decision making, problem solving, and escalating topics that are beyond the project manager's authority; and
- ▶ Reviewing and approving changes to the project, and product changes that are beyond the authority of the project manager.

2.4 MANAGEMENT ELEMENTS

Management elements are the components that comprise the key functions or principles of general management in the organization. The general management elements are allocated within the organization according to its governance framework and the organizational structure type selected.

The key functions or principles of management include but are not limited to:

- ▶ Division of work using specialized skills and availability to perform work;
- ▶ Authority given to perform work;
- ▶ Responsibility to perform work appropriately assigned based on such attributes as skill and experience;
- ▶ Discipline of action (e.g., respect for authority, people, and rules);
- ▶ Unity of command (e.g., only one person gives orders for any action or activity to an individual);
- ▶ Unity of direction (e.g., one plan and one head for a group of activities with the same objective);
- ▶ General goals of the organization take precedence over individual goals;

- ▶ Paid fairly for work performed;

- ▶ Optimal use of resources;

- ▶ Clear communication channels;

- ▶ Right materials to the right person for the right job at the right time;

- ▶ Fair and equal treatment of people in the workplace;

- ▶ Clear security of work positions;

- ▶ Safety of people in the workplace;

- ▶ Open contribution to planning and execution by each person; and

- ▶ Optimal morale.

Performance of these management elements are assigned to selected individuals within the organization. These individuals may perform the noted functions within various organizational structures. For example, in a hierarchical structure, there are horizontal and vertical levels within the organization. These hierarchical levels range from the line management level through to the executive management level. The responsibility, accountability, and authority assigned to the hierarchical level indicate how the individual may perform the noted function within that organizational structure.

2.5 ORGANIZATIONAL STRUCTURES

Determination of the appropriate organizational structure type is a result of the study of trade-offs between two key variables. The variables are the organizational structure types available for use and how to optimize them for a given organization. There is not a one-size-fits-all structure for any given organization. The final structure for a given organization is unique due to the numerous variables to be considered.

2.5.1 ORGANIZATIONAL STRUCTURE TYPES

Organizational structures take many forms or types. Table 2-1 compares several types of organizational structures and their influence on projects.

Table 2-1. Influences of Organizational Structures on Projects

Organizational Structure Type	Project Characteristics					
	Work Groups Arranged by:	Project Manager's Authority	Project Manager's Role	Resource Availability	Who Manages the Project Budget?	Project Management Administrative Staff
Organic or Simple	Flexible; people working side by side	Little or none	Part-time; may or may not be a designated job role like coordinator	Little or none	Owner or operator	Little or none
Functional (centralized)	Job being done (e.g., engineering, manufacturing)	Little or none	Part-time; may or may not be a designated job role like coordinator	Little or none	Functional manager	Part-time
Multidivisional (may replicate functions for each division with little centralization)	One of: product; production processes; portfolio; program; geographic region; customer type	Little or none	Part-time; may or may not be a designated job role like coordinator	Little or none	Functional manager	Part-time
Matrix – strong	By job function, with project manager as a function	Moderate to high	Full-time designated job role	Moderate to high	Project manager	Full-time
Matrix – weak	Job function	Low	Part-time; done as part of another job and not a designated job role like coordinator	Low	Functional manager	Part-time
Matrix – balanced	Job function	Low to moderate	Part-time; embedded in the functions as a skill and may not be a designated job role like coordinator	Low to moderate	Mixed	Part-time
Project-oriented (composite, hybrid)	Project	High to almost total	Full-time designated job role	High to almost total	Project manager	Full-time
Virtual	Network structure with nodes at points of contact with other people	Low to moderate	Full-time or part-time	Low to moderate	Mixed	Could be full-time or part-time
Hybrid	Mix of other types	Mixed	Mixed	Mixed	Mixed	Mixed
PMO*	Mix of other types	High to almost total	Full-time designated job role	High to almost total	Project manager	Full-time

*PMO refers to a portfolio, program, or project management office or organization.

Process Groups: A Practice Guide

2.5.2 FACTORS IN ORGANIZATIONAL STRUCTURE SELECTION

Each organization considers numerous factors for establishing its organizational structure. Each factor may carry a different level of importance in the final analysis. The combination of the factor, its value, and relative importance provides the organization's decision makers with the right information for inclusion in the analysis.

Factors to consider in selecting an organizational structure include but are not limited to:

▶ Degree of alignment with organizational objectives;

▶ Efficiency of performance;

▶ Specialization capabilities;

▶ Span of control, efficiency, and effectiveness;

▶ Clear path for escalation of decisions;

▶ Clear line and scope of authority;

▶ Delegation capabilities;

▶ Accountability assignment;

▶ Responsibility assignment;

▶ Adaptability of design;

▶ Simplicity of design;

▶ Cost considerations;

▶ Physical locations (e.g., colocated, regional, and virtual); and

▶ Clear communication (e.g., policies, status of work, and organization's vision).

2.6 PROJECT MANAGEMENT OFFICE

A project management office (PMO) is an organizational structure that standardizes the project-related governance processes and facilitates the sharing of resources, methodologies, tools, and techniques. The responsibilities of a PMO can range from providing project management support functions to the direct management of one or more projects.

Types of PMOs

There are several types of PMOs in organizations. Each type varies in the degree of control and influence it has on projects within the organization, such as:

▶ **Supportive.** Supportive PMOs provide a consultative role to projects by supplying templates, best practices, training, access to information, and lessons learned from other projects. This type of PMO serves as a project repository. The degree of control provided by the PMO is low.

▶ **Controlling.** Controlling PMOs provide support and require compliance through various means. The degree of control provided by the PMO is moderate. Compliance may involve:

  ▷ Adoption of project management frameworks or methodologies;

  ▷ Use of specific templates, forms, and tools; and

  ▷ Conformance to governance frameworks.

▶ **Directive.** Directive PMOs take control of the projects by directly managing the projects. Project managers are assigned by and report to the PMO. The degree of control provided by the PMO is high.

The project management office may have an organization-wide responsibility. It may play a role in supporting strategic alignment and delivering organizational value. The PMO integrates data and information from organizational strategic projects and evaluates how higher-level strategic objectives are being fulfilled. The PMO is the natural liaison between the organization's portfolios, programs, projects, and the organizational measurement systems (e.g., balanced scorecard).

The projects supported or administered by the PMO may not be related other than by being managed together. The specific form, function, and structure of a PMO are dependent upon the needs of the organization that it supports.

A PMO may have the authority to act as an integral stakeholder and a key decision maker throughout the life of each project in order to keep it aligned with the business objectives. The PMO may:

▶ Make recommendations,

▶ Lead knowledge transfer,

▶ Terminate projects, and

▶ Take other actions, as required.

A primary function of a PMO is to support project managers in a variety of ways, which may include but are not limited to:

▶ Managing shared resources across all projects administered by the PMO;

▶ Identifying and developing project management methodology, best practices, and standards;

▶ Coaching, mentoring, training, and oversight;

▶ Monitoring compliance with project management standards, policies, procedures, and templates by means of project audits;

▶ Developing and managing project policies, procedures, templates, and other shared documentation (organizational process assets); and

▶ Coordinating communication across projects.

Role of the Project Manager

A project manager plays a critical role in the leadership of a project team in order to achieve the project's objectives. This role is clearly visible throughout the project. Many project managers become involved in a project from its initiation through closing. However, in some organizations, a project manager may be involved in evaluation and analysis activities prior to project initiation. These activities may include consulting with executive and business unit leaders on ideas for advancing strategic objectives, improving organizational performance, or meeting customer needs. In some organizational settings, the project manager may also be called upon to manage or assist in business analysis, business case development, and aspects of portfolio management for a project. A project manager may also be involved in follow-on activities related to realizing business benefits from the project. The role of a project manager may vary from organization to organization. Ultimately, the project management role is tailored to fit the organization in the same way that the project management processes are tailored to fit the project.

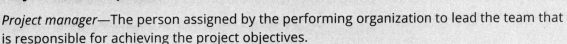

Project Leadership Roles

Project manager—The person assigned by the performing organization to lead the team that is responsible for achieving the project objectives.

Functional manager—The functional manager focuses on providing management oversight for a functional or business unit.

Operations manager—Operations managers are responsible for ensuring that business operations are efficient.

- **Project team and roles.** A large project comprises many members, each playing a different role. A large project may have more than 100 project members led by a project manager. Team members may fulfill many different roles, such as design, manufacturing, and facilities management. They may represent multiple business units or groups within an organization. The project members make up each leader's team.

- **Responsibility for team.** The project manager is responsible for what the team produces—the *project outcome*. The project manager needs to take a holistic view of the team's products in order to plan, coordinate, and complete them. This is accomplished by reviewing the vision, mission, and objectives of the organization to ensure alignment with their products. The project manager then establishes an interpretation of the vision, mission, and objectives involved in successfully completing their products, and uses this interpretation to communicate and motivate the team toward the successful completion of their objectives.

- **Knowledge and skills.** The project manager is not expected to perform every role on the project, but should possess project management knowledge, technical knowledge, understanding, and experience. The project manager provides the project team with leadership, planning, and coordination through communications. The project manager provides written communications (e.g., documented plans and schedules) and communicates in real time with the team using meetings and verbal or nonverbal cues.

3.1 THE PROJECT MANAGER'S SPHERE OF INFLUENCE

Project managers fulfill numerous roles within their sphere of influence. These roles reflect the project manager's capabilities and are representative of the value and contributions of the project management profession. This section highlights the roles of the project manager in the various spheres of influence shown in Figure 3-1.

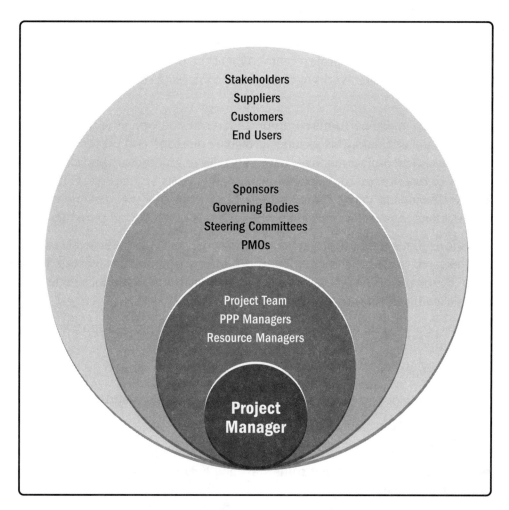

Figure 3-1. Example of Project Manager's Sphere of Influence

3.1.1 THE PROJECT

The project manager leads the project team to meet the project's objectives and stakeholders' expectations. The project manager works to balance the competing constraints on the project with the available resources.

The project manager also performs communication roles between the project sponsor, team members, and other stakeholders. This includes providing direction and presenting the vision of success for the project. The project manager uses soft skills (e.g., interpersonal skills and the ability to manage people) to balance the conflicting and competing goals of the project stakeholders in order to achieve consensus. In this context, consensus means that the relevant stakeholders support the project decisions and actions even when there is not 100% agreement.

Research shows that successful project managers consistently and effectively use certain essential skills. Research reveals that the top 2% of project managers, as designated by their bosses and team members, distinguish themselves by demonstrating superior relationship and communication skills while displaying a positive attitude.

The ability to communicate with stakeholders, including the team and sponsors, applies across multiple aspects of the project including, but not limited to the following:

▶ Developing finely tuned skills using multiple methods (e.g., verbal, written, and nonverbal);

▶ Creating, maintaining, and adhering to communications plans and schedules;

▶ Communicating predictably and consistently;

▶ Seeking to understand the project stakeholders' communication needs (communication may be the only deliverable that some stakeholders receive until the project's end product or service is completed);

▶ Making communications concise, clear, complete, simple, relevant, and tailored;

▶ Including important positive and negative news;

▶ Incorporating feedback channels; and

▶ Relationship skills involving the development of extensive networks of people throughout the project manager's spheres of influence. These networks include formal networks such as organizational reporting structures. However, the informal networks that project managers develop, maintain, and nurture are more important. Informal networks include the use of established relationships with individuals such as subject matter experts and influential leaders. Use of these formal and informal networks allows the project manager to engage multiple people in solving problems and navigating the bureaucracies encountered in a project.

3.1.2 THE ORGANIZATION

The project manager proactively interacts with other project managers. Other independent projects or projects that are part of the same program may impact a project due to, but not limited to, the following:

▶ Demands on the same resources,

▶ Priorities of funding,

▶ Receipt or distribution of deliverables, and

▶ Alignment of project goals and objectives with those of the organization.

Interacting with other project managers helps to create a positive influence for fulfilling the various needs of the project. These needs may be in the form of human, technical, or financial resources and deliverables required by the team for project completion. The project manager seeks ways to develop relationships that assist the team in achieving the goals and objectives of the project.

In addition, the project manager maintains a strong advocacy role within the organization. The project manager proactively interacts with managers within the organization throughout the project. The project manager also works with the project sponsor to address internal political and strategic issues that may impact the team or the viability or quality of the project.

The project manager may work toward increasing the project management competency and capability within the organization as a whole and is involved in both tacit and explicit knowledge transfer or integration initiatives. The project manager also works to:

▶ Demonstrate the value of project management,

▶ Increase acceptance of project management in the organization, and

▶ Advance the efficacy of the PMO when one exists in the organization.

Depending on the organizational structure, a project manager may report to a functional manager. In other cases, a project manager may be one of several project managers who report to a PMO or a portfolio or program manager who is ultimately responsible for one or more organization-wide projects. The project manager works closely with all relevant managers to achieve the project objectives and to ensure the project management plan aligns with the portfolio or program plan. The project manager also works closely and in collaboration with other roles, such as organizational managers, subject matter experts, and those involved with business analysis. In some situations, the project manager may be an external consultant placed in a temporary management role.

3.1.3 THE INDUSTRY

The project manager stays informed about current industry trends. The project manager takes this information and sees how it may impact or apply to the current projects. These trends include but are not limited to:

▶ Product and technology development;

▶ New and changing market niches;

▶ Standards (e.g., project management, quality management, information security management);

▶ Technical support tools;

▶ Economic forces that impact the immediate project;

▶ Influences affecting the project management discipline; and

▶ Process improvement and sustainability strategies.

3.1.4 PROJECT STAKEHOLDERS

A stakeholder is an individual, group, or organization that may affect, be affected by, or perceive itself to be affected by a decision, activity, or outcome of a project. Project stakeholders may be internal or external to the project, and they may be actively involved, passively involved, or unaware of the project. Project stakeholders may have a positive or negative impact on the project, or they may be positively or negatively impacted by the project. Examples of stakeholders include but are not limited to:

- **Internal stakeholders:**
  - Sponsor,
  - Resource manager,
  - Project management office (PMO),
  - Portfolio steering committee,
  - Program manager,
  - Project managers of other projects, and
  - Team members.
- **External stakeholders:**
  - Customers,
  - End users,
  - Suppliers,
  - Shareholders,
  - Regulatory bodies, and
  - Competitors.

Stakeholder involvement may range from occasional contributions in surveys and focus groups to full project sponsorship that includes the provision of financial, political, or other types of support. The type and level of project involvement can change over the course of the project's life cycle. Therefore, successfully identifying, analyzing, and engaging stakeholders and effectively managing their project expectations and participation throughout the project life cycle is critical to project success.

3.2 PROJECT MANAGER COMPETENCES

Recent PMI studies applied the *Project Manager Competency Development (PMCD) Framework* [6] to the skills needed by project managers through the use of the PMI Talent Triangle® shown in Figure 3-2. The Talent Triangle focuses on three key skill sets: Ways of Working, Business Acumen, and Power Skills.

Figure 3-2. The PMI Talent Triangle®

3.2.1 WAYS OF WORKING

It is important for project managers to master diverse and creative ways of getting the job done. Project managers should understand and adopt many ways of working, including predictive, agile, design thinking, or other new practices still to be developed. This will allow individuals to quickly shift their way of working as new challenges arise. This enables success when the right solutions at the right moment in time are applied.

3.2.2 BUSINESS ACUMEN

Business acumen is the ability to make good judgments and quick decisions while understanding the many factors of influence across an organization or industry. Professionals at every level should actively develop business acumen, whether through experience, training, courses, certifications, or self-guided learning, to achieve the highest level of success. This enables a deeper knowledge of how any project aligns with the broader organizational strategy and global trends, enabling efficient and effective decision making.

3.2.3 POWER SKILLS

Beyond the traditional top-down leadership skills, power skills (formerly known as "soft skills") are the critical interpersonal skills of professionals at every level that enable them to apply influence, inspire change, and build relationships. Power skills include collaborative leadership skills, communication skills, having an innovative mindset, having a for-purpose orientation, and exercising empathy. Mastering these power skills allows professionals to be powerful, influential stakeholders who can instigate change and make ideas a reality.

3.3 QUALITIES AND SKILLS OF A LEADER

Research shows that the qualities and skills of a leader include but are not limited to:

▶ Being a visionary (e.g., help to describe the products, goals, and objectives of the project; able to dream and translate those dreams for others);

▶ Being optimistic and positive;

▶ Being collaborative;

▶ Managing relationships and conflict by:

   ▷ Building trust;

   ▷ Satisfying concerns;

   ▷ Seeking consensus;

   ▷ Balancing competing and opposing goals;

   ▷ Applying persuasion, negotiation, compromise, and conflict resolution skills;

   ▷ Developing and nurturing personal and professional networks;

   ▷ Taking a long-term view that relationships are just as important as the project; and

   ▷ Continuously developing and applying political acumen.

▶ Communicating by:

   ▷ Spending sufficient time communicating (research shows that top project managers spend about 90% of their time on a project in communicating);

   ▷ Managing expectations;

   ▷ Accepting feedback graciously;

   ▷ Giving feedback constructively; and

   ▷ Asking and listening.

▶ Being respectful (helping others retain their autonomy), courteous, friendly, kind, honest, trustworthy, loyal, and ethical;

- ▶ Exhibiting integrity and being culturally sensitive, courageous, a problem solver, and decisive;

- ▶ Giving credit to others where due;

- ▶ Being a lifelong learner who is results- and action-oriented;

- ▶ Focusing on the important things, including:

    - ▷ Continuously prioritizing work by reviewing and adjusting as necessary;

    - ▷ Finding and using a prioritization method that works for them and the project;

    - ▷ Differentiating high-level strategic priorities, especially those related to critical success factors for the project;

    - ▷ Maintaining vigilance on primary project constraints;

    - ▷ Remaining flexible on tactical priorities; and

    - ▷ Being able to sift through massive amounts of information to obtain the most important information.

- ▶ Having a holistic and systemic view of the project, taking internal and external factors into account equally;

- ▶ Being able to apply critical thinking (e.g., application of analytical methods to reach decisions) and identify themself as a change agent; and

- ▶ Being able to build effective teams, be service oriented, and have fun and share humor effectively with team members.

3.3.1 LEADERSHIP STYLES

Project managers may lead their teams in many ways. The style a project manager selects may be a personal preference, or the result of the combination of multiple factors associated with the project. The style a project manager uses may change over time based on the factors in play. Major factors to consider include but are not limited to:

- ▶ Leader characteristics (e.g., attitudes, moods, needs, values, ethics);

- ▶ Team member characteristics (e.g., attitudes, moods, needs, values, ethics);

- ▶ Organizational characteristics (e.g., its purpose, structure, and type of work performed); and

- ▶ Environmental characteristics (e.g., social situation, economic state, and political elements).

Research describes numerous leadership styles that a project manager can adopt. Some of the most common examples of these styles include but are not limited to:

- ▶ *Laissez-faire* (e.g., allowing the team to make their own decisions and establish their own goals, also referred to as taking a hands-off style);

- ▶ *Transactional* (e.g., focus on goals, feedback, and accomplishment to determine rewards; management by exception);

- ▶ *Servant leader* (e.g., demonstrates commitment to serve and put other people first; focuses on other people's growth, learning, development, autonomy, and well-being; concentrates on relationships, community, and collaboration; leadership is secondary and emerges after service);

- ▶ *Transformational* (e.g., empowering followers through idealized attributes and behaviors, inspirational motivation, encouragement for innovation and creativity, and individual consideration);

- ▶ *Charismatic* (e.g., able to inspire; is high-energy, enthusiastic, self-confident; holds strong convictions); and

- ▶ *Interactional* (e.g., a combination of transactional, transformational, and charismatic).

3.3.2 LEADERSHIP COMPARED TO MANAGEMENT

The words *leadership* and *management* are often used interchangeably. However, they are not synonymous. The word *management* is more closely associated with directing another person to get from one point to another using a known set of expected behaviors. In contrast, leadership involves working with others through discussion or debate in order to guide them from one point to another.

The method that a project manager chooses to employ reveals a distinct difference in behavior, self-perception, and project role. Table 3-1 compares management and leadership on several important levels.

Project managers need to employ both leadership and management in order to be successful. The skill is in finding the right balance for each situation. The way in which management and leadership are employed often shows up in the project manager's leadership style.

Table 3-1. Team Management and Team Leadership Compared

Management	Leadership
Direct using positional power	Guide, influence, and collaborate using relational power
Maintain	Develop
Administrate	Innovate
Focus on systems and structure	Focus on relationships with people
Rely on control	Inspire trust
Focus on near-term goals	Focus on long-range vision
Ask how and when	Ask what and why
Focus on bottom line	Focus on the horizon
Accept status quo	Challenge status quo
Do things right	Do the right things
Focus on operational issues and problem solving	Focus on vision, alignment, motivation, and inspiration

3.3.3 POLITICS, POWER, AND GETTING THINGS DONE

Leadership and management are ultimately about being able to get things done. The skills and qualities noted help the project manager to achieve project goals and objectives. At the root of many of these skills and qualities is the ability to deal with politics. Politics involves influence, negotiation, autonomy, and power.

The project manager observes and collects data about the project and organizational landscapes. The data then needs to be reviewed in the context of the project, the people involved, the organization, and the environment as a whole. This review yields the information and knowledge necessary for the project manager to plan and implement the most appropriate action. The project manager's action is a result of selecting the right kind of power to influence and negotiate with others. Exercise of power also carries with it the responsibility of being sensitive to and respectful of other people. The effective action of the project manager maintains the autonomy of those involved. The project manager's action results in the right people performing the activities necessary to fulfill the project's objectives.

Power can originate with traits exhibited by the individual or the organization. Power is often supported by other people's perceptions of the leader. It is essential for project managers to be aware of their relationships with other people. Relationships enable project managers to get things done on the project. There are numerous forms of power at the disposal of project managers. Power and its use can be complex given its nature and the various factors at play in a project. Various forms of power include but are not limited to:

▶ Positional (sometimes called formal, authoritative, legitimate) (e.g., formal position granted in the organization or team);

▶ Informational (e.g., control of gathering or distribution);

▶ Referent (e.g., respect or admiration others hold for the individual, credibility gained);

▶ Situational (e.g., gained due to unique situation such as a specific crisis);

▶ Personal or charismatic (e.g., charm, attraction);

▶ Relational (e.g., participates in networking, connections, and alliances);

▶ Expert (e.g., skill, information possessed; experience, training, education, certification);

▶ Reward-oriented (e.g., ability to give praise, monetary rewards, or other desired items);

▶ Punitive or coercive (e.g., ability to invoke discipline or negative consequences);

▶ Ingratiating (e.g., application of flattery or other common ground to win favor or cooperation);

▶ Pressure-based (e.g., limit freedom of choice or movement for the purpose of gaining compliance to desired action);

- Guilt-based (e.g., imposition of obligation or sense of duty);

- Persuasive (e.g., ability to provide arguments that move people to a desired course of action); and

- Avoiding (e.g., refusing to participate).

Top project managers are proactive and intentional when it comes to power. These project managers will work to acquire the power and authority they need within the boundaries of organizational policies, protocols, and procedures rather than wait for it to be granted.

3.3.4 PERSONALITY

Personality refers to the individual differences in characteristic patterns of thinking, feeling, and behaving. Personality characteristics or traits include but are not limited to:

- Authentic (e.g., accepts others for what and who they are, shows open concern);

- Courteous (e.g., ability to apply appropriate behavior and etiquette);

- Creative (e.g., ability to think abstractly, to see things differently, to innovate);

- Cultural (e.g., measure of sensitivity to other cultures including values, norms, and beliefs);

- Emotional (e.g., ability to perceive emotions and the information they present and to manage them; measure of interpersonal skills);

- Intellectual (e.g., measure of human intelligence over multiple aptitudes);

- Managerial (e.g., measure of management practice and potential);

- Political (e.g., measure of political intelligence and making things happen);

- Service-oriented (e.g., evidence of willingness to serve other people);

- Social (e.g., ability to understand and manage people); and

- Systemic (e.g., drive to understand and build systems).

An effective project manager will have some level of ability with each of these characteristics in order to be successful. Each project, organization, and situation requires the project manager to emphasize different aspects of personality.

3.4 PERFORMING INTEGRATION

The role of the project manager is twofold when performing integration on the project:

▶ Project managers play a key role in working with the project sponsor to understand the strategic objectives and ensure the alignment of the project objectives and results with those of the portfolio, program, and business areas. In this way, project managers contribute to the integration and execution of the strategy.

▶ Project managers are responsible for guiding the team to work together to focus on what is really essential at the project level. This is achieved through the integration of processes, knowledge, and people.

Integration is a critical skill for project managers and takes place at three different levels: the process, cognitive, and context levels.

3.4.1 PERFORMING INTEGRATION AT THE PROCESS LEVEL

Project management may be seen as a set of processes and activities that are undertaken to achieve the project objectives. Some of these processes may take place once (e.g., the initial creation of the project charter), but many others overlap and occur several times throughout the project. One example of this process overlap and multiple occurrences is a change in a requirement that impacts scope, schedule, or budget and requires a change request. Several project management processes such as the Control Scope process and the Perform Integrated Change Control process may involve a change request. The Perform Integrated Change Control process occurs throughout the project for integrating change requests.

Although there is no stated definition on how to integrate the project processes, it is clear that a project has a small chance of meeting its objective if the project manager fails to integrate the project processes where they interact.

3.4.2 INTEGRATION AT THE COGNITIVE LEVEL

There are many different ways to manage a project. The method selected typically depends on the specific characteristics of the project including its size, how complicated the project or organization may be, and the culture of the performing organization. It is clear that the personal skills and abilities of the project manager are closely related to the way in which the project is managed.

The project manager applies experience, insight, ways of working, power skills, and business acumen to the project. It is through the project manager's ability to integrate the applicable project management processes, which makes it possible to achieve the desired project results.

3.4.3 INTEGRATION AT THE CONTEXT LEVEL

There have been many changes in the context in which business and projects take place today compared to a few decades ago. New technologies have been introduced. Social networks, multicultural aspects, virtual teams, and new values are part of the new reality of projects. One example is knowledge and people integration in the context of a large, cross-functional project implementation involving multiple organizations. The project manager considers the implications of this context in communications planning and knowledge management to guide the project team.

Project managers need to be cognizant of the project context and these new aspects when managing the integration. Then project managers can decide how to best use these new elements of the environment in their projects to achieve success.

3.4.4 INTEGRATION AND COMPLEXITY

Some projects may be referred to as complex and considered difficult to manage. In simple terms, complex and complicated are concepts often used to describe what is considered to be intricate.

Three Dimensions of Complexity

Complexity within projects is a result of the organization's system behavior, human behavior, and the uncertainty at work in the organization or its environment. In *Navigating Complexity: A Practice Guide* [7], these three dimensions of complexity are defined as:

▶ **System behavior.** The interdependencies of components and systems.

▶ **Human behavior.** The interplay between diverse individuals and groups.

▶ **Ambiguity.** Uncertainty of emerging issues and lack of understanding or confusion.

Complexity itself is a perception of an individual based on personal experience, observation, and skill. Rather than being complex, a project is more accurately described as containing complexity. Portfolios, programs, and projects may contain elements of complexity.

When approaching the integration of a project, the project manager should consider elements that are both inside and outside of the project. The project manager should examine the characteristics or properties of the project. Complexity as a characteristic or property of a project is typically defined as:

▶ Containing multiple parts,

▶ Possessing a number of connections between the parts,

▶ Exhibiting dynamic interactions between the parts, and

▶ Exhibiting behavior, produced as a result of those interactions, which cannot be explained as the simple sum of the parts (e.g., emergent behavior).

Examining these various items that appear to make the project complex should help the project manager identify key areas when planning, managing, and controlling the project to ensure integration.

Initiating Process Group

The processes in the Initiating Process Group are shown in Table 4-1.

Table 4-1. Initiating Process Group Processes

Initiating Processes	
4.1 Develop Project Charter	4.2 Identify Stakeholders

These processes define a new project or a new phase of an existing project by obtaining authorization to start the project or phase. The purpose of this Process Group is to align stakeholder expectations and the project purpose, inform stakeholders of the scope and objectives, and discuss how their participation in the project and its associated phases can help to ensure their expectations are met. The initial scope is defined and initial financial resources are committed. Stakeholders who will interact and influence the overall outcome of the project are identified. The project manager is appointed if not already assigned. This information is captured in the project charter and stakeholder register. When the project charter is approved, the project is officially authorized, and the project manager is authorized to apply organizational resources to the project activities.

The key benefits of this Process Group are that only projects that are aligned with the organization's strategic objectives are authorized and the business case, benefits, and stakeholders are considered from the start of the project. In some organizations, the project manager is involved in developing the business case and defining the benefits. In those organizations, the project manager generally helps write the project charter; in other organizations, the pre-project work is done by the project sponsor, project management office (PMO), portfolio steering committee, or other stakeholder group. This practice guide assumes the project has been approved by the sponsor or other governing body and the business documents have been reviewed prior to authorizing the project. In most cases, business documents originate outside of the project, but are used as inputs to the project.

Business documents are documents that are generally originated outside of the project but are used as inputs to the project. Examples of business documents include the business case and benefits management plan. Figure 4-1 shows the sponsor and the business documents in relation to the Initiating Processes.

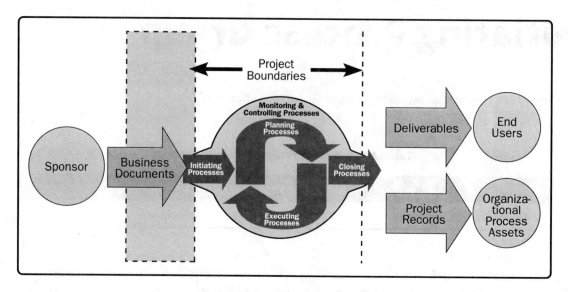

Figure 4-1. Project Boundaries

Projects are often divided into phases. When this is done, information from processes in the Initiating Process Group is reexamined to determine if the information is still valid. Revisiting the Initiating processes at the start of each phase helps keep the project focused on the business need that the project was undertaken to address. The project charter, business documents, and success criteria are verified. The influence drivers, expectations, and objectives of the project stakeholders are reviewed.

Involve Stakeholders

Involving the sponsors, customers, and other stakeholders during initiation creates a shared understanding of success criteria. It also increases the likelihood of deliverable acceptance when the project is complete and stakeholder satisfaction throughout the project.

4.1 DEVELOP PROJECT CHARTER

Develop Project Charter is the process for developing the document that formally authorizes the existence of a project and provides the project manager with the authority to apply organizational resources to project activities. The key benefits of this process are:

▶ Provides a direct link between the project and the strategic objectives of the organization,

▶ Creates a formal record of the project, and

▶ Shows the organizational commitment to the project.

This process is performed once or at predefined points in the project. The inputs, tools and techniques, and outputs are shown in Figure 4-2. Figure 4-3 presents the data flow diagram for this process.

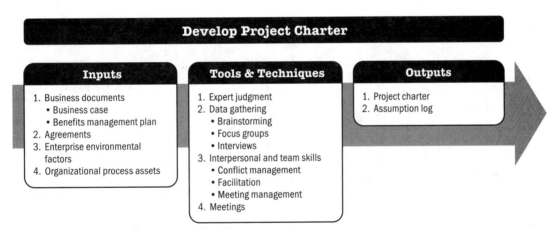

Note: This figure provides the inputs, tools and techniques, and outputs that may be used for this process. Descriptions for inputs and outputs appear in Section 9. Descriptions for tools and techniques appear in Section 10.

Figure 4-2. Develop Project Charter: Inputs, Tools & Techniques, and Outputs

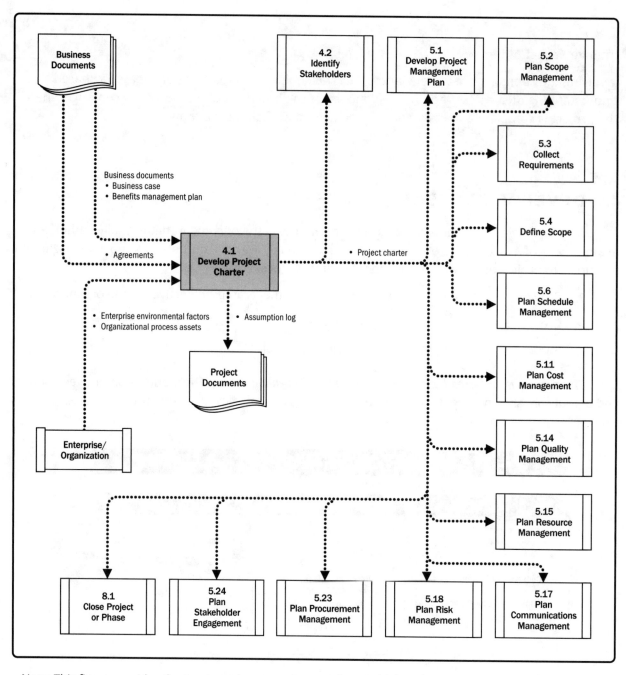

Note: This figure provides the inputs and outputs that may be used for this process. Descriptions for inputs and outputs appear in Section 9.

Figure 4-3. Develop Project Charter: Data Flow Diagram

The project charter establishes a partnership between the performing and requesting organizations. In the case of external projects, a formal contract is typically the preferred way to establish an agreement. A project charter may still be used to establish internal agreements within an organization to ensure proper delivery under the contract. The approved project charter formally initiates the project. A project manager is identified and assigned as early in the project as is feasible, preferably while the project charter is being developed and always prior to the start of planning. The project charter can be developed by the sponsor or the project manager in collaboration with the initiating entity. This collaboration allows the project manager to have a better understanding of the project purpose, objectives, and expected benefits. This understanding will better allow for efficient resource allocation to project activities. The project charter provides the project manager with the authority to plan, execute, and control the project.

Projects are initiated by an entity external to the project such as a sponsor, program, or project management office (PMO), or a portfolio governing body chairperson or authorized representative. The project initiator or sponsor should be at a level that is appropriate to procure funding and commit resources to the project. Projects are initiated due to internal business needs or external influences. These needs or influences often trigger the creation of a needs analysis, feasibility study, business case, or description of the situation that the project will address. Chartering a project validates alignment of the project to the strategy and ongoing work of the organization. A project charter is not considered to be a contract because there is no consideration or money promised or exchanged in its creation.

4.2 IDENTIFY STAKEHOLDERS

Identify Stakeholders is the process of identifying project stakeholders regularly and analyzing and documenting relevant information regarding their interests, involvement, interdependencies, influence, and potential impact on project success. The key benefit of this process is that it enables the project team to identify the appropriate focus for engagement of each stakeholder or group of stakeholders.

This process is performed periodically throughout the project as needed. The inputs, tools and techniques, and outputs are shown in Figure 4-4. Figure 4-5 presents the data flow diagram for this process.

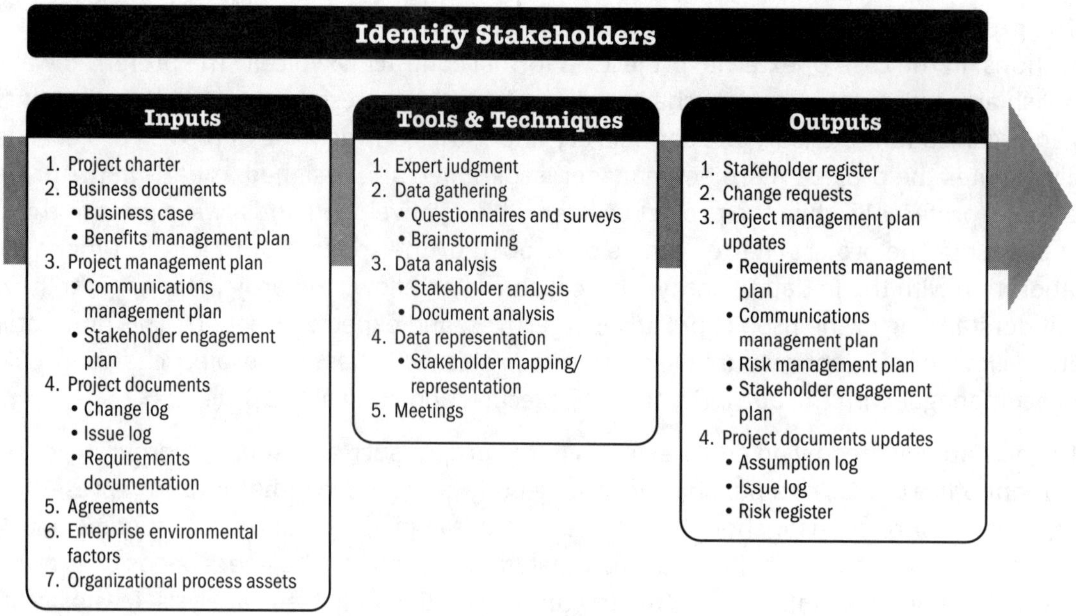

Identify Stakeholders

Inputs	Tools & Techniques	Outputs

1. Project charter
2. Business documents
  • Business case
  • Benefits management plan
3. Project management plan
  • Communications management plan
  • Stakeholder engagement plan
4. Project documents
  • Change log
  • Issue log
  • Requirements documentation
5. Agreements
6. Enterprise environmental factors
7. Organizational process assets
	1. Expert judgment
	2. Data gathering
	  • Questionnaires and surveys
	  • Brainstorming
	3. Data analysis
	  • Stakeholder analysis
	  • Document analysis
	4. Data representation
	  • Stakeholder mapping/representation
	5. Meetings
		1. Stakeholder register
		2. Change requests
		3. Project management plan updates
		  • Requirements management plan
		  • Communications management plan
		  • Risk management plan
		  • Stakeholder engagement plan
		4. Project documents updates
		  • Assumption log
		  • Issue log
		  • Risk register

Note: This figure provides the inputs, tools and techniques, and outputs that may be used for this process. Descriptions for inputs and outputs appear in Section 9. Descriptions for tools and techniques appear in Section 10.

Figure 4-4. Identify Stakeholders: Inputs, Tools & Techniques, and Outputs

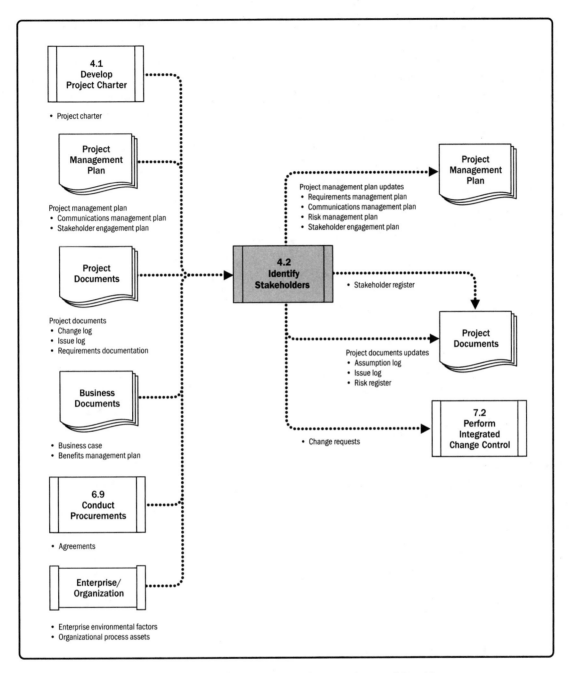

Note: This figure provides the inputs and outputs that may be used for this process. Descriptions for inputs and outputs appear in Section 9.

Figure 4-5. Identify Stakeholders: Data Flow Diagram

This process frequently occurs for the first time in a project either prior to or at the same time the project charter is developed and approved. It is repeated as necessary but should be performed at the start of each phase and when a significant change in the project or the organization occurs. Each time the identification process is repeated, the project management plan components and project documents should be consulted to identify relevant project stakeholders.

Planning Process Group

The processes in the Planning Process Group are shown in Table 5-1.

Table 5-1. Planning Process Group Processes

Planning Processes	
5.1 Develop Project Management Plan	5.13 Determine Budget
5.2 Plan Scope Management	5.14 Plan Quality Management
5.3 Collect Requirements	5.15 Plan Resource Management
5.4 Define Scope	5.16 Estimate Activity Resources
5.5 Create WBS	5.17 Plan Communications Management
5.6 Plan Schedule Management	5.18 Plan Risk Management
5.7 Define Activities	5.19 Identify Risks
5.8 Sequence Activities	5.20 Perform Qualitative Risk Analysis
5.9 Estimate Activity Durations	5.21 Perform Quantitative Risk Analysis
5.10 Develop Schedule	5.22 Plan Risk Responses
5.11 Plan Cost Management	5.23 Plan Procurement Management
5.12 Estimate Costs	5.24 Plan Stakeholder Engagement

The Planning Process Group consists of those processes that establish the total scope of the effort, define and refine the objectives, and develop the course of action required to attain those objectives. The processes in the Planning Process Group develop the components of the project management plan and the project documents used to carry out the project. The nature of a project may require the use of repeated feedback loops for additional analysis. As more project information or characteristics are gathered and understood, additional planning will likely be required. Significant changes that occur throughout the project life cycle may initiate a need to revisit one or more of the planning processes and, possibly, one or both of the Initiating processes. This ongoing refinement of the project management plan is called progressive elaboration, indicating that planning and documentation are iterative or ongoing activities. The key benefit of this Process Group is to define the course of action to successfully complete the project or phase.

The project management team seeks input and encourages involvement from relevant stakeholders while planning the project and developing the project management plan and project documents. When the initial planning effort is completed, the approved version of the project management plan is considered a baseline. Throughout the project, the Monitoring and Controlling processes compare the project performance to the baselines.

The Planning Process Group project management processes are described in Sections 5.1 through 5.24.

5.1 DEVELOP PROJECT MANAGEMENT PLAN

Develop Project Management Plan is the process of defining, preparing, and coordinating all plan components and consolidating them into an integrated project management plan. The key benefit of this process is the production of a comprehensive document that defines the basis of all project work and how the work will be performed.

This process is performed once or at predefined points in the project. The inputs, tools and techniques, and outputs are shown in Figure 5-1. Figure 5-2 presents the data flow diagram for this process.

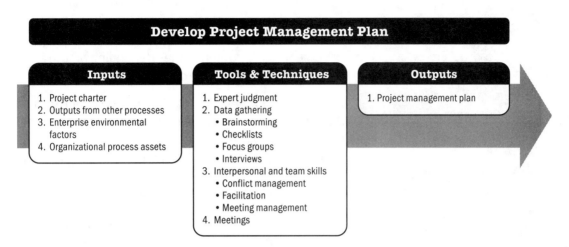

Note: This figure provides the inputs, tools and techniques, and outputs that may be used for this process. Descriptions for inputs and outputs appear in Section 9. Descriptions for tools and techniques appear in Section 10.

Figure 5-1. Develop Project Management Plan: Inputs, Tools & Techniques, and Outputs

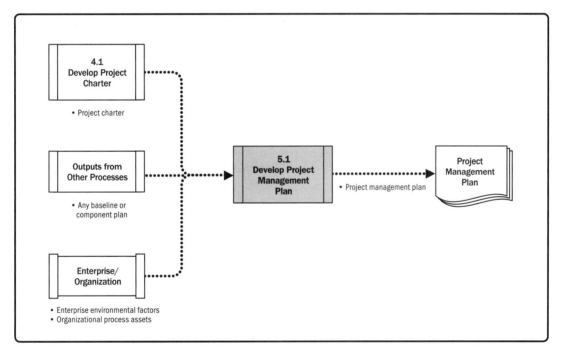

Note: This figure provides the inputs and outputs that may be used for this process. Descriptions for inputs and outputs appear in Section 9.

Figure 5-2. Develop Project Management Plan: Data Flow Diagram

Projects that exist in the context of a program or portfolio should develop a project management plan that is consistent with the program or portfolio management plan. For example, if the program management plan indicates all changes exceeding a specified cost need to be reviewed by the change control board (CCB), then this process and cost threshold need to be defined in the project management plan.

The project management plan defines how the project is executed, monitored and controlled, and closed. The project management plan's content varies depending on the application area and complexity of the project.

The project management plan may be either summary level or detailed. Each component plan is described to the extent required by the specific project. The project management plan should be robust enough to respond to an ever-changing project environment. This agility may result in more accurate information as the project progresses.

The project management plan should be baselined; that is, it is necessary to define at least the project references for scope, time, and cost, so that the project execution can be measured and compared to those references and performance can be managed. Before the baselines are defined, the project management plan may be updated as many times as necessary. No formal process is required at that time. But, once it is baselined, it may only be changed through the Perform Integrated Change Control process. Consequently, change requests will be generated and decided upon whenever a change is requested. This results in a project management plan that is progressively elaborated by controlled and approved updates extending through project closure.

5.2 PLAN SCOPE MANAGEMENT

Plan Scope Management is the process of creating a scope management plan that documents how the project and product scope will be defined, validated, and controlled. The key benefit of this process is that it provides guidance and direction on how scope will be managed throughout the project.

This process is performed once or at predefined points in the project. The inputs, tools and techniques, and outputs are shown in in Figure 5-3. Figure 5-4 presents the data flow diagram for this process.

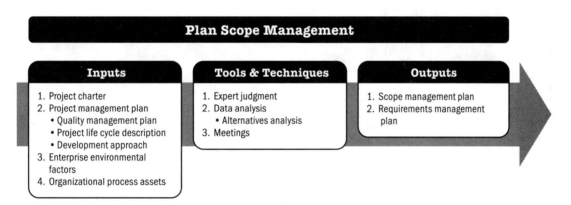

Plan Scope Management		
Inputs	**Tools & Techniques**	**Outputs**

1. Project charter
2. Project management plan
  • Quality management plan
  • Project life cycle description
  • Development approach
3. Enterprise environmental factors
4. Organizational process assets
	1. Expert judgment
	2. Data analysis
	  • Alternatives analysis
	3. Meetings
		1. Scope management plan
		2. Requirements management plan

Note: This figure provides the inputs, tools and techniques, and outputs that may be used for this process. Descriptions for inputs and outputs appear in Section 9. Descriptions for tools and techniques appear in Section 10.

Figure 5-3. Plan Scope Management: Inputs, Tools & Techniques, and Outputs

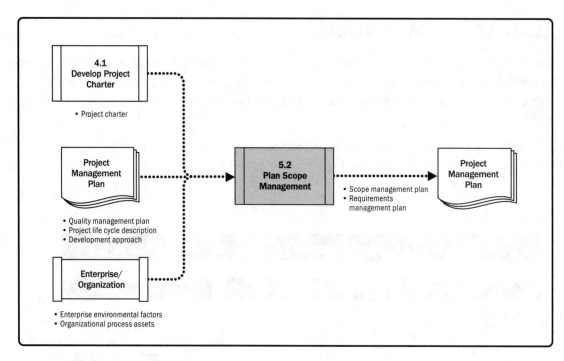

Note: This figure provides the inputs and outputs that may be used for this process. Descriptions for inputs and outputs appear in Section 9.

Figure 5-4. Plan Scope Management: Data Flow Diagram

The scope management plan is a component of the project or program management plan that describes how the scope will be defined, developed, monitored, controlled, and validated. The development of the scope management plan and the detailing of the project scope begin with the analysis of information contained in the project charter, the latest approved subsidiary plans of the project management plan, historical information contained in the organizational process assets, and any other relevant enterprise environmental factors.

5.3 COLLECT REQUIREMENTS

Collect Requirements is the process of determining, documenting, and managing stakeholder needs and requirements to meet objectives. The key benefit of this process is that it provides the basis for defining the product scope and project scope.

This process is performed once or at predefined points in the project. The inputs, tools and techniques, and outputs are shown in Figure 5-5. Figure 5-6 presents the data flow diagram for this process.

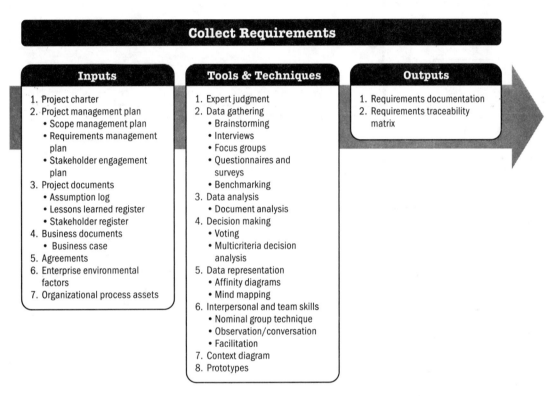

Note: This figure provides the inputs, tools and techniques, and outputs that may be used for this process. Descriptions for inputs and outputs appear in Section 9. Descriptions for tools and techniques appear in Section 10.

Figure 5-5. Collect Requirements: Inputs, Tools & Techniques, and Outputs

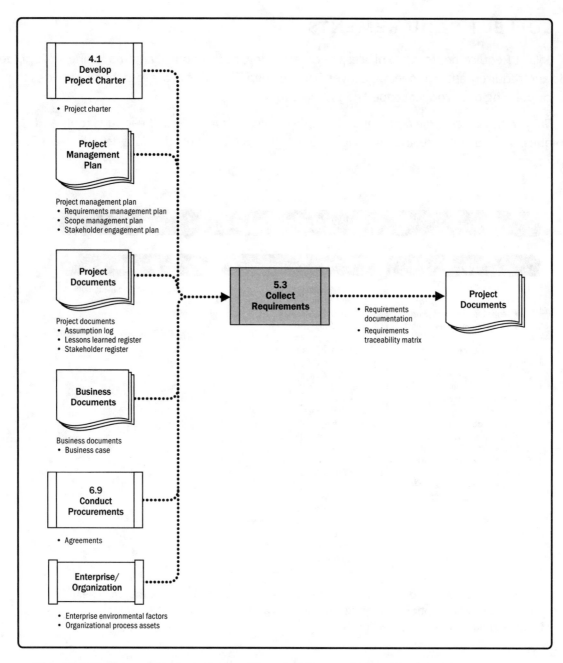

Note: This figure provides the inputs and outputs that may be used for this process. Descriptions for inputs and outputs appear in Section 9.

Figure 5-6. Collect Requirements: Data Flow Diagram

This practice guide does not specifically address product requirements since those are industry specific. Note that *Business Analysis for Practitioners: A Practice Guide* [3] provides more in-depth information about product requirements. A project's success is directly influenced by active stakeholder involvement in the discovery and decomposition of needs into project and product requirements and by the care taken in determining, documenting, and managing the requirements of the product, service, or result of the project. Requirements include conditions or capabilities that are required to be present in a product, service, or result to satisfy an agreement or other formally imposed specification. Requirements include the quantified and documented needs and expectations of the sponsor, customer, and other stakeholders. These requirements need to be elicited, analyzed, and recorded in enough detail to be included in the scope baseline and to be measured once project execution begins. Requirements become the foundation of the work breakdown structure (WBS). Cost, schedule, quality planning, and procurement are all based on these requirements.

5.4 DEFINE SCOPE

Define Scope is the process of developing a detailed description of the project and product. The key benefit of this process is that it describes the product, service, or result boundaries and acceptance criteria.

This process is performed once or at predefined points in the project. The inputs, tools and techniques, and outputs are shown in Figure 5-7. Figure 5-8 presents the data flow diagram for this process.

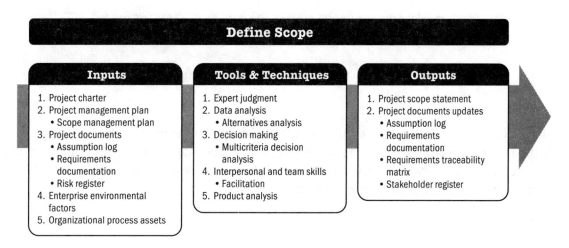

Note: This figure provides the inputs, tools and techniques, and outputs that may be used for this process. Descriptions for inputs and outputs appear in Section 9. Descriptions for tools and techniques appear in Section 10.

Figure 5-7. Define Scope: Inputs, Tools & Techniques, and Outputs

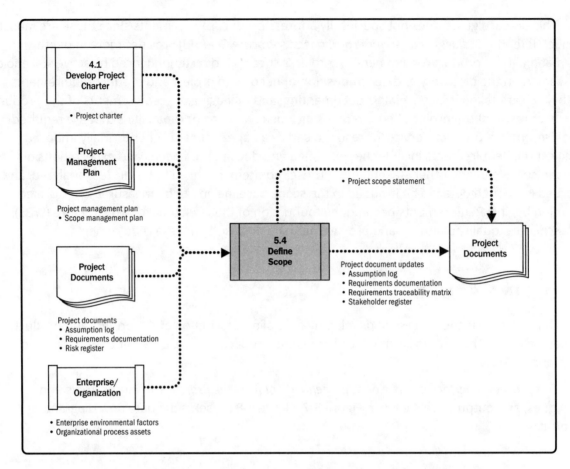

Note: This figure provides the inputs and outputs that may be used for this process. Descriptions for inputs and outputs appear in Section 9.

Figure 5-8. Define Scope: Data Flow Diagram

Since all of the requirements identified in Collect Requirements may not be included in the project, the Define Scope process results in the selection of the final project requirements from the requirements documentation developed during the Collect Requirements process. It then develops a detailed description of the project and product, service, or result.

The preparation of a detailed project scope statement builds upon the high-level project description that is documented during project initiation. During project planning, the project scope is defined and described with greater specificity as more information about the project is known. Existing risks, assumptions, and constraints are analyzed for completeness and added or updated as necessary. The Define Scope process can be highly iterative. In iterative life cycle projects, a high-level vision will be developed for the overall project, but the detailed scope is determined one iteration at a time, and the detailed planning for the next iteration is carried out as work progresses on the current project scope and deliverables.

5.5 CREATE WBS

Create WBS is the process of subdividing project deliverables and project work into smaller, more manageable components. The key benefit of this process is that it provides a framework of what has to be delivered.

This process is performed once or at predefined points in the project. The inputs, tools and techniques, and outputs are shown in Figure 5-9. Figure 5-10 presents the data flow diagram for this process.

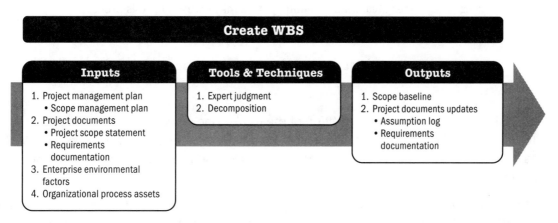

Note: This figure provides the inputs, tools and techniques, and outputs that may be used for this process. Descriptions for inputs and outputs appear in Section 9. Descriptions for tools and techniques appear in Section 10.

Figure 5-9. Create WBS: Inputs, Tools & Techniques, and Outputs

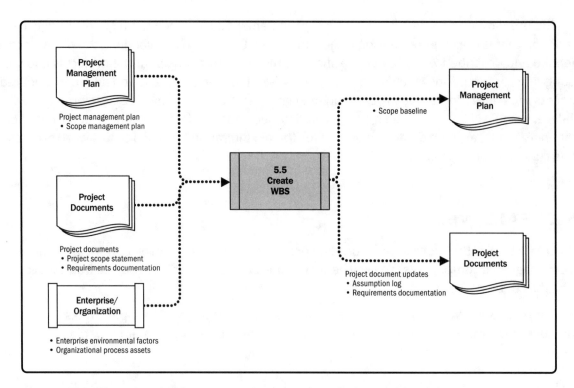

Note: This figure provides the inputs and outputs that may be used for this process. Descriptions for inputs and outputs appear in Section 9.

Figure 5-10. Create WBS: Data Flow Diagram

The WBS is a hierarchical decomposition of the total scope of work to be carried out by the project team to accomplish the project objectives and create the required deliverables. The WBS organizes and defines the total scope of the project and represents the work specified in the current approved project scope statement.

The planned work is contained within the lowest level of WBS components, which are called work packages. A work package can be used to group the activities where work is scheduled and estimated, monitored, and controlled. In the context of the WBS, work refers to work products or deliverables that are the result of activity and not to the activity itself.

5.6 PLAN SCHEDULE MANAGEMENT

Plan Schedule Management is the process of establishing the policies, procedures, and documentation for planning, developing, managing, executing, and controlling the project schedule. The key benefit of this process is that it provides guidance and direction on how the project schedule will be managed throughout the project.

This process is performed once or at predefined points in the project. The inputs, tools and techniques, and outputs are shown in Figure 5-11. Figure 5-12 presents the data flow diagram for this process.

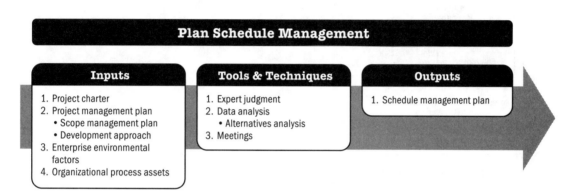

Note: This figure provides the inputs, tools and techniques, and outputs that may be used for this process. Descriptions for inputs and outputs appear in Section 9. Descriptions for tools and techniques appear in Section 10.

Figure 5-11. Plan Schedule Management: Inputs, Tools & Techniques, and Outputs

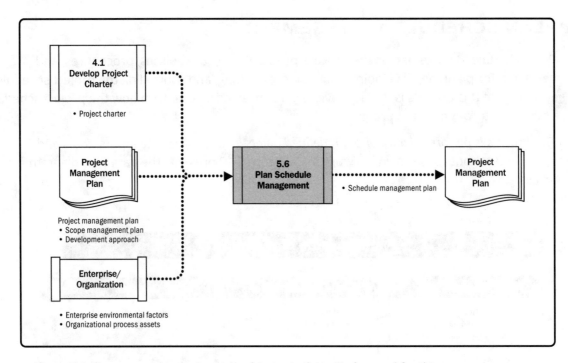

Note: This figure provides the inputs and outputs that may be used for this process. Descriptions for inputs and outputs appear in Section 9.

Figure 5-12. Plan Schedule Management: Data Flow Diagram

5.7 DEFINE ACTIVITIES

Define Activities is the process of identifying and documenting the specific actions to be performed to produce the project deliverables. The key benefit of this process is that it decomposes work packages into schedule activities that provide a basis for estimating, scheduling, executing, monitoring, and controlling the project work.

This process is performed throughout the project. The inputs, tools and techniques, and outputs are shown in Figure 5-13. Figure 5-14 presents the data flow diagram for this process.

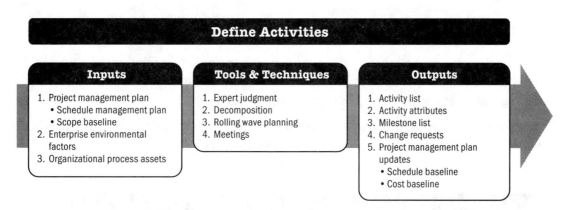

Note: This figure provides the inputs, tools and techniques, and outputs that may be used for this process. Descriptions for inputs and outputs appear in Section 9. Descriptions for tools and techniques appear in Section 10.

Figure 5-13. Define Activities: Inputs, Tools & Techniques, and Outputs

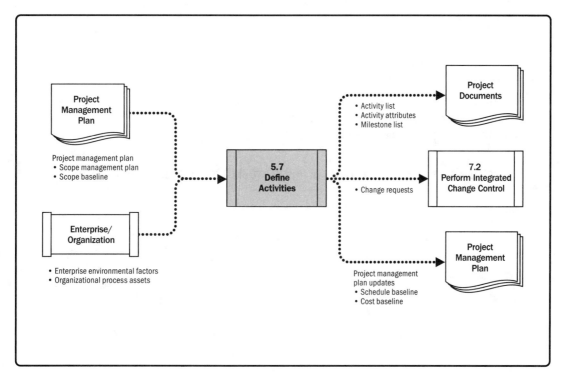

Note: This figure provides the inputs and outputs that may be used for this process. Descriptions for inputs and outputs appear in Section 9.

Figure 5-14. Define Activities: Data Flow Diagram

5.8 SEQUENCE ACTIVITIES

Sequence Activities is the process of identifying and documenting relationships among the project activities. The key benefit of this process is that it defines the logical sequence of work to obtain the greatest efficiency given all project constraints.

This process is performed throughout the project. The inputs, tools and techniques, and outputs are shown in Figure 5-15. Figure 5-16 presents the data flow diagram for this process.

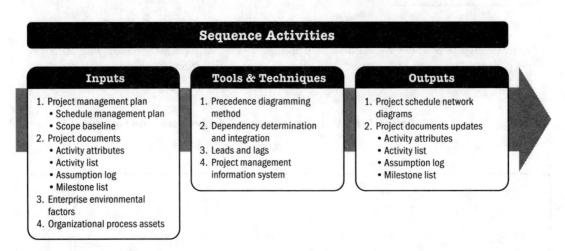

Note: This figure provides the inputs, tools and techniques, and outputs that may be used for this process. Descriptions for inputs and outputs appear in Section 9. Descriptions for tools and techniques appear in Section 10.

Figure 5-15. Sequence Activities: Inputs, Tools & Techniques, and Outputs

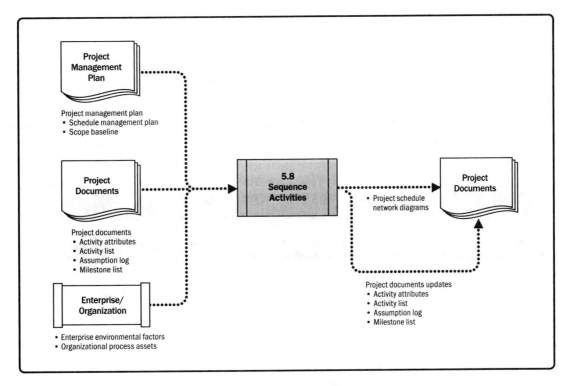

Note: This figure provides the inputs and outputs that may be used for this process. Descriptions for inputs and outputs appear in Section 9.

Figure 5-16. Sequence Activities: Data Flow Diagram

Every activity except the first and last should be connected to at least one predecessor and at least one successor activity with an appropriate logical relationship. Logical relationships should be designed to create a realistic project schedule. It may be necessary to use lead or lag time between activities to support a realistic and achievable project schedule (see leads and lags in Section 10). Sequencing can be performed by using project management software or by using manual or automated techniques. The Sequence Activities process concentrates on converting the project activities from a list to a diagram to act as a first step to publish the schedule baseline.

5.9 ESTIMATE ACTIVITY DURATIONS

Estimate Activity Durations is the process of estimating the number of work periods needed to complete individual activities with estimated resources. The key benefit of this process is that it provides the amount of time each activity will take to complete.

This process is performed throughout the project. The inputs, tools and techniques, and outputs are shown in Figure 5-17. Figure 5-18 presents the data flow diagram for this process.

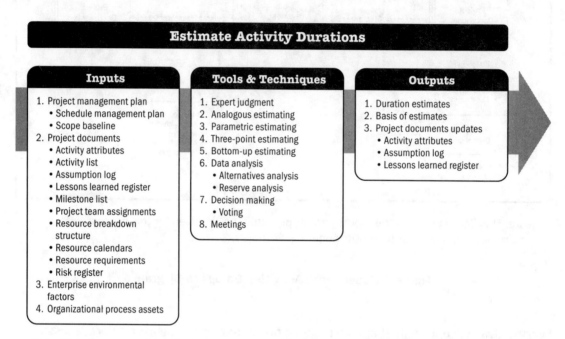

Note: This figure provides the inputs, tools and techniques, and outputs that may be used for this process. Descriptions for inputs and outputs appear in Section 9. Descriptions for tools and techniques appear in Section 10.

Figure 5-17. Estimate Activity Durations: Inputs, Tools & Techniques, and Outputs

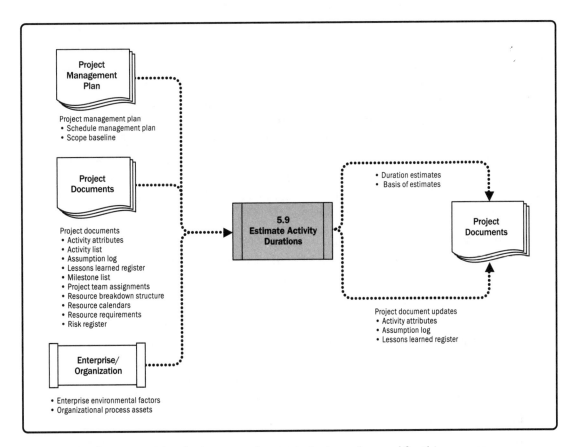

Note: This figure provides the inputs and outputs that may be used for this process. Descriptions for inputs and outputs appear in Section 9.

Figure 5-18. Estimate Activity Durations: Data Flow Diagram

Estimating activity durations uses information from the scope of work, required resource types or skill levels, estimated resource quantities, and resource calendars. Other factors that may influence the duration estimates include constraints imposed on the duration, effort involved, or type of resources (e.g., fixed duration, fixed effort or work, fixed number of resources), as well as the schedule network analysis technique used. The inputs for the estimates of duration originate from the person or gro up on the project team who is most familiar with the nature of the work in the specific activity. The duration estimate is progressively elaborated, and the process considers the quality and availability of the input data. For example, as more detailed and precise data are available about the project engineering and design work, the accuracy and quality of the duration estimates improve.

The Estimate Activity Durations process requires an estimation of the amount of work effort required to complete the activity and the amount of available resources estimated to complete the activity. These estimates are used to approximate the number of work periods (activity duration) needed to complete the activity using the appropriate project and resource calendars. In many cases, the number of resources that are expected to be available to accomplish an activity, along with the skill proficiency of those resources, may determine the activity's duration. A change to a driving resource allocated to the activity will usually have an effect on the duration, but this is not a simple "straight-line" or linear relationship. Sometimes, the intrinsic nature of the work (i.e., constraints imposed on the duration, effort involved, or number of resources) will take a predetermined amount of time to complete regardless of the resource allocation (e.g., a 24-hour stress test). Other factors for consideration when estimating duration include:

▶ **Law of diminishing returns.** When one factor (e.g., resource) used to determine the effort required to produce a unit of work is increased while all other factors remain fixed, a point will eventually be reached at which additions of that one factor start to yield progressively smaller or diminishing increases in output.

▶ **Number of resources.** Increasing the number of resources to twice the original number of the resources does not always reduce the time by half, as it may increase extra duration due to risk, and at some point adding too many resources to the activity may increase duration due to knowledge transfer, learning curve, additional coordination, and other factors involved.

▶ **Advances in technology.** This may also play an important role in determining duration estimates. For example, an increase in the output of a manufacturing plant may be achieved by procuring the latest advances in technology, which may impact duration and resource needs.

▶ **Motivation of staff.** The project manager also needs to be aware of Student Syndrome—or procrastination—when people start to apply themselves only at the last possible moment before the deadline, and Parkinson's Law where work expands to fill the time available for its completion.

All data and assumptions that support duration estimating are documented for each activity duration estimate.

5.10 DEVELOP SCHEDULE

Develop Schedule is the process of analyzing activity sequences, durations, resource requirements, and schedule constraints to create a schedule model for project execution and monitoring and controlling. The key benefit of this process is that it generates a schedule model with planned dates for completing project activities.

This process is performed throughout the project. The inputs, tools and techniques, and outputs are shown in Figure 5-19. Figure 5-20 presents the data flow diagram for this process.

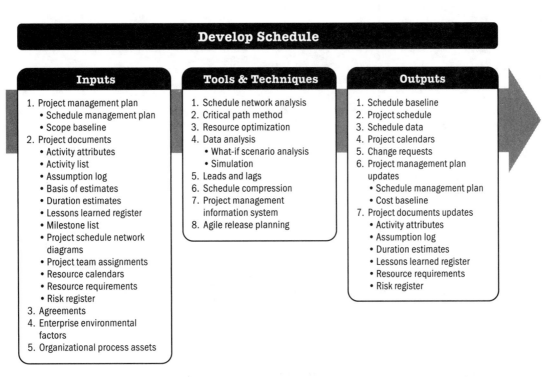

Develop Schedule

Inputs	Tools & Techniques	Outputs

1. Project management plan
  • Schedule management plan
  • Scope baseline
2. Project documents
  • Activity attributes
  • Activity list
  • Assumption log
  • Basis of estimates
  • Duration estimates
  • Lessons learned register
  • Milestone list
  • Project schedule network diagrams
  • Project team assignments
  • Resource calendars
  • Resource requirements
  • Risk register
3. Agreements
4. Enterprise environmental factors
5. Organizational process assets
	1. Schedule network analysis
	2. Critical path method
	3. Resource optimization
	4. Data analysis
	  • What-if scenario analysis
	  • Simulation
	5. Leads and lags
	6. Schedule compression
	7. Project management information system
	8. Agile release planning
		1. Schedule baseline
		2. Project schedule
		3. Schedule data
		4. Project calendars
		5. Change requests
		6. Project management plan updates
		  • Schedule management plan
		  • Cost baseline
		7. Project documents updates
		  • Activity attributes
		  • Assumption log
		  • Duration estimates
		  • Lessons learned register
		  • Resource requirements
		  • Risk register

Note: This figure provides the inputs, tools and techniques, and outputs that may be used for this process. Descriptions for inputs and outputs appear in Section 9. Descriptions for tools and techniques appear in Section 10.

Figure 5-19. Develop Schedule: Inputs, Tools & Techniques, and Outputs

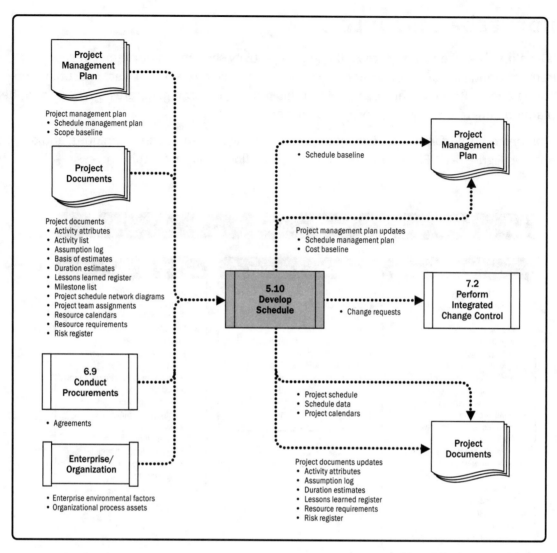

Note: This figure provides the inputs and outputs that may be used for this process. Descriptions for inputs and outputs appear in Section 9.

Figure 5-20. Develop Schedule: Data Flow Diagram

Developing an acceptable project schedule is an iterative process. The schedule model is used to determine the planned start and finish dates for project activities and milestones based on the best available information. Schedule development can require the review and revision of duration estimates, resource estimates, and schedule reserves to establish an approved project schedule that can serve as a baseline to track progress. Key steps include defining the project milestones, identifying and sequencing activities, and estimating durations. Once the activity start and finish dates have been determined, it is common to have the project staff assigned to the activities review their assigned activities. The staff confirms that the start and finish dates present no conflict with resource calendars or assigned activities on other projects or tasks and thus are still valid. The schedule is then analyzed to determine conflicts with logical relationships and if resource leveling is required before the schedule is approved and baselined. Revising and maintaining the project schedule model to sustain a realistic schedule continues throughout the duration of the project.

For more specific information regarding scheduling, refer to the *Practice Standard for Scheduling* [8].

5.11 PLAN COST MANAGEMENT

Plan Cost Management is the process of defining how the project costs will be estimated, budgeted, managed, monitored, and controlled. The key benefit of this process is that it provides guidance and direction on how the project costs will be managed throughout the project.

This process is performed once or at predefined points in the project. The inputs, tools and techniques, and outputs are shown in Figure 5-21. Figure 5-22 presents the data flow diagram for this process.

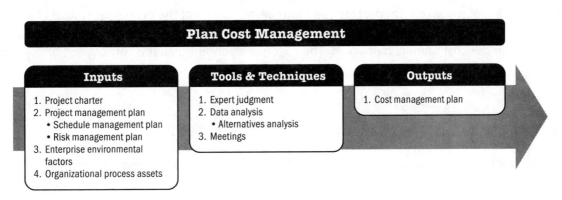

Note: This figure provides the inputs, tools and techniques, and outputs that may be used for this process. Descriptions for inputs and outputs appear in Section 9. Descriptions for tools and techniques appear in Section 10.

Figure 5-21. Plan Cost Management: Inputs, Tools & Techniques, and Outputs

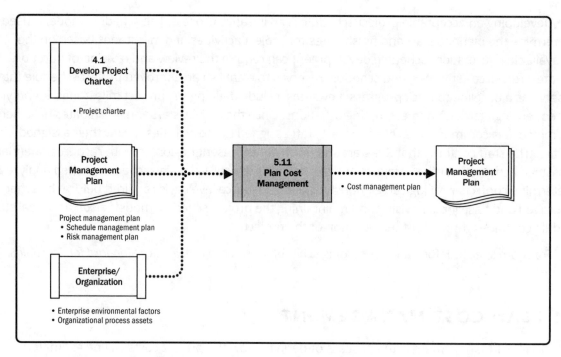

Note: This figure provides the inputs and outputs that may be used for this process. Descriptions for inputs and outputs appear in Section 9.

Figure 5-22. Plan Cost Management: Data Flow Diagram

The cost management planning effort occurs early in project planning and sets the framework for each of the cost management processes so that performance of the processes will be efficient and coordinated. The cost management processes and their associated tools and techniques are documented in the cost management plan. The cost management plan is a component of the project management plan.

5.12 ESTIMATE COSTS

Estimate Costs is the process of developing an approximation of the cost of resources needed to complete project work. The key benefit of this process is that it determines the monetary resources required for the project.

This process is performed periodically throughout the project as needed. The inputs, tools and techniques, and outputs are shown in Figure 5-23. Figure 5-24 presents the data flow diagram for this process.

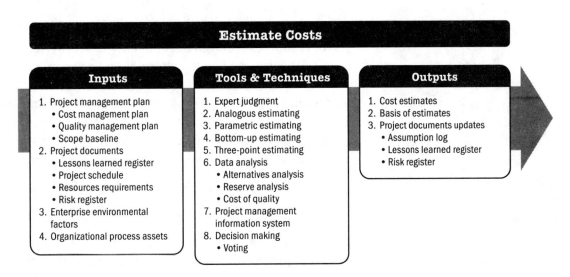

Note: This figure provides the inputs, tools and techniques, and outputs that may be used for this process. Descriptions for inputs and outputs appear in Section 9. Descriptions for tools and techniques appear in Section 10.

Figure 5-23. Estimate Costs: Inputs, Tools & Techniques, and Outputs

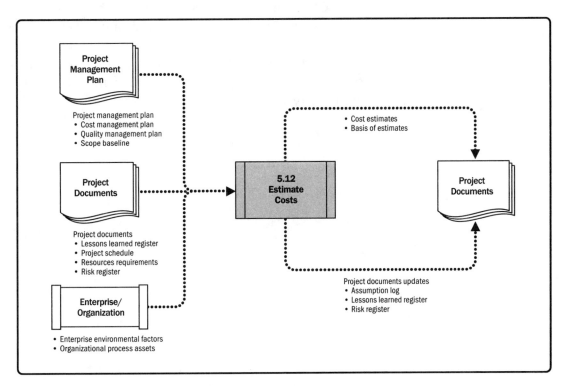

Note: This figure provides the inputs and outputs that may be used for this process. Descriptions for inputs and outputs appear in Section 9.

Figure 5-24. Estimate Costs: Data Flow Diagram

Cost estimates are generally expressed in units of some currency (i.e., dollars, euros, yen, etc.), although in some instances other units of measure, such as staff hours or staff days, are used to facilitate comparisons by eliminating the effects of currency fluctuations.

A cost estimate is a quantitative assessment of the likely costs for resources required to complete the activity. It is a prediction that is based on the information known at a given point in time. Cost estimates include the identification and consideration of costing alternatives to initiate and complete the project. Cost trade-offs and risks should be considered, such as make versus buy, buy versus lease, and the sharing of resources in order to achieve optimal costs for the project.

Cost estimates should be reviewed and refined during the course of the project to reflect additional detail as it becomes available and assumptions are tested. The accuracy of a project estimate will increase as the project progresses through the project life cycle. For example, a project in the start-up phase may have a rough order of magnitude (ROM) estimate in the range of −25% to +75%. Later in the project, as more information is known, definitive estimates could narrow the range of accuracy to −5% to +10%. In some organizations, there are guidelines for when such refinements can be made and the degree of confidence or accuracy that is expected.

Costs are estimated for all resources that will be charged to the project. This includes but is not limited to labor, materials, equipment, services, and facilities, as well as special categories such as an inflation allowance, cost of financing, or contingency costs. Cost estimates may be presented at the activity level or in summary form.

5.13 DETERMINE BUDGET

Determine Budget is the process of aggregating the estimated costs of individual activities or work packages to establish an authorized cost baseline. The key benefit of this process is that it determines the cost baseline against which project performance can be monitored and controlled.

This process is performed once or at predefined points in the project. The inputs, tools and techniques, and outputs are shown in Figure 5-25. Figure 5-26 presents the data flow diagram for this process.

A project budget includes all of the funds authorized to execute the project. The cost baseline is the approved version of the time-phased project budget that includes contingency reserves but excludes management reserves.

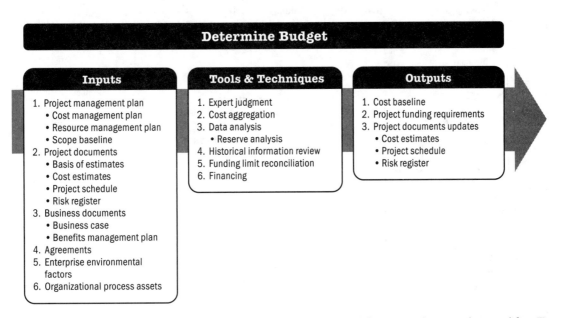

Note: This figure provides the inputs, tools and techniques, and outputs that may be used for this process. Descriptions for inputs and outputs appear in Section 9. Descriptions for tools and techniques appear in Section 10.

Figure 5-25. Determine Budget: Inputs, Tools & Techniques, and Outputs

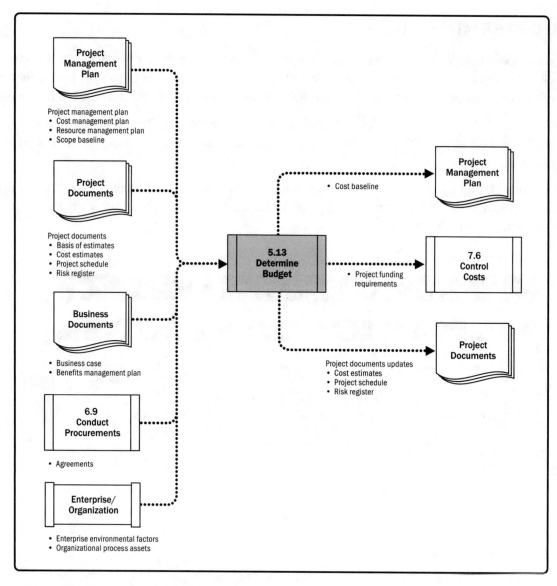

Note: This figure provides the inputs and outputs that may be used for this process. Descriptions for inputs and outputs appear in Section 9.

Figure 5-26. Determine Budget: Data Flow Diagram

5.14 PLAN QUALITY MANAGEMENT

Plan Quality Management is the process of identifying quality requirements and/or standards for the project and its deliverables. This process documents how the project will demonstrate compliance with quality requirements and/or standards. The key benefit of this process is that it provides guidance and direction on how quality will be managed and verified throughout the project.

This process is performed once or at predefined points in the project. The inputs, tools and techniques, and outputs are shown in Figure 5-27. Figure 5-28 presents the data flow diagram for this process.

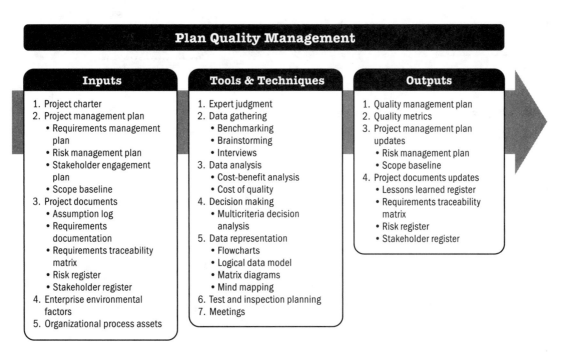

Plan Quality Management

Inputs	Tools & Techniques	Outputs
1. Project charter	1. Expert judgment	1. Quality management plan
2. Project management plan	2. Data gathering	2. Quality metrics
• Requirements management plan	• Benchmarking	3. Project management plan updates
• Risk management plan	• Brainstorming	• Risk management plan
• Stakeholder engagement plan	• Interviews	• Scope baseline
• Scope baseline	3. Data analysis	4. Project documents updates
3. Project documents	• Cost-benefit analysis	• Lessons learned register
• Assumption log	• Cost of quality	• Requirements traceability matrix
• Requirements documentation	4. Decision making	• Risk register
• Requirements traceability matrix	• Multicriteria decision analysis	• Stakeholder register
• Risk register	5. Data representation	
• Stakeholder register	• Flowcharts	
4. Enterprise environmental factors	• Logical data model	
5. Organizational process assets	• Matrix diagrams	
	• Mind mapping	
	6. Test and inspection planning	
	7. Meetings	

Note: This figure provides the inputs, tools and techniques, and outputs that may be used for this process. Descriptions for inputs and outputs appear in Section 9. Descriptions for tools and techniques appear in Section 10.

Figure 5-27. Plan Quality Management: Inputs, Tools & Techniques, and Outputs

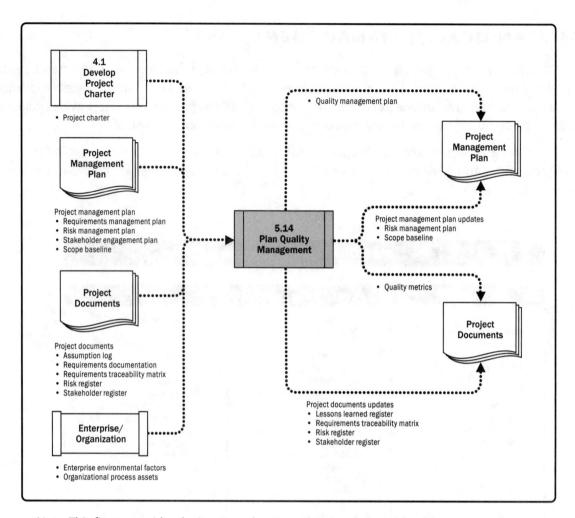

Note: This figure provides the inputs and outputs that may be used for this process. Descriptions for inputs and outputs appear in Section 9.

Figure 5-28. Plan Quality Management: Data Flow Diagram

Quality planning should be performed in parallel with the other planning processes. For example, changes proposed in the deliverables in order to meet identified quality standards may require cost or schedule adjustments and a detailed risk analysis of the impact to plans.

The quality planning techniques discussed here are those used most frequently on projects. There are many others that may be useful on certain projects or in specific application areas.

5.15 PLAN RESOURCE MANAGEMENT

Plan Resource Management is the process of defining how to estimate, acquire, manage, and use team and physical resources. The key benefit of this process is that it establishes the approach and level of management effort needed for managing project resources based on the type and complexity of the project.

This process is performed once or at predefined points in the project. The inputs, tools and techniques, and outputs are shown in Figure 5-29. Figure 5-30 presents the data flow diagram for this process.

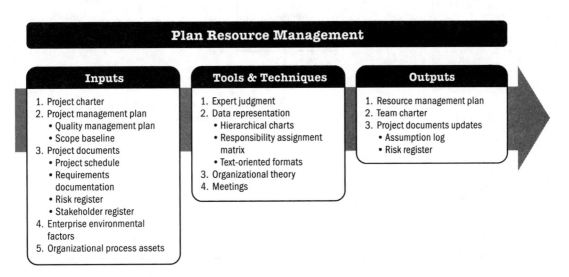

Plan Resource Management		
Inputs	**Tools & Techniques**	**Outputs**

1. Project charter
2. Project management plan
  • Quality management plan
  • Scope baseline
3. Project documents
  • Project schedule
  • Requirements documentation
  • Risk register
  • Stakeholder register
4. Enterprise environmental factors
5. Organizational process assets
	1. Expert judgment
	2. Data representation
	  • Hierarchical charts
	  • Responsibility assignment matrix
	  • Text-oriented formats
	3. Organizational theory
	4. Meetings
		1. Resource management plan
		2. Team charter
		3. Project documents updates
		  • Assumption log
		  • Risk register

Note: This figure provides the inputs, tools and techniques, and outputs that may be used for this process. Descriptions for inputs and outputs appear in Section 9. Descriptions for tools and techniques appear in Section 10.

Figure 5-29. Plan Resource Management: Inputs, Tools & Techniques, and Outputs

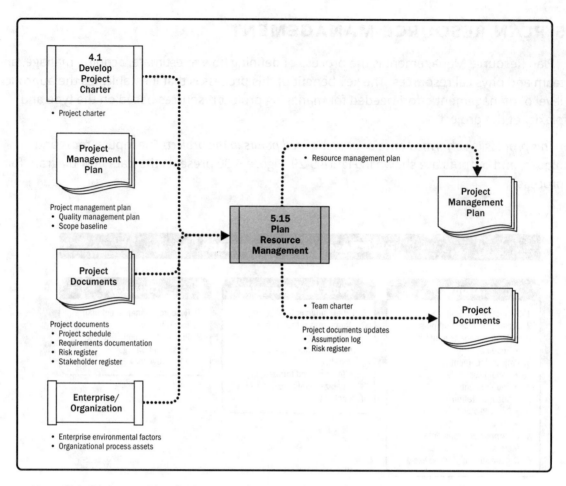

Note: This figure provides the inputs and outputs that may be used for this process. Descriptions for inputs and outputs appear in Section 9.

Figure 5-30. Plan Resource Management: Data Flow Diagram

Resource planning is used to determine and identify an approach to ensure that sufficient resources are available for the successful completion of the project. Project resources may include team members, supplies, materials, equipment, services, and facilities. Effective resource planning should consider and plan for the availability of, or competition for, scarce resources.

Project resources can be obtained from the organization's internal assets or from outside the organization through a procurement process. Other projects may be competing for the same resources required for the project at the same time and location. This may significantly impact project costs, schedules, risks, quality, and other project areas.

5.16 ESTIMATE ACTIVITY RESOURCES

Estimate Activity Resources is the process of estimating team resources and the type and quantities of materials, equipment, and supplies necessary to perform project work. The key benefit of this process is that it identifies the type, quantity, and characteristics of resources required to complete the project.

This process is performed periodically throughout the project as needed. The inputs, tools and techniques, and outputs are shown in Figure 5-31. Figure 5-32 presents the data flow diagram for this process.

Estimate Activity Resources

Inputs	Tools & Techniques	Outputs
1. Project management plan • Resource management plan • Scope baseline 2. Project documents • Activity attributes • Activity list • Assumption log • Cost estimates • Resource calendars • Risk register 3. Enterprise environmental factors 4. Organizational process assets	1. Expert judgment 2. Bottom-up estimating 3. Analogous estimating 4. Parametric estimating 5. Data analysis • Alternatives analysis 6. Project management information system 7. Meetings	1. Resource requirements 2. Basis of estimates 3. Resource breakdown structure 4. Project documents updates • Activity attributes • Assumption log • Lessons learned register

Note: This figure provides the inputs, tools and techniques, and outputs that may be used for this process. Descriptions for inputs and outputs appear in Section 9. Descriptions for tools and techniques appear in Section 10.

Figure 5-31. Estimate Activity Resources: Inputs, Tools & Techniques, and Outputs

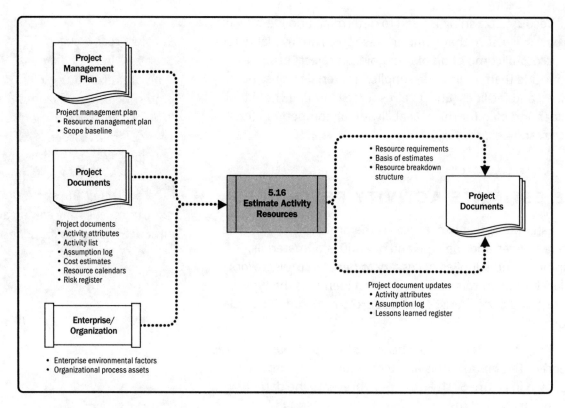

Note: This figure provides the inputs and outputs that may be used for this process. Descriptions for inputs and outputs appear in Section 9.

Figure 5-32. Estimate Activity Resources: Data Flow Diagram

The Estimate Activity Resources process is closely coordinated with other processes, such as the Estimate Costs process. For example:

▶ A construction project team will need to be familiar with local building codes. Such knowledge is often readily available from local sellers. If the internal labor pool lacks experience with unusual or specialized construction techniques, the additional cost for a consultant may be the most effective way to secure knowledge of the local building codes.

▶ An automotive design team will need to be familiar with the latest automated assembly techniques. The requisite knowledge could be obtained by hiring a consultant, by sending a designer to a seminar on robotics, or by including someone from manufacturing as a member of the project team.

5.17 PLAN COMMUNICATIONS MANAGEMENT

Plan Communications Management is the process of developing an appropriate approach and plan for project communications activities based on the information needs of each stakeholder or group, available organizational assets, and the needs of the project. The key benefit of this process is a documented approach to effectively and efficiently engage stakeholders by presenting relevant information in a timely manner.

This process is performed periodically throughout the project as needed. The inputs, tools and techniques, and outputs are shown in Figure 5-33. Figure 5-34 presents the data flow diagram for the process.

Plan Communications Management

Inputs	Tools & Techniques	Outputs
1. Project charter 2. Project management plan • Resource management plan • Stakeholder engagement plan 3. Project documents • Requirements documentation • Stakeholder register 4. Enterprise environmental factors 5. Organizational process assets	1. Expert judgment 2. Communication requirements analysis 3. Communication technology 4. Communication models 5. Communication methods 6. Interpersonal and team skills • Communication styles assessment • Political awareness • Cultural awareness 7. Data representation • Stakeholder engagement assessment matrix 8. Meetings	1. Communications management plan 2. Project management plan updates • Stakeholder engagement plan 3. Project documents updates • Project schedule • Stakeholder register

Note: This figure provides the inputs, tools and techniques, and outputs that may be used for this process. Descriptions for inputs and outputs appear in Section 9. Descriptions for tools and techniques appear in Section 10.

Figure 5-33. Plan Communications Management: Inputs, Tools & Techniques, and Outputs

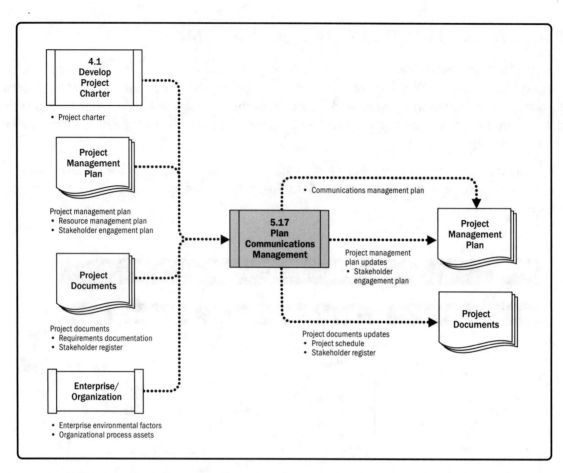

Note: This figure provides the inputs and outputs that may be used for this process. Descriptions for inputs and outputs appear in Section 9.

Figure 5-34. Plan Communications Management: Data Flow Diagram

An effective communications management plan that recognizes the diverse information needs of the project's stakeholders is developed early in the project life cycle. It should be reviewed regularly and modified when necessary, when the stakeholder community changes or at the start of each new project phase.

On most projects, communications planning is performed very early, during stakeholder identification and project management plan development.

While all projects share the need to communicate project information, the information needs and methods of distribution may vary widely. In addition, the methods of storage, retrieval, and ultimate disposition of the project information need to be considered and documented during this process. The results of the Plan Communications Management process should be reviewed regularly throughout the project and revised as needed to ensure continued applicability

5.18 PLAN RISK MANAGEMENT

Plan Risk Management is the process of defining how to conduct risk management activities for a project. The key benefit of this process is that it ensures that the degree, type, and visibility of risk management are proportionate to both risks and the importance of the project to the organization and other stakeholders.

This process is performed once or at predefined points in the project. The inputs, tools and techniques, and outputs are shown in Figure 5-35. Figure 5-36 presents the data flow diagram for this process.

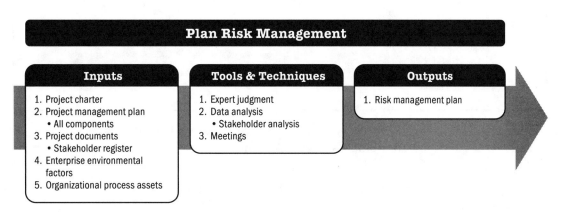

Note: This figure provides the inputs, tools and techniques, and outputs that may be used for this process. Descriptions for inputs and outputs appear in Section 9. Descriptions for tools and techniques appear in Section 10.

Figure 5-35. Plan Risk Management: Inputs, Tools & Techniques, and Outputs

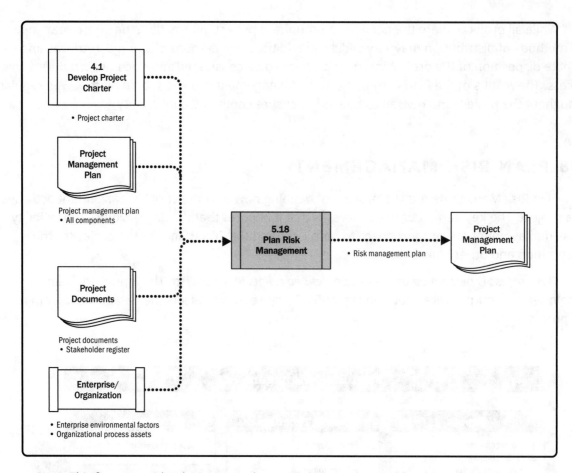

Note: This figure provides the inputs and outputs that may be used for this process. Descriptions for inputs and outputs appear in Section 9.

Figure 5-36. Plan Risk Management: Data Flow Diagram

The Plan Risk Management process should begin when a project is conceived and should be completed early in the project. It may be necessary to revisit this process later in the project life cycle, for example at a major phase change, if the project scope changes significantly, or if a subsequent review of risk management effectiveness determines that the Plan Risk Management process requires modification.

5.19 IDENTIFY RISKS

Identify Risks is the process of identifying individual project risks as well as sources of overall project risk and documenting their characteristics. The key benefit of this process is the documentation of existing individual project risks and the sources of overall project risk. It also brings together information so the project team can respond appropriately to identified risks.

This process is performed throughout the project. The inputs, tools and techniques, and outputs are shown in Figure 5-37. Figure 5-38 presents the data flow diagram for this process.

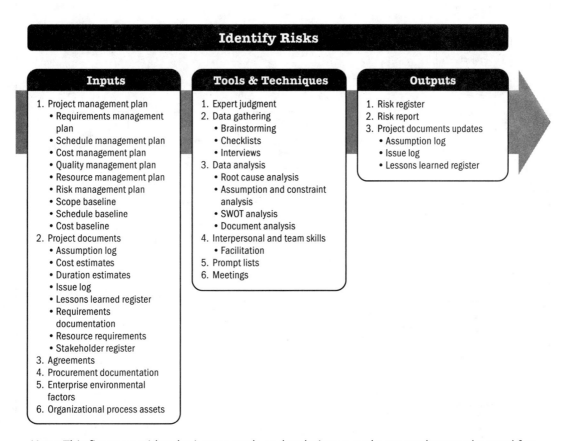

Note: This figure provides the inputs, tools and techniques, and outputs that may be used for this process. Descriptions for inputs and outputs appear in Section 9. Descriptions for tools and techniques appear in Section 10.

Figure 5-37. Identify Risks: Inputs, Tools & Techniques, and Outputs

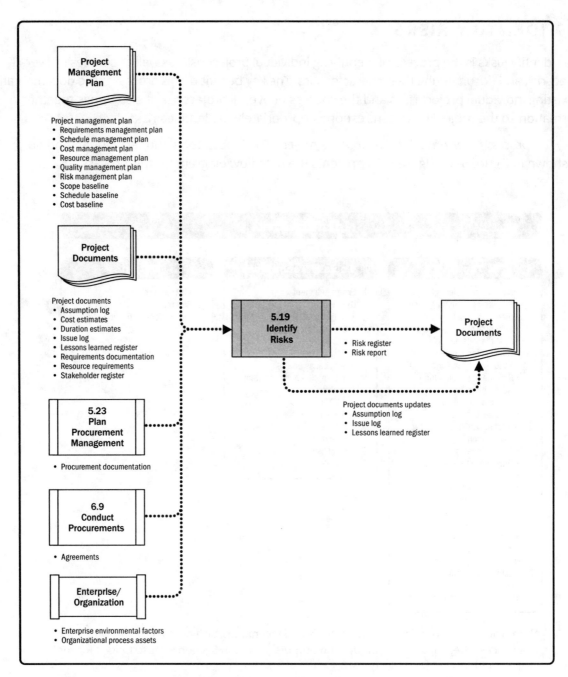

Note: This figure provides the inputs and outputs that may be used for this process. Descriptions for inputs and outputs appear in Section 9.

Figure 5-38. Identify Risks: Data Flow Diagram

Identify Risks considers both individual project risks and sources of overall project risk. Participants in risk identification activities may include the following: project manager, project team members, business analyst, project risk specialist (if assigned), customers, subject matter experts from outside the project team, end users, other project managers, operations managers, stakeholders, and risk management experts within the organization. While these personnel are often key participants for risk identification, all project stakeholders should be encouraged to identify individual project risks. It is particularly important to involve the project team so they can develop and maintain a sense of ownership and responsibility for identified individual project risks, the level of overall project risk, and associated risk response actions.

When describing and recording individual project risks, a consistent format should be used for risk statements to ensure that each risk is understood clearly and unambiguously in order to support effective analysis and risk response development. Risk owners for individual project risks may be nominated as part of the Identify Risks process and will be confirmed during the Perform Qualitative Risk Analysis process. Preliminary risk responses may also be identified and recorded and will be reviewed and confirmed as part of the Plan Risk Responses process.

Identify Risks is an iterative process, since new individual project risks may emerge as the project progresses through its life cycle and the level of overall project risk will also change. The frequency of iteration and participation in each risk identification cycle will vary by situation, and this will be defined in the risk management plan.

5.20 PERFORM QUALITATIVE RISK ANALYSIS

Perform Qualitative Risk Analysis is the process of prioritizing individual project risks for further analysis or action by assessing their probability of occurrence and impact as well as other characteristics. The key benefit of this process is that it focuses efforts on high-priority risks.

This process is performed throughout the project. The inputs, tools and techniques, and outputs are shown in Figure 5-39. Figure 5-40 presents the data flow diagram for this process.

Perform Qualitative Risk Analysis

Inputs	Tools & Techniques	Outputs

1. Project management plan
  • Risk management plan
2. Project documents
  • Assumption log
  • Risk register
  • Stakeholder register
3. Enterprise environmental factors
4. Organizational process assets
	1. Expert judgment
	2. Data gathering
	  • Interviews
	3. Data analysis
	  • Risk data quality assessment
	  • Risk probability and impact assessment
	  • Assessment of other risk parameters
	4. Interpersonal and team skills
	  • Facilitation
	5. Risk categorization
	6. Data representation
	  • Probability and impact matrix
	  • Hierarchical charts
	7. Meetings
		1. Project documents updates
		  • Assumption log
		  • Issue log
		  • Risk register
		  • Risk report

Note: This figure provides the inputs, tools and techniques, and outputs that may be used for this process. Descriptions for inputs and outputs appear in Section 9. Descriptions for tools and techniques appear in Section 10.

Figure 5-39. Perform Qualitative Risk Analysis: Inputs, Tools & Techniques, and Outputs

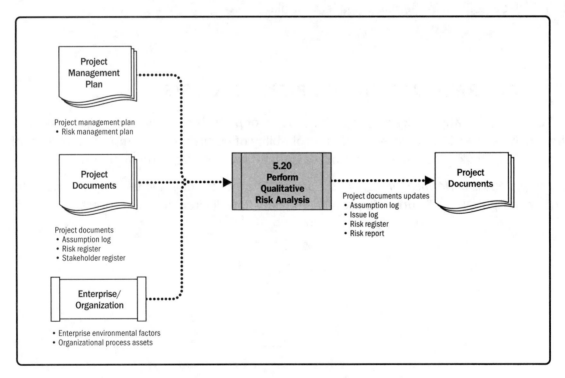

Note: This figure provides the inputs and outputs that may be used for this process. Descriptions for inputs and outputs appear in Section 9.

Figure 5-40. Perform Qualitative Risk Analysis: Data Flow Diagram

Perform Qualitative Risk Analysis assesses the priority of identified individual project risks using their probability of occurrence, the corresponding impact on project objectives if the risks occur, and other factors. Such assessments are subjective as they are based on perceptions of risk by the project team and other stakeholders. Effective assessment therefore requires explicit identification and management of the risk attitudes of key participants in the Perform Qualitative Risk Analysis process. Risk perception introduces bias into the assessment of identified risks, so attention should be paid to identifying bias and correcting for it. Where a facilitator is used to support the Perform Qualitative Risk Analysis process, addressing bias is a key part of the facilitator's role. An evaluation of the quality of the available information on individual project risks also helps to clarify the assessment of each risk's importance to the project.

Perform Qualitative Risk Analysis establishes the relative priorities of individual project risks for Plan Risk Responses. It identifies a risk owner for each risk who will take responsibility for planning an appropriate risk response and ensuring that it is implemented. Perform Qualitative Risk Analysis also lays the foundation for Perform Quantitative Risk Analysis if this process is required.

The Perform Qualitative Risk Analysis process is performed regularly throughout the project life cycle, as defined in the risk management plan. Often, in an agile development environment, the Perform Qualitative Risk Analysis process is conducted before the start of each iteration.

5.21 PERFORM QUANTITATIVE RISK ANALYSIS

Perform Quantitative Risk Analysis is the process of numerically analyzing the combined effect of identified individual project risks and other sources of uncertainty on overall project objectives. The key benefit of this process is that it quantifies overall project risk exposure, and it can also provide additional quantitative risk information to support risk response planning.

This process is not required for every project, but where it is used, it is performed throughout the project. The inputs and outputs are shown in Figure 5-41. Figure 5-42 presents the data flow diagram for this process.

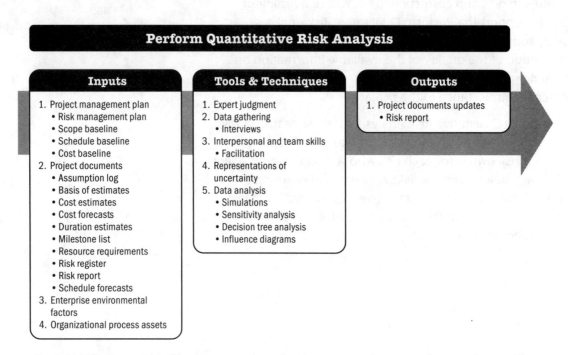

Note: This figure provides the inputs, tools and techniques, and outputs that may be used for this process. Descriptions for inputs and outputs appear in Section 9. Descriptions for tools and techniques appear in Section 10.

Figure 5-41. Perform Quantitative Risk Analysis: Inputs, Tools & Techniques, and Outputs

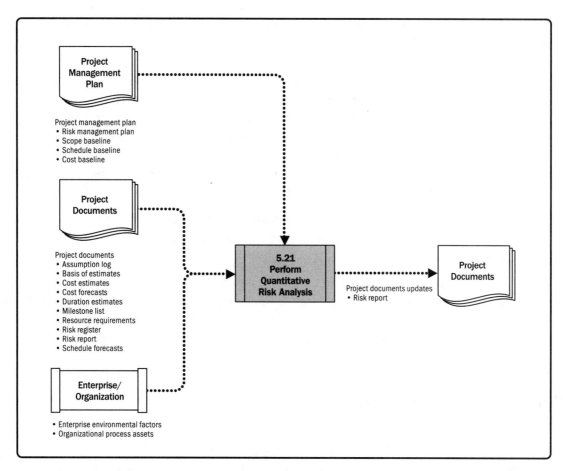

Note: This figure provides the inputs and outputs that may be used for this process. Descriptions for inputs and outputs appear in Section 9.

Figure 5-42. Perform Quantitative Risk Analysis: Data Flow Diagram

Perform Quantitative Risk Analysis is not required for all projects. Undertaking a robust analysis depends on the availability of high-quality data about individual project risks and other sources of uncertainty, as well as a sound underlying project baseline for scope, schedule, and cost. Quantitative risk analysis usually requires specialized risk software and expertise in the development and interpretation of risk models. It also consumes additional time and cost. The use of quantitative risk analysis for a project will be specified in the project's risk management plan. It is most likely appropriate for large or complex projects, strategically important projects, projects for which it is a contractual requirement, or projects in which a key stakeholder requires it. Quantitative risk analysis is the only reliable method to assess overall project risk through evaluating the aggregated effect on project outcomes of all individual project risks and other sources of uncertainty.

Perform Quantitative Risk Analysis uses information on individual project risks that have been assessed by the Perform Qualitative Risk Analysis process as having a significant potential to affect the project's objectives.

Outputs from Perform Quantitative Risk Analysis are used as inputs to the Plan Risk Responses process, particularly in recommending responses to the level of overall project risk and key individual risks. A quantitative risk analysis may also be undertaken following the Plan Risk Responses process to determine the likely effectiveness of planned responses in reducing overall project risk exposure.

5.22 PLAN RISK RESPONSES

Plan Risk Responses is the process of developing options, selecting strategies, and agreeing on actions to address overall project risk exposure as well as to treat individual project risks. The key benefit of this process is that it identifies appropriate ways to address overall project risk and individual project risks. This process also allocates resources and inserts activities into project documents and the project management plan as needed.

This process is performed throughout the project. The inputs, tools and techniques, and outputs are shown in Figure 5-43. Figure 5-44 presents the data flow diagram for this process.

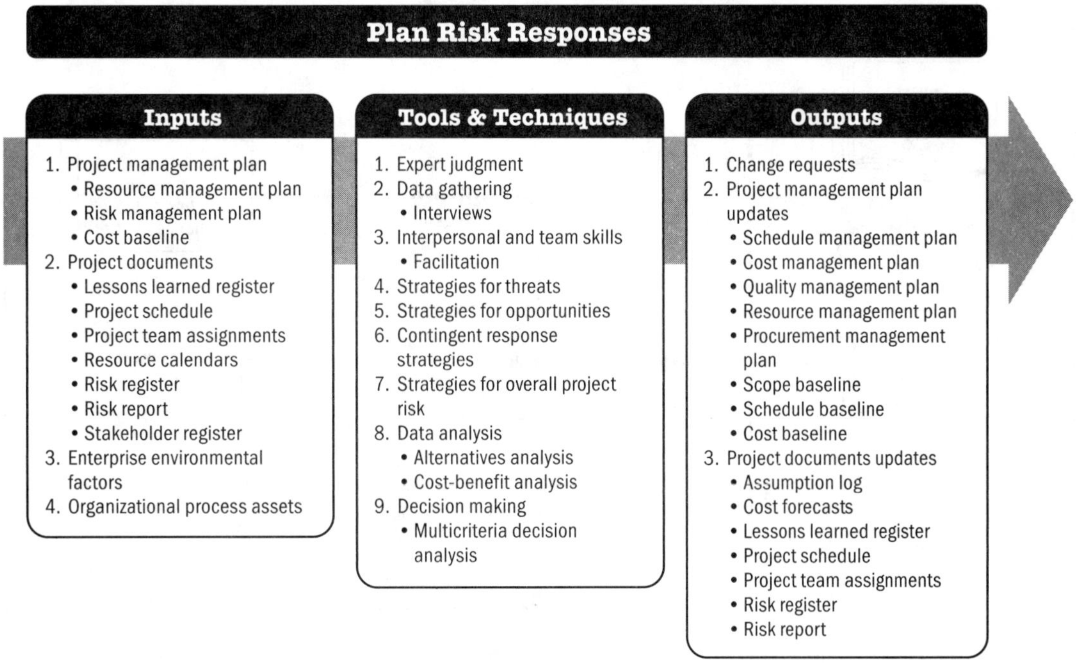

Plan Risk Responses

Inputs	Tools & Techniques	Outputs

1. Project management plan
  • Resource management plan
  • Risk management plan
  • Cost baseline
2. Project documents
  • Lessons learned register
  • Project schedule
  • Project team assignments
  • Resource calendars
  • Risk register
  • Risk report
  • Stakeholder register
3. Enterprise environmental factors
4. Organizational process assets
	1. Expert judgment
	2. Data gathering
	  • Interviews
	3. Interpersonal and team skills
	  • Facilitation
	4. Strategies for threats
	5. Strategies for opportunities
	6. Contingent response strategies
	7. Strategies for overall project risk
	8. Data analysis
	  • Alternatives analysis
	  • Cost-benefit analysis
	9. Decision making
	  • Multicriteria decision analysis
		1. Change requests
		2. Project management plan updates
		  • Schedule management plan
		  • Cost management plan
		  • Quality management plan
		  • Resource management plan
		  • Procurement management plan
		  • Scope baseline
		  • Schedule baseline
		  • Cost baseline
		3. Project documents updates
		  • Assumption log
		  • Cost forecasts
		  • Lessons learned register
		  • Project schedule
		  • Project team assignments
		  • Risk register
		  • Risk report

Note: This figure provides the inputs, tools and techniques, and outputs that may be used for this process. Descriptions for inputs and outputs appear in Section 9. Descriptions for tools and techniques appear in Section 10.

Figure 5-43. Plan Risk Responses: Inputs, Tools & Techniques, and Outputs

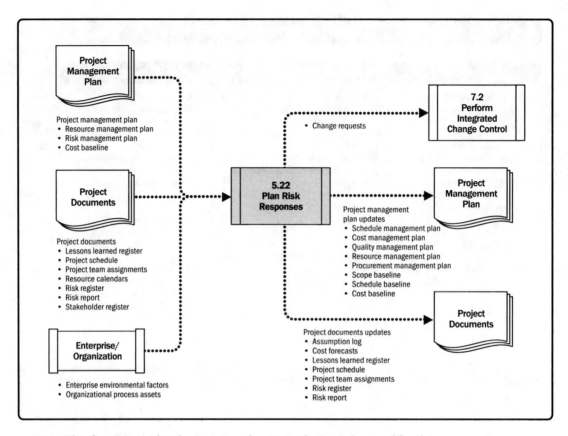

Note: This figure provides the inputs and outputs that may be used for this process. Descriptions for inputs and outputs appear in Section 9.

Figure 5-44. Plan Risk Responses: Data Flow Diagram

Effective and appropriate risk responses can minimize individual threats, maximize individual opportunities, and reduce overall project risk exposure. Unsuitable risk responses can have the converse effect. Once risks have been identified, analyzed, and prioritized, plans should be developed by the nominated risk owner for addressing every individual project risk the project team considers to be sufficiently important, either because of the threat it poses to the project objectives or the opportunity it offers. The project manager should also consider how to respond appropriately to the current level of overall project risk.

Risk responses should be appropriate for the significance of the risk, cost effective in meeting the challenge, realistic within the project context, agreed upon by all parties involved, and owned by a responsible person. Selecting the optimal risk response from several options is often required. The strategy or mix of strategies most likely to be effective should be selected for each risk. Structured decision-making techniques may be used to choose the most appropriate response. For large or complex projects, it may be appropriate to use a mathematical optimization model or real options analysis as a basis for a more robust economic analysis of alternative risk response strategies.

Specific actions are developed to implement the agreed-upon risk response strategy, including primary and backup strategies, as necessary. A contingency plan (or fallback plan) can be developed for implementation if the selected strategy turns out not to be fully effective or if an accepted risk occurs. Secondary risks should also be identified. Secondary risks are risks that arise as a direct result of implementing a risk response. A contingency reserve is often allocated for time or cost. If developed, it may include identification of the conditions that trigger its use.

5.23 PLAN PROCUREMENT MANAGEMENT

Plan Procurement Management is the process of documenting project procurement decisions, specifying the approach, and identifying potential sellers. The key benefit of this process is that it determines whether to acquire goods and services from outside the project and, if so, what to acquire as well as how and when to acquire it. Goods and services may be procured from other parts of the performing organization or from external sources.

This process is performed once or at predefined points in the project. The inputs, tools and techniques, and outputs are shown in Figure 5-45. Figure 5-46 presents the data flow diagram for this process.

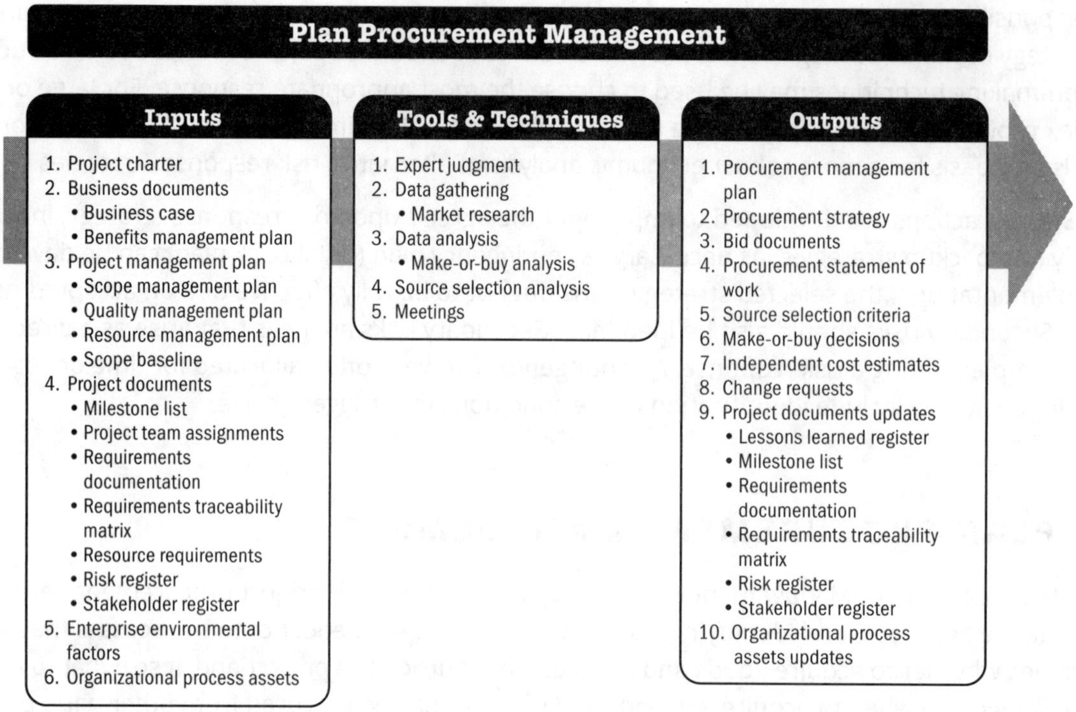

Plan Procurement Management

Inputs	Tools & Techniques	Outputs

1. Project charter
2. Business documents
  • Business case
  • Benefits management plan
3. Project management plan
  • Scope management plan
  • Quality management plan
  • Resource management plan
  • Scope baseline
4. Project documents
  • Milestone list
  • Project team assignments
  • Requirements documentation
  • Requirements traceability matrix
  • Resource requirements
  • Risk register
  • Stakeholder register
5. Enterprise environmental factors
6. Organizational process assets
	1. Expert judgment
	2. Data gathering
	  • Market research
	3. Data analysis
	  • Make-or-buy analysis
	4. Source selection analysis
	5. Meetings
		1. Procurement management plan
		2. Procurement strategy
		3. Bid documents
		4. Procurement statement of work
		5. Source selection criteria
		6. Make-or-buy decisions
		7. Independent cost estimates
		8. Change requests
		9. Project documents updates
		  • Lessons learned register
		  • Milestone list
		  • Requirements documentation
		  • Requirements traceability matrix
		  • Risk register
		  • Stakeholder register
		10. Organizational process assets updates

Note: This figure provides the inputs, tools and techniques, and outputs that may be used for this process. Descriptions for inputs and outputs appear in Section 9. Descriptions for tools and techniques appear in Section 10.

Figure 5-45. Plan Procurement Management: Inputs, Tools & Techniques, and Outputs

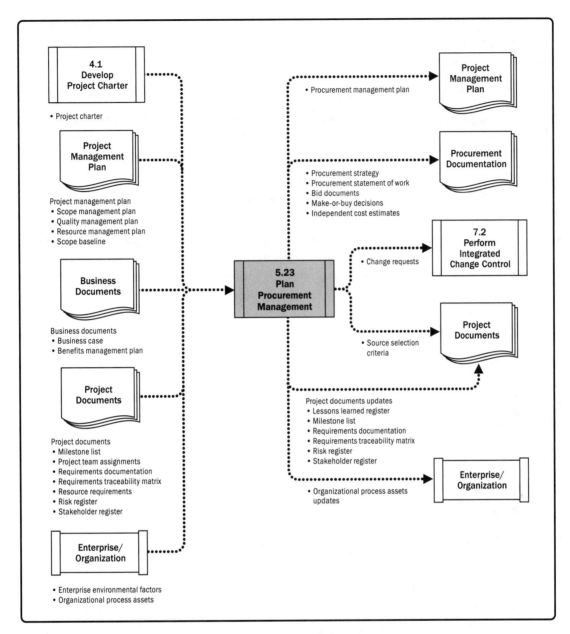

Note: This figure provides the inputs and outputs that may be used for this process. Descriptions for inputs and outputs appear in Section 9.

Figure 5-46. Plan Procurement Management: Data Flow Diagram

Typical Steps in the Plan Procurement Management Process

▶ Prepare the procurement statement of work (SOW) or terms of reference (TOR).

▶ Prepare a high-level cost estimate to determine the budget.

▶ Advertise the opportunity.

▶ Identify a short list of qualified sellers.

▶ Prepare and issue bid documents.

▶ Prepare and submit proposals by the seller.

▶ Conduct a technical evaluation of the proposals including quality.

▶ Perform a cost evaluation of the proposals.

▶ Prepare the final combined quality and cost evaluation to select the winning proposal.

▶ Finalize negotiations and sign contract between the buyer and the seller.

Defining roles and responsibilities related to procurement should be done early in the Plan Procurement Management process. The project manager should ensure that the project team is staffed with procurement expertise at the level required for the project. Participants in the procurement process may include personnel from the purchasing or procurement department as well as personnel from the buying organization's legal department. These responsibilities should be documented in the procurement management plan.

The requirements of the project schedule can significantly influence the strategy during the Plan Procurement Management process. Decisions made in developing the procurement management plan can also influence the project schedule and are integrated with the Develop Schedule process, the Estimate Activity Resources process, and make-or-buy decisions.

5.24 PLAN STAKEHOLDER ENGAGEMENT

Plan Stakeholder Engagement is the process of developing approaches to involve project stakeholders based on their needs, expectations, interests, and potential impact on the project. The key benefit is that it provides an actionable plan to interact effectively with stakeholders.

This process is performed periodically throughout the project as needed. The inputs, tools and techniques, and outputs are shown in Figure 5-47. Figure 5-48 presents the data flow diagram for this process.

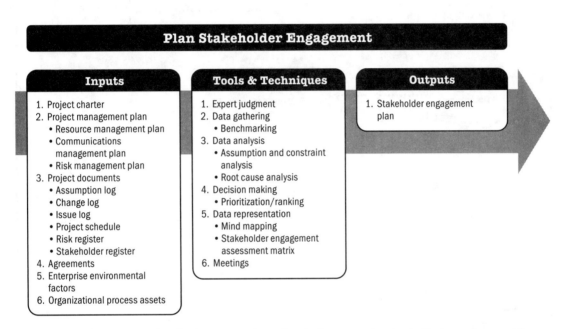

Note: This figure provides the inputs, tools and techniques, and outputs that may be used for this process. Descriptions for inputs and outputs appear in Section 9. Descriptions for tools and techniques appear in Section 10.

Figure 5-47. Plan Stakeholder Engagement: Inputs, Tools & Techniques, and Outputs

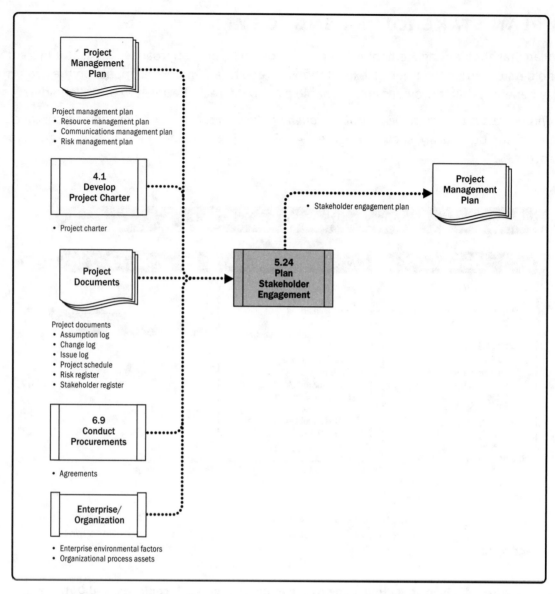

Note: This figure provides the inputs and outputs that may be used for this process. Descriptions for inputs and outputs appear in Section 9.

Figure 5-48. Plan Stakeholder Engagement: Data Flow Diagram

Process Groups: A Practice Guide

An effective plan that recognizes the diverse information needs of the project's stakeholders is developed early in the project life cycle and is reviewed and updated regularly as the stakeholder community changes. The first version of the stakeholder engagement plan is developed after the initial stakeholder community has been identified by the Identify Stakeholder process. The stakeholder engagement plan is updated regularly to reflect changes to the stakeholder community.

Situations Requiring Updates to the Stakeholder Engagement Plan

Typical trigger situations requiring updates to the plan include, but are not limited to:

▶ The start of a new phase of the project;

▶ Changes to the organizational structure or changes within the industry;

▶ New individuals or groups become stakeholders, current stakeholders are no longer part of the stakeholder community, or there are changes regarding the importance of particular stakeholders to the project's success; and

▶ Outputs of other project processes, such as change management, risk management, or issue management, require a review of stakeholder engagement strategies.

Executing Process Group

The processes in the Executing Process Group are shown in Table 6-1.

Table 6-1. Executing Process Group Processes

Executing Processes	
6.1 Direct and Manage Project Work	6.6 Manage Team
6.2 Manage Project Knowledge	6.7 Manage Communications
6.3 Manage Quality	6.8 Implement Risk Responses
6.4 Acquire Resources	6.9 Conduct Procurements
6.5 Develop Team	6.10 Manage Stakeholder Engagement

The Executing Process Group consists of those processes performed to complete the work defined in the project management plan to satisfy the project requirements. This Process Group involves coordinating resources, managing stakeholder engagement, and integrating and performing the activities of the project in accordance with the project management plan. The key benefit of this Process Group is that the work needed to meet the project requirements and objectives is performed according to plan. A large portion of the project budget, resources, and time is expended in performing the Executing Process Group processes. The processes in the Executing Process Group may generate change requests. If approved, the change requests may trigger one or more Planning processes that result in a modified management plan, project documents, and possibly new baselines. The Executing Process Group includes the project management processes identified in Sections 6.1 through 6.10.

6.1 DIRECT AND MANAGE PROJECT WORK

Direct and Manage Project Work is the process of leading and performing the work defined in the project management plan and implementing approved changes to achieve the project's objectives. The key benefit of this process is that it provides overall management of the project work and deliverables, thus improving the probability of project success.

This process is performed throughout the project. The inputs, tools and techniques, and outputs are shown in Figure 6-1. Figure 6-2 presents the data flow diagram for this process.

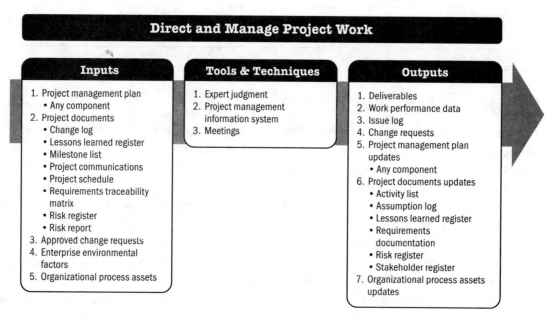

Direct and Manage Project Work

Inputs	Tools & Techniques	Outputs

1. Project management plan
  • Any component
2. Project documents
  • Change log
  • Lessons learned register
  • Milestone list
  • Project communications
  • Project schedule
  • Requirements traceability matrix
  • Risk register
  • Risk report
3. Approved change requests
4. Enterprise environmental factors
5. Organizational process assets
	1. Expert judgment
	2. Project management information system
	3. Meetings
		1. Deliverables
		2. Work performance data
		3. Issue log
		4. Change requests
		5. Project management plan updates
		  • Any component
		6. Project documents updates
		  • Activity list
		  • Assumption log
		  • Lessons learned register
		  • Requirements documentation
		  • Risk register
		  • Stakeholder register
		7. Organizational process assets updates

Note: This figure provides the inputs, tools and techniques, and outputs that may be used for this process. Descriptions for inputs and outputs appear in Section 9. Descriptions for tools and techniques appear in Section 10.

Figure 6-1. Direct and Manage Project Work: Inputs, Tools & Techniques, and Outputs

Process Groups: A Practice Guide

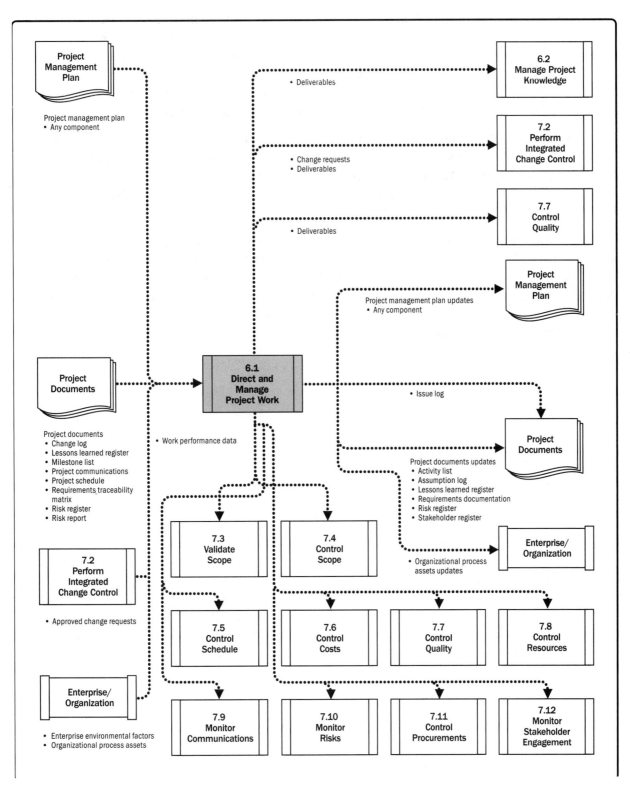

Note: This figure provides the inputs and outputs that may be used for this process. Descriptions for inputs and outputs appear in Section 9.

Figure 6-2. Direct and Manage Project Work: Data Flow Diagram

Direct and Manage Project Work involves executing the planned project activities to complete project deliverables and accomplish established objectives. Available resources are allocated, their efficient use is managed, and changes in project plans stemming from analyzing work performance data and information are carried out. The Direct and Manage Project Work process is directly affected by the project application area. Deliverables are produced as outputs from processes performed to accomplish the project work as planned and scheduled in the project management plan.

The project manager, along with the project management team, directs the performance of the planned project activities and manages the various technical and organizational interfaces that exist in the project. Direct and Manage Project Work also requires review of the impact of all project changes and the implementation of approved changes: corrective action, preventive action, and/or defect repair.

During project execution, the work performance data are collected and communicated to the applicable controlling processes for analysis. Work performance data analysis provides information about the completion status of deliverables and other relevant details about project performance. The work performance data will also be used as an input to the Monitoring and Controlling Process Group. Work performance data can also be used as feedback into lessons learned to improve the performance of future work packages.

6.2 MANAGE PROJECT KNOWLEDGE

Manage Project Knowledge is the process of using existing knowledge and creating new knowledge to achieve the project's objectives and contribute to organizational learning. The key benefits of this process are that prior organizational knowledge is leveraged to produce or improve the project outcomes, and knowledge created by the project is available to support organizational operations and future projects or phases.

This process is performed throughout the project. The inputs, tools and techniques, and outputs are shown in Figure 6-3. Figure 6-4 presents the data flow diagram for this process.

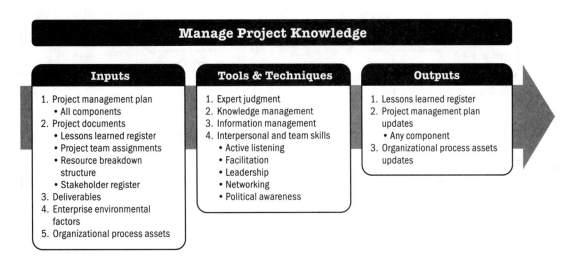

Note: This figure provides the inputs, tools and techniques, and outputs that may be used for this process. Descriptions for inputs and outputs appear in Section 9. Descriptions for tools and techniques appear in Section 10.

Figure 6-3. Manage Project Knowledge: Inputs, Tools & Techniques, and Outputs

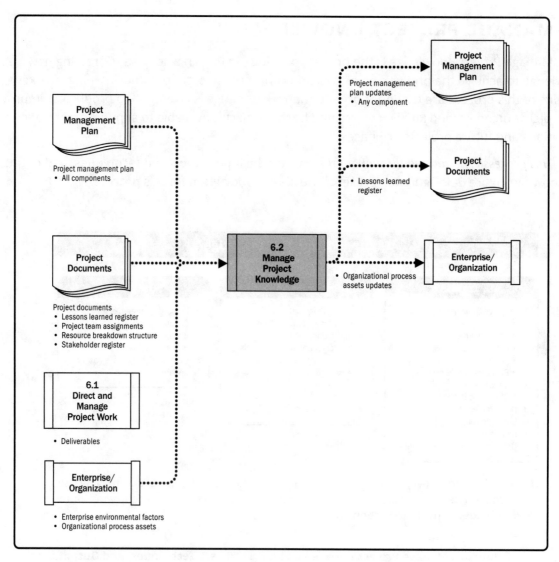

Note: This figure provides the inputs and outputs that may be used for this process. Descriptions for inputs and outputs appear in Section 9.

Figure 6-4. Manage Project Knowledge: Data Flow Diagram

Knowledge is commonly split into "explicit" (knowledge that can be readily codified using words, pictures, and numbers) and "tacit" (knowledge that is personal and difficult to express, such as beliefs, insights, experience, and "know-how"). Knowledge management is concerned with managing both tacit and explicit knowledge for two purposes: reusing existing knowledge and creating new knowledge. The key activities that underpin both purposes are knowledge sharing and knowledge integration (of knowledge from different domains, contextual knowledge, and project management knowledge).

It is a common misconception that managing knowledge involves just documenting it so it can be shared. Another common misconception is that managing knowledge involves just obtaining lessons learned at the end of the project in order to use it in the future projects. Only codified explicit knowledge can be shared in this way. But codified explicit knowledge lacks context and is open to different interpretations, so even though it can easily be shared, it isn't always understood or applied in the right way. Tacit knowledge has context built in but is very difficult to codify. It resides in the minds of individual experts or in social groups and situations, and is normally shared through conversations and interactions between people.

Create an Atmosphere of Trust

From an organizational perspective, knowledge management is about making sure the skills, experience, and expertise of the project team and other stakeholders are used before, during, and after the project. Because knowledge resides in the minds of people and people cannot be forced to share what they know (or to pay attention to others' knowledge), the most important part of knowledge management is creating an atmosphere of trust so that people are motivated to share their knowledge. Even the best knowledge management tools and techniques will not work if people are not motivated to share what they know or to pay attention to what others know. In practice, knowledge is shared using a mixture of knowledge management tools and techniques (interactions between people) and information management tools and techniques (in which people codify part of their explicit knowledge by documenting it so it can be shared).

6.3 MANAGE QUALITY

Manage Quality is the process of translating the quality management plan into executable quality activities that incorporate the organization's quality policies into the project. The key benefits of this process are that it increases the probability of meeting the quality objectives as well as identifying ineffective processes and causes of poor quality. Manage Quality uses the data and results from the Control Quality process to reflect the overall quality status of the project to the stakeholders.

This process is performed throughout the project. The inputs, tools and techniques, and outputs are shown in Figure 6-5. Figure 6-6 presents the data flow diagram for this process.

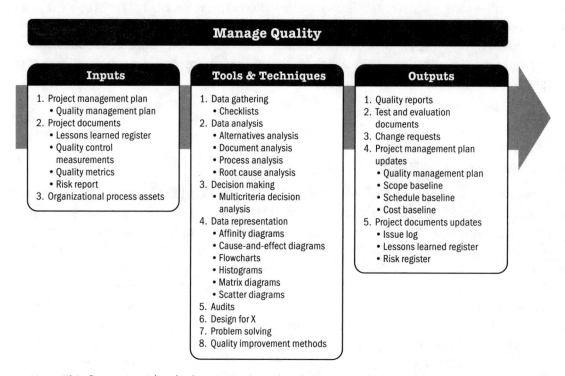

Note: This figure provides the inputs, tools and techniques, and outputs that may be used for this process. Descriptions for inputs and outputs appear in Section 9. Descriptions for tools and techniques appear in Section 10.

Figure 6-5. Manage Quality: Inputs, Tools & Techniques, and Outputs

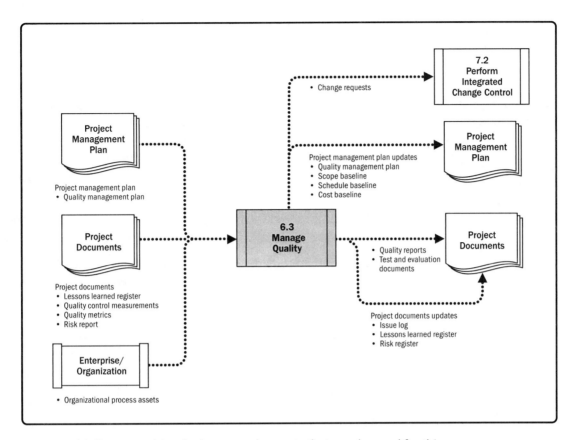

Note: This figure provides the inputs and outputs that may be used for this process. Descriptions for inputs and outputs appear in Section 9.

Figure 6-6. Manage Quality: Data Flow Diagram

Manage Quality is sometimes called quality assurance, although Manage Quality has a broader definition than quality assurance as it is used in non-project work. In project management, the focus of quality assurance is on the processes used in the project. Quality assurance is about using project processes effectively. It involves following and meeting standards to assure stakeholders that the final product will meet their needs, expectations, and requirements. Manage Quality includes all the quality assurance activities and is also concerned with the product design aspects and process improvements. Manage Quality work will fall under the conformance work category in the cost of quality framework.

> *In agile projects, quality management is performed by all team members throughout the project. In traditional projects, quality management is often the responsibility of specific team members.*

The Manage Quality process implements a set of planned and systematic acts and processes defined within the project's quality management plan that helps to:

▶ Design an optimal and mature product by implementing specific design guidelines that address specific aspects of the product,

▶ Build confidence that a future output will be completed in a manner that meets the specified requirements and expectations through quality assurance tools and techniques such as quality audits and failure analysis,

▶ Confirm that the quality processes are used and that their use meets the quality objectives of the project, and

▶ Improve the efficiency and effectiveness of processes and activities to achieve better results and performance and enhance stakeholders' satisfaction.

The project manager and project team may use the organization's quality assurance department, or other organizational functions, to execute some of the Manage Quality activities such as failure analysis, design of experiments, and quality improvement. Quality assurance departments usually have cross-organizational experience in using quality tools and techniques and are a good resource for the project.

Manage Quality is Considered the Work of Everybody

The project manager, the project team, the project sponsor, the management of the performing organization, and even the customer are all involved in this process. These roles have responsibilities for managing quality in the project, though the roles differ in size and effort. The level of participation in the quality management effort may differ between industries and project management styles.

6.4 ACQUIRE RESOURCES

Acquire Resources is the process of obtaining team members, facilities, equipment, materials, supplies, and other resources necessary to complete project work. The key benefit of this process is that it outlines and guides the selection of resources and assigns them to their respective activities.

This process is performed periodically throughout the project as needed. The inputs, tools and techniques, and outputs are shown in Figure 6-7. Figure 6-8 presents the data flow diagram for this process.

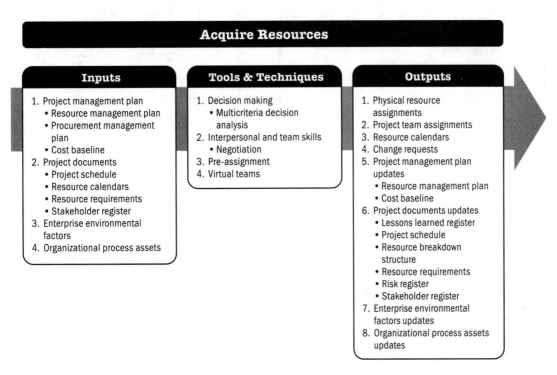

Acquire Resources

Inputs	Tools & Techniques	Outputs

1. Project management plan
  • Resource management plan
  • Procurement management plan
  • Cost baseline
2. Project documents
  • Project schedule
  • Resource calendars
  • Resource requirements
  • Stakeholder register
3. Enterprise environmental factors
4. Organizational process assets
	1. Decision making
	  • Multicriteria decision analysis
	2. Interpersonal and team skills
	  • Negotiation
	3. Pre-assignment
	4. Virtual teams
		1. Physical resource assignments
		2. Project team assignments
		3. Resource calendars
		4. Change requests
		5. Project management plan updates
		  • Resource management plan
		  • Cost baseline
		6. Project documents updates
		  • Lessons learned register
		  • Project schedule
		  • Resource breakdown structure
		  • Resource requirements
		  • Risk register
		  • Stakeholder register
		7. Enterprise environmental factors updates
		8. Organizational process assets updates

Note: This figure provides the inputs, tools and techniques, and outputs that may be used for this process. Descriptions for inputs and outputs appear in Section 9. Descriptions for tools and techniques appear in Section 10.

Figure 6-7. Acquire Resources: Inputs, Tools & Techniques, and Outputs

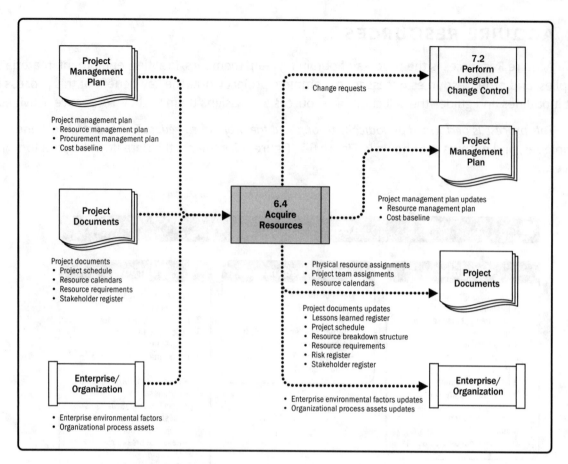

Note: This figure provides the inputs and outputs that may be used for this process. Descriptions for inputs and outputs appear in Section 9.

Figure 6-8. Acquire Resources: Data Flow Diagram

The resources needed for a project can be internal or external to the project-performing organization. Internal resources are acquired (assigned) from functional or resource managers. External resources are acquired through the procurement processes.

The project management team may or may not have direct control over resource selection because of collective bargaining agreements, use of subcontractor personnel, a matrix project environment, internal or external reporting relationships, or other reasons. It is important that the following factors are considered during the process of acquiring the project resources:

- ▶ The project manager or project team should effectively negotiate and influence others who are in a position to provide the required team and physical resources for the project.

- ▶ Failure to acquire the necessary resources for the project may affect project schedules, budgets, customer satisfaction, quality, and risks. Insufficient resources or capabilities decrease the probability of success and, in a worst-case scenario, could result in project cancellation.

- ▶ If the team resources are not available due to constraints such as economic factors or assignment to other projects, the project manager or project team may be required to assign alternative resources, perhaps with different competencies or costs. Alternative resources are allowed provided there is no violation of legal, regulatory, mandatory, or other specific criteria.

These factors should be considered and accounted for in the planning stages of the project. The project manager or project management team will be required to document the impact of the unavailability of required resources in the project schedule, project budget, project risks, project quality, training plans, and other project management plans.

6.5 DEVELOP TEAM

Develop Team is the process of improving competencies, team member interaction, and the overall team environment to enhance project performance. The key benefit of this process is that it results in improved teamwork, enhanced interpersonal skills and competencies, motivated employees, reduced attrition, and improved overall project performance.

This process is performed throughout the project. The inputs, tools and techniques, and outputs are shown in Figure 6-9. Figure 6-10 presents the data flow diagram for this process.

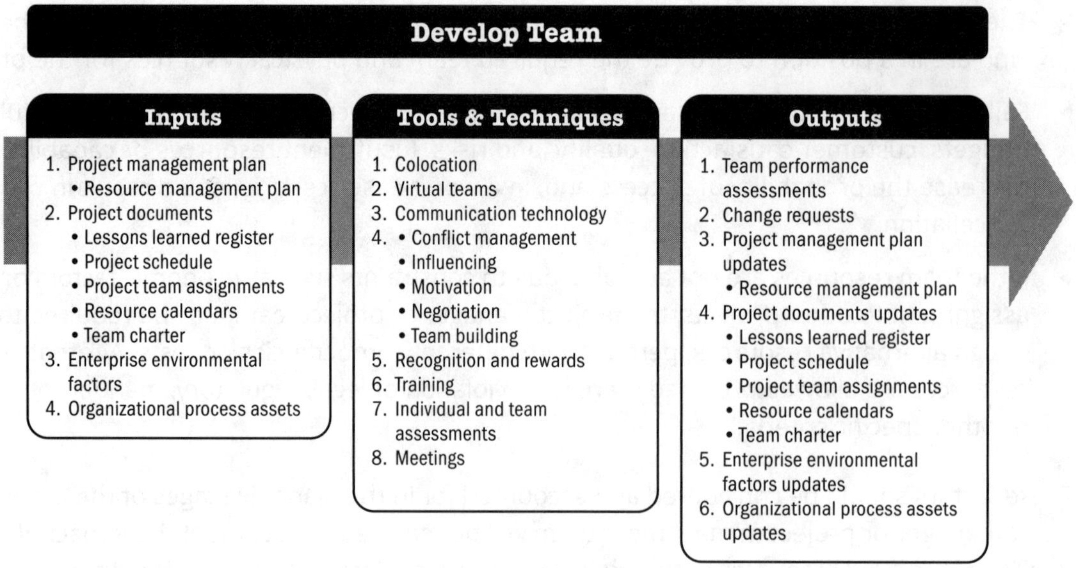

Develop Team

Inputs	Tools & Techniques	Outputs

1. Project management plan
  • Resource management plan
2. Project documents
  • Lessons learned register
  • Project schedule
  • Project team assignments
  • Resource calendars
  • Team charter
3. Enterprise environmental factors
4. Organizational process assets
	1. Colocation
	2. Virtual teams
	3. Communication technology
	4. • Conflict management
	  • Influencing
	  • Motivation
	  • Negotiation
	  • Team building
	5. Recognition and rewards
	6. Training
	7. Individual and team assessments
	8. Meetings
		1. Team performance assessments
		2. Change requests
		3. Project management plan updates
		  • Resource management plan
		4. Project documents updates
		  • Lessons learned register
		  • Project schedule
		  • Project team assignments
		  • Resource calendars
		  • Team charter
		5. Enterprise environmental factors updates
		6. Organizational process assets updates

Note: This figure provides the inputs, tools and techniques, and outputs that may be used for this process. Descriptions for inputs and outputs appear in Section 9. Descriptions for tools and techniques appear in Section 10.

Figure 6-9. Develop Team: Inputs, Tools & Techniques, and Outputs

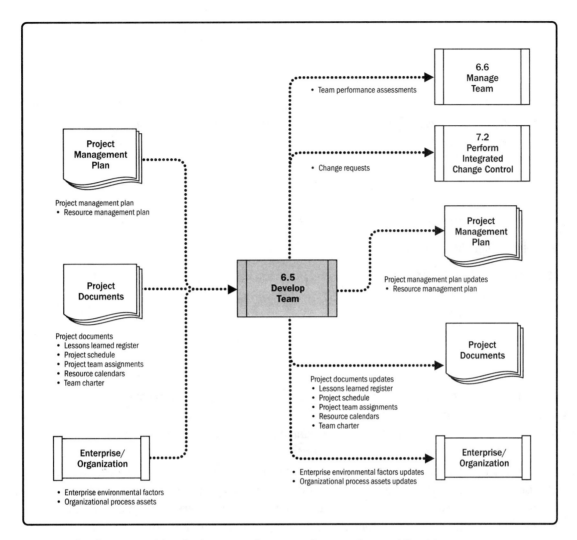

Note: This figure provides the inputs and outputs that may be used for this process. Descriptions for inputs and outputs appear in Section 9.

Figure 6-10. Develop Team: Data Flow Diagram

Project managers require the skills to identify, build, maintain, motivate, lead, and inspire project teams to achieve high team performance and meet the project's objectives. Teamwork is a critical factor for project success. Developing effective project teams is one of the project manager's primary responsibilities.

High-Performing Teams

Project managers should create an environment that facilitates teamwork and continually motivates the team by providing challenges and opportunities, providing timely feedback and support as needed, and recognizing and rewarding good performance. High team performance can be achieved by employing these behaviors:

▶ Use open and effective communication.

▶ Create team-building opportunities.

▶ Develop trust among team members.

▶ Manage conflicts in a constructive manner.

▶ Encourage collaborative problem solving.

▶ Encourage collaborative decision making.

Project managers operate in a global environment and work on projects characterized by cultural diversity. Team members often have diverse industry experience, communicate in multiple languages, and sometimes work with a "team language" or cultural norm that may be different from their native one. The project management team should capitalize on cultural differences, focus on developing and sustaining the project team throughout the project life cycle, and promote working together interdependently in a climate of mutual trust. Developing the project team improves the people skills, technical competencies, and overall team environment and project performance. It requires clear, timely, effective, and efficient communication between team members throughout the life of the project. Objectives of developing a project team include but are not limited to:

▶ Improve the knowledge and skills of team members to increase their ability to complete project deliverables, while lowering costs, reducing schedules, and improving quality.

▶ Improve feelings of trust and agreement among team members to raise morale, lower conflict, and increase teamwork.

Process Groups: A Practice Guide

▶ Create a dynamic, cohesive, and collaborative team culture to: (1) improve individual and team productivity, team spirit, and cooperation; and (2) allow cross-training and mentoring between team members to share knowledge and expertise.

▶ Empower the team to participate in decision making and take ownership of the provided solutions to improve team productivity for more effective and efficient results.

One of the models used to describe team development is the Tuckman ladder, which includes five stages of development that teams may go through. Although it is common for these stages to occur in order, it is not uncommon for a team to get stuck in a particular stage or regress to an earlier stage. Projects with team members who worked together in the past might skip a stage.

▶ **Forming.** This phase is where the team members meet and learn about the project and their formal roles and responsibilities. Team members tend to be independent and not as open in this phase.

▶ **Storming.** During this phase, the team begins to address the project work, technical decisions, and the project management approach. If team members are not collaborative or open to differing ideas and perspectives, the environment can become counterproductive.

▶ **Norming.** In this phase, team members begin to work together and adjust their work habits and behaviors to support the team. The team members learn to trust each other.

▶ **Performing.** Teams that reach the performing stage function as a well-organized unit. They are interdependent and work through issues smoothly and effectively.

▶ **Adjourning.** In this phase, the team completes the work and moves on from the project. This typically occurs when staff is released from the project as deliverables are completed or as part of the Close Project or Phase process.

The duration of a particular stage depends upon team dynamics, team size, and team leadership. Project managers should have a good understanding of team dynamics in order to move their team members through all stages in an effective manner.

6.6 MANAGE TEAM

Manage Team is the process of tracking team member performance, providing feedback, resolving issues, and managing team changes to optimize project performance. The key benefit of this process is that it influences team behavior, manages conflict, and resolves issues.

This process is performed throughout the project. The inputs, tools and techniques, and outputs are shown in Figure 6-11. Figure 6-12 presents the data flow diagram for this process.

Managing a project team requires a variety of management and leadership skills for fostering teamwork and integrating the efforts of team members to create high-performance teams. Team management involves a combination of skills with special emphasis on communication, conflict management, negotiation, and leadership. Project managers should provide challenging assignments to team members and give recognition for high performance.

> A project manager needs to be sensitive to both the willingness and the ability of team members to perform their work and adjust their management and leadership styles accordingly. Team members with low-skill abilities will require more intensive oversight than those who have demonstrated ability and experience.

Manage Team

Inputs	Tools & Techniques	Outputs

1. Project management plan
  • Resource management plan
2. Project documents
  • Issue log
  • Lessons learned register
  • Project team assignments
  • Team charter
3. Work performance reports
4. Team performance assessments
5. Enterprise environmental factors
6. Organizational process assets
	1. Interpersonal and team skills
	  • Conflict management
	  • Decision making
	  • Emotional intelligence
	  • Influencing
	  • Leadership
	2. Project management information system
		1. Change requests
		2. Project management plan updates
		  • Resource management plan
		  • Schedule baseline
		  • Cost baseline
		3. Project documents updates
		  • Issue log
		  • Lessons learned register
		  • Project team assignments
		4. Enterprise environmental factors updates

Note: This figure provides the inputs, tools and techniques, and outputs that may be used for this process. Descriptions for inputs and outputs appear in Section 9. Descriptions for tools and techniques appear in Section 10.

Figure 6-11. Manage Team: Inputs, Tools & Techniques, and Outputs

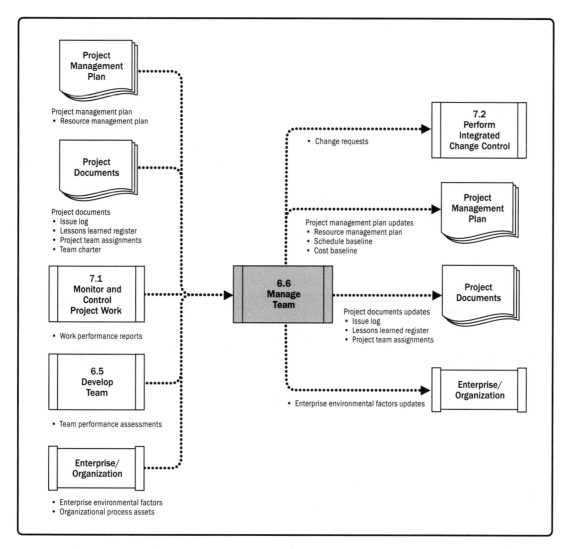

Note: This figure provides the inputs and outputs that may be used for this process. Descriptions for inputs and outputs appear in Section 9.

Figure 6-12. Manage Team: Data Flow Diagram

6.7 MANAGE COMMUNICATIONS

Manage Communications is the process of ensuring timely and appropriate collection, creation, distribution, storage, retrieval, management, monitoring, and the ultimate disposition of project information. The key benefit of this process is that it enables an efficient and effective information flow between the project team and the stakeholders.

The Manage Communications process identifies all aspects of effective communication, including choice of appropriate technologies, methods, and techniques. In addition, it should allow for flexibility in the communications activities, allowing adjustments in the methods and techniques to accommodate the changing needs of stakeholders and the project.

This process is performed throughout the project. The inputs, tools and techniques, and outputs are shown in Figure 6-13. Figure 6-14 presents the data flow diagram for this process.

Manage Communications

Inputs	Tools & Techniques	Outputs

1. Project management plan
  • Resource management plan
  • Communications management plan
  • Stakeholder engagement plan
2. Project documents
  • Change log
  • Issue log
  • Lessons learned register
  • Quality report
  • Risk report
  • Stakeholder register
3. Work performance reports
4. Enterprise environmental factors
5. Organizational process assets
	1. Communication technology
	2. Communication methods
	3. Communication skills
	  • Communication competence
	  • Feedback
	  • Nonverbal
	  • Presentations
	4. Project management information system
	5. Project reporting
	6. Interpersonal and team skills
	  • Active listening
	  • Conflict management
	  • Cultural awareness
	  • Meeting management
	  • Networking
	  • Political awareness
	7. Meetings
		1. Project communications
		2. Project management plan updates
		  • Communications management plan
		  • Stakeholder engagement plan
		3. Project documents updates
		  • Issue log
		  • Lessons learned register
		  • Project schedule
		  • Risk register
		  • Stakeholder register
		4. Organizational process assets updates

Note: This figure provides the inputs, tools and techniques, and outputs that may be used for this process. Descriptions for inputs and outputs appear in Section 9. Descriptions for tools and techniques appear in Section 10.

Figure 6-13. Manage Communications: Inputs, Tools & Techniques, and Outputs

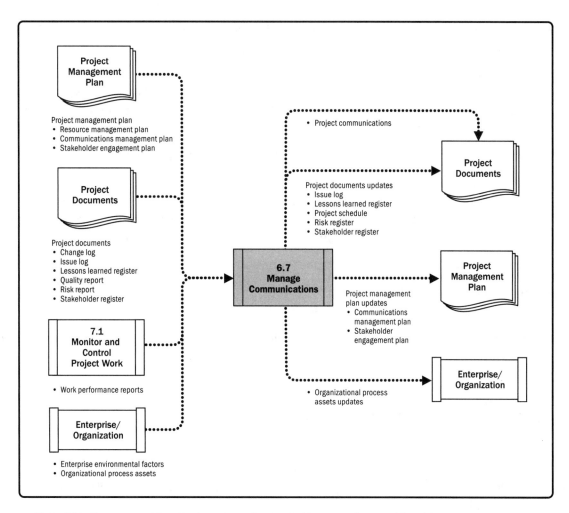

Note: This figure provides the inputs and outputs that may be used for this process. Descriptions for inputs and outputs appear in Section 9.

Figure 6-14. Manage Communications: Data Flow Diagram

This process goes beyond the distribution of relevant information and seeks to ensure that the information being communicated to project stakeholders has been appropriately generated and formatted and received by the intended audience. It also provides opportunities for stakeholders to make requests for further information, clarification, and discussion. Techniques and considerations for effective communications management include but are not limited to:

- ▶ **Sender-receiver models.** Incorporate feedback loops to provide opportunities for interaction/participation and remove barriers to effective communication.

- ▶ **Choice of media.** Make decisions about the application of communications artifacts to meet specific project needs, such as when to communicate in writing versus orally, when to prepare an informal memo versus a formal report, and when to use push/pull options and the choice of appropriate technology.

- ▶ **Writing style.** Use active versus passive voice, sentence structure, and word choice in the appropriate manner.

- ▶ **Meeting management.** Prepare an agenda, invite essential participants, and ensure they attend. Deal with conflicts within the meeting or those conflicts that result from inadequate follow-up of minutes and actions or attendance of the wrong people.

- ▶ **Presentations.** Be aware of the impact of body language and design of visual aids.

- ▶ **Facilitation.** Build consensus and overcome obstacles, such as difficult group dynamics, and maintain interest and enthusiasm among group members.

- ▶ **Active listening.** Listen actively by acknowledging, clarifying and confirming, understanding, and removing barriers that adversely affect comprehension.

6.8 IMPLEMENT RISK RESPONSES

Implement Risk Responses is the process of implementing agreed-upon risk response plans. The key benefit of this process is that it ensures that agreed-upon risk responses are executed as planned in order to address overall project risk exposure, minimize individual project threats, and maximize individual project opportunities.

This process is performed throughout the project. The inputs, tools and techniques, and outputs are shown in Figure 6-15. Figure 6-16 presents the data flow diagram for this process.

Implement Risk Responses

Inputs	Tools & Techniques	Outputs

1. Project management plan
  • Risk management plan
2. Project documents
  • Lessons learned register
  • Risk register
  • Risk report
3. Organizational process assets
	1. Expert judgment
	2. Interpersonal and team skills
	  • Influencing
	3. Project management
	  information system
		1. Change requests
		2. Project documents updates
		  • Issue log
		  • Lessons learned register
		  • Project team assignments
		  • Risk register
		  • Risk report

Note: This figure provides the inputs, tools and techniques, and outputs that may be used for this process. Descriptions for inputs and outputs appear in Section 9. Descriptions for tools and techniques appear in Section 10.

Figure 6-15. Implement Risk Responses: Inputs, Tools & Techniques, and Outputs

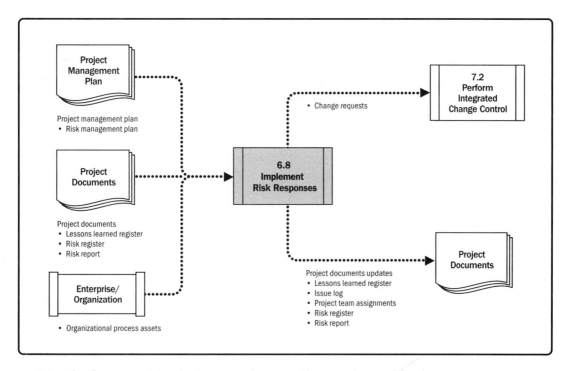

Note: This figure provides the inputs and outputs that may be used for this process. Descriptions for inputs and outputs appear in Section 9.

Figure 6-16. Implement Risk Responses: Data Flow Diagram

Only when risk owners give the required level of effort to implement the agreed-upon responses will the overall risk exposure of the project and individual threats and opportunities be managed proactively.

Proper attention to the Implement Risk Responses process will ensure that agreed-upon risk responses are actually executed. A common problem is that project teams spend time and effort to identify and analyze risks and develop risk responses, then risk responses are agreed upon and documented in the risk register and risk report, but no action is taken to manage the risk.

6.9 CONDUCT PROCUREMENTS

Conduct Procurements is the process of obtaining seller responses, selecting a seller, and awarding a contract. The key benefit of this process is that it selects a qualified seller and implements the legal agreement for delivery. The end results of the process are the established agreements, including formal contracts.

This process is performed periodically throughout the project as needed. The inputs, tools and techniques, and outputs are shown in Figure 6-17. Figure 6-18 presents the data flow diagram for this process.

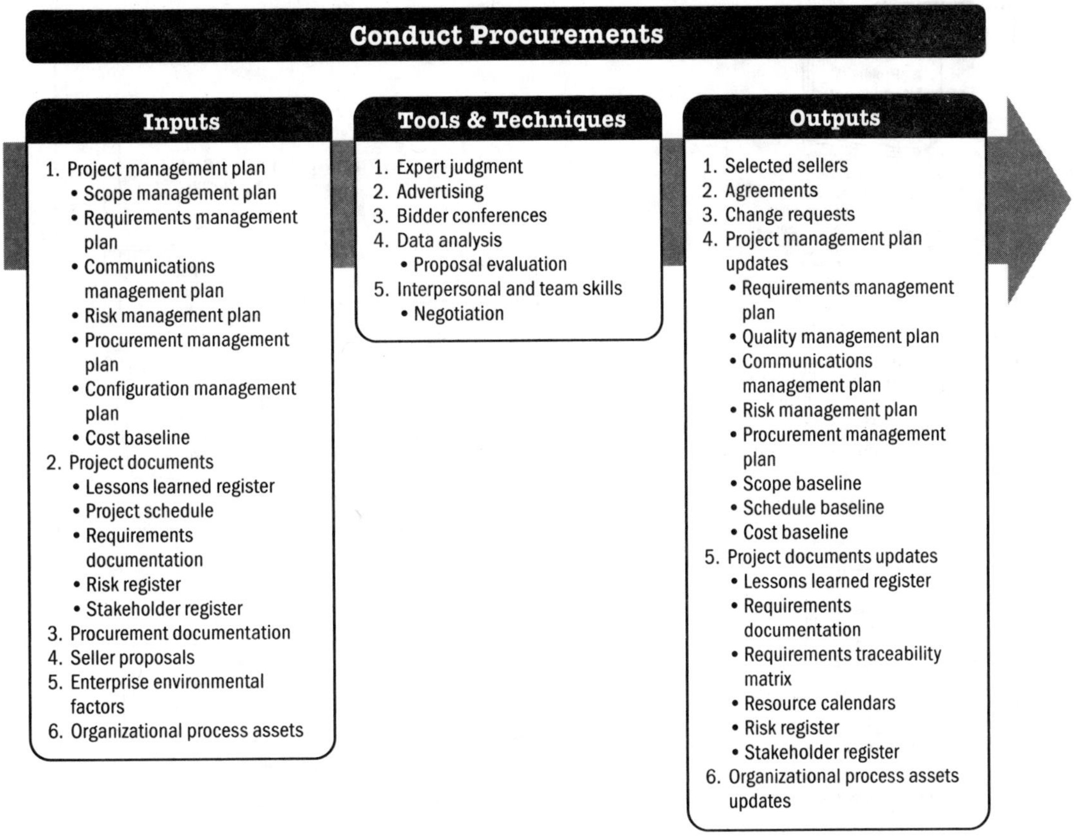

Conduct Procurements

Inputs	Tools & Techniques	Outputs

1. Project management plan
  • Scope management plan
  • Requirements management plan
  • Communications management plan
  • Risk management plan
  • Procurement management plan
  • Configuration management plan
  • Cost baseline
2. Project documents
  • Lessons learned register
  • Project schedule
  • Requirements documentation
  • Risk register
  • Stakeholder register
3. Procurement documentation
4. Seller proposals
5. Enterprise environmental factors
6. Organizational process assets
	1. Expert judgment
	2. Advertising
	3. Bidder conferences
	4. Data analysis
	  • Proposal evaluation
	5. Interpersonal and team skills
	  • Negotiation
		1. Selected sellers
		2. Agreements
		3. Change requests
		4. Project management plan updates
		  • Requirements management plan
		  • Quality management plan
		  • Communications management plan
		  • Risk management plan
		  • Procurement management plan
		  • Scope baseline
		  • Schedule baseline
		  • Cost baseline
		5. Project documents updates
		  • Lessons learned register
		  • Requirements documentation
		  • Requirements traceability matrix
		  • Resource calendars
		  • Risk register
		  • Stakeholder register
		6. Organizational process assets updates

Note: This figure provides the inputs, tools and techniques, and outputs that may be used for this process. Descriptions for inputs and outputs appear in Section 9. Descriptions for tools and techniques appear in Section 10.

Figure 6-17. Conduct Procurements: Inputs, Tools & Techniques, and Outputs

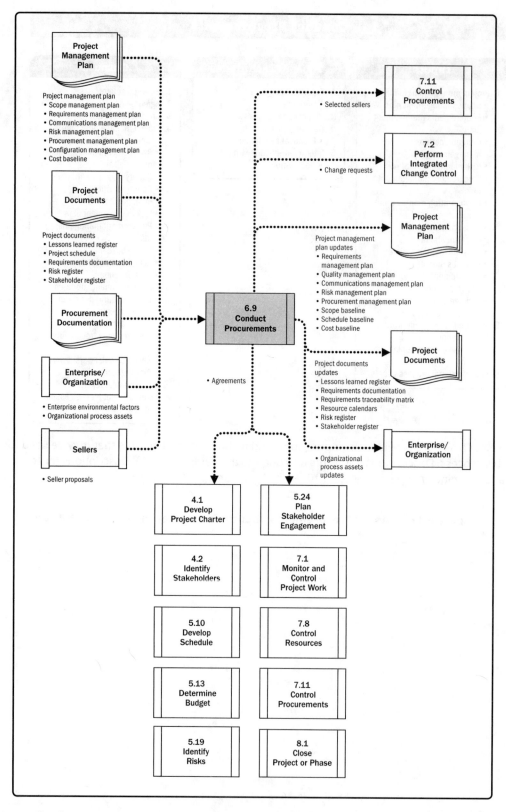

Project management plan
• Scope management plan
• Requirements management plan
• Communications management plan
• Risk management plan
• Procurement management plan
• Configuration management plan
• Cost baseline

Project documents
• Lessons learned register
• Project schedule
• Requirements documentation
• Risk register
• Stakeholder register

• Enterprise environmental factors
• Organizational process assets

• Seller proposals

• Selected sellers

• Change requests

Project management plan updates
• Requirements management plan
• Quality management plan
• Communications management plan
• Risk management plan
• Procurement management plan
• Scope baseline
• Schedule baseline
• Cost baseline

Project documents updates
• Lessons learned register
• Requirements documentation
• Requirements traceability matrix
• Resource calendars
• Risk register
• Stakeholder register

• Organizational process assets updates

• Agreements

Note: This figure provides the inputs and outputs that may be used for this process.
Descriptions for inputs and outputs appear in Section 9.

Figure 6-18. Conduct Procurements: Data Flow Diagram

Process Groups: A Practice Guide

6.10 MANAGE STAKEHOLDER ENGAGEMENT

Manage Stakeholder Engagement is the process of communicating and working with stakeholders to meet their needs and expectations, address issues, and foster appropriate stakeholder involvement. The key benefit of this process is that it allows the project manager to increase support and minimize resistance from stakeholders.

This process is performed throughout the project. The inputs, tools and techniques, and outputs are shown in Figure 6-19. Figure 6-20 presents the data flow diagram for this process.

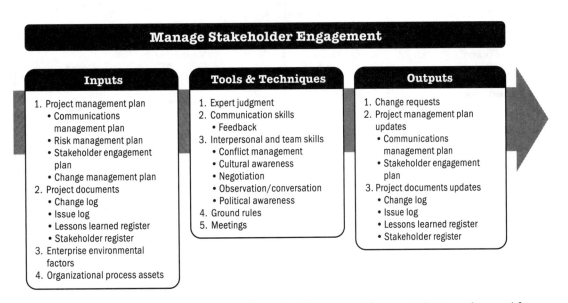

Note: This figure provides the inputs, tools and techniques, and outputs that may be used for this process. Descriptions for inputs and outputs appear in Section 9. Descriptions for tools and techniques appear in Section 10.

Figure 6-19. Manage Stakeholder Engagement: Inputs, Tools & Techniques, and Outputs

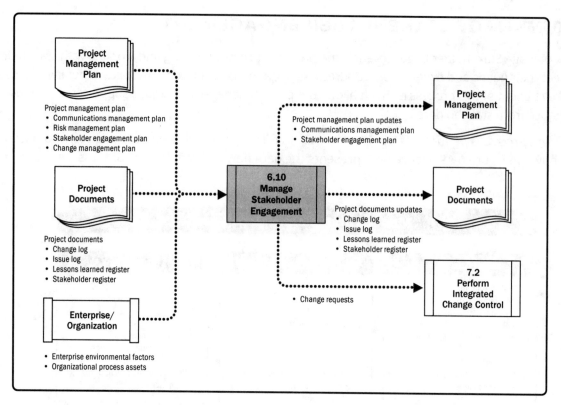

Note: This figure provides the inputs and outputs that may be used for this process. Descriptions for inputs and outputs appear in Section 9.

Figure 6-20. Manage Stakeholder Engagement: Data Flow Diagram

Manage Stakeholder Engagement involves activities such as:

▶ Engage stakeholders at appropriate project stages to obtain, confirm, or maintain their continued commitment to the success of the project.

▶ Manage stakeholder expectations through negotiation and communication.

▶ Address any risks or potential concerns related to stakeholder management and anticipate future issues that may be raised by stakeholders.

▶ Clarify and resolve issues that have been identified.

Managing stakeholder engagement helps to ensure that stakeholders clearly understand the project goals, objectives, benefits, and risks for the project, as well as how their contribution will enhance project success.

Monitoring and Controlling Process Group

7

The processes in the Monitoring and Controlling Process Group are shown in Table 7-1.

Table 7-1. Monitoring and Controlling Process Group Processes

Monitoring and Controlling Processes	
7.1 Monitor and Control Project Work	7.7 Control Quality
7.2 Perform Integrated Change Control	7.8 Control Resources
7.3 Validate Scope	7.9 Monitor Communications
7.4 Control Scope	7.10 Monitor Risks
7.5 Control Schedule	7.11 Control Procurements
7.6 Control Costs	7.12 Monitor Stakeholder Engagement

The Monitoring and Controlling Process Group consists of those processes required to track, review, and regulate the progress and performance of the project; identify any areas in which changes to the plan are required; and initiate the corresponding changes. Monitoring is collecting project performance data, producing performance measures, and reporting and disseminating performance information. Controlling is comparing actual performance with planned performance, analyzing variances, assessing trends to effect process improvements, evaluating possible alternatives, and recommending appropriate corrective action as needed.

The key benefit of this Process Group is that project performance is measured and analyzed at regular intervals, appropriate events, or when exception conditions occur in order to identify and correct variances from the project management plan. The Monitoring and Controlling Process Group also involves the following activities:

▶ Evaluate change requests and decide on the appropriate response.

▶ Recommend corrective or preventive action in anticipation of possible problems.

▶ Monitor the ongoing project activities against the project management plan and project baselines.

▶ Influence the factors that could circumvent the change control process so only approved changes are implemented.

Continuous monitoring provides the project team and other stakeholders with insight into the status of the project and identifies any areas that require additional attention. The Monitoring and Controlling Process Group monitors and controls the work being done within each Process Group, each life cycle phase, and the project as a whole. The Monitoring and Controlling Process Group includes the project management processes identified in Sections 7.1 through 7.12.

7.1 MONITOR AND CONTROL PROJECT WORK

Monitor and Control Project Work is the process of tracking, reviewing, and reporting the overall progress to meet the performance objectives defined in the project management plan. The key benefits of this process are that it allows stakeholders to understand the current state of the project, to recognize the actions taken to address any performance issues, and to have visibility into the future project status with cost and schedule forecasts.

This process is performed throughout the project. The inputs, tools and techniques, and outputs are shown in Figure 7-1. Figure 7-2 presents the data flow diagram for this process.

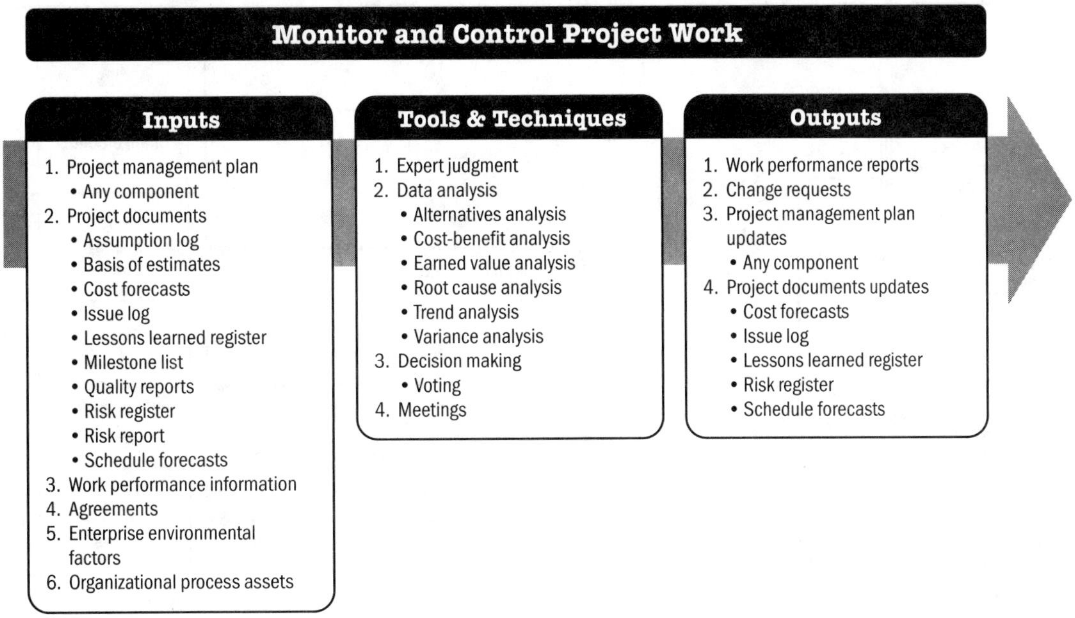

Monitor and Control Project Work

Inputs	Tools & Techniques	Outputs

1. Project management plan
  • Any component
2. Project documents
  • Assumption log
  • Basis of estimates
  • Cost forecasts
  • Issue log
  • Lessons learned register
  • Milestone list
  • Quality reports
  • Risk register
  • Risk report
  • Schedule forecasts
3. Work performance information
4. Agreements
5. Enterprise environmental factors
6. Organizational process assets
	1. Expert judgment
	2. Data analysis
	  • Alternatives analysis
	  • Cost-benefit analysis
	  • Earned value analysis
	  • Root cause analysis
	  • Trend analysis
	  • Variance analysis
	3. Decision making
	  • Voting
	4. Meetings
		1. Work performance reports
		2. Change requests
		3. Project management plan updates
		  • Any component
		4. Project documents updates
		  • Cost forecasts
		  • Issue log
		  • Lessons learned register
		  • Risk register
		  • Schedule forecasts

Note: This figure provides the inputs, tools and techniques, and outputs that may be used for this process. Descriptions for inputs and outputs appear in Section 9. Descriptions for tools and techniques appear in Section 10.

Figure 7-1. Monitor and Control Project Work: Inputs, Tools & Techniques, and Outputs

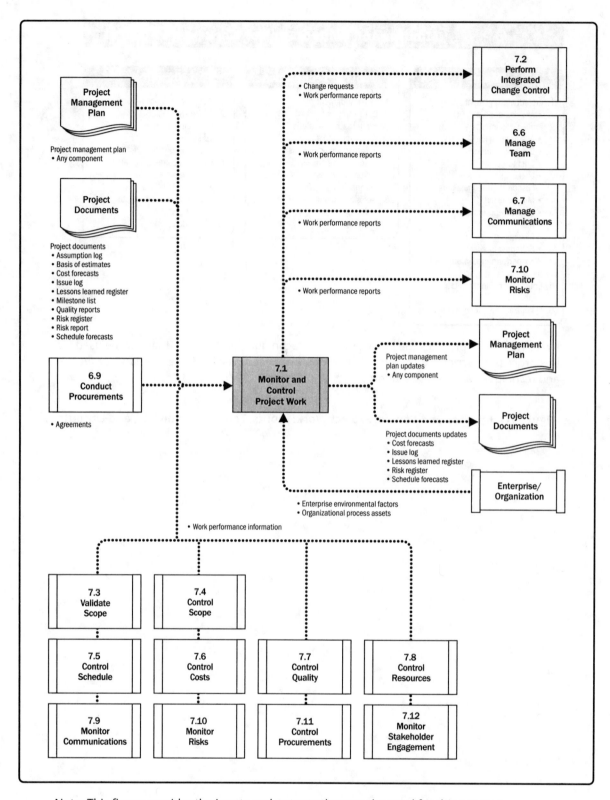

Note: This figure provides the inputs and outputs that may be used for this process.
Descriptions for inputs and outputs appear in Section 9.

Figure 7-2. Monitor and Control Project Work: Data Flow Diagram

Monitoring is an aspect of project management performed throughout the project. Monitoring includes collecting, measuring, and assessing measurements and trends to effect process improvements. Continuous monitoring gives the project management team insight into the health of the project and identifies any areas that may require special attention. Control includes determining corrective or preventive actions or replanning and following up on action plans to determine whether the actions taken resolved the performance issue. The Monitor and Control Project Work process is concerned with:

▶ Comparing actual project performance against the project management plan;

▶ Assessing performance periodically to determine whether any corrective or preventive actions are indicated, and then recommending those actions as necessary;

▶ Checking the status of individual project risks;

▶ Maintaining an accurate, timely information base concerning the project's product(s) and their associated documentation through project completion;

▶ Providing information to support status reporting, progress measurement, and forecasting;

▶ Providing forecasts to update current cost and current schedule information;

▶ Monitoring implementation of approved changes as they occur;

▶ Providing appropriate reporting on project progress and status to program management when the project is part of an overall program; and

▶ Ensuring that the project stays aligned with the business needs.

7.2 PERFORM INTEGRATED CHANGE CONTROL

Perform Integrated Change Control is the process of reviewing all change requests; approving changes and managing changes to deliverables, project documents, and the project management plan; and communicating the decisions. This process reviews all requests for changes to project documents, deliverables, or the project management plan and determines the resolution of the change requests. The key benefit of this process is that it allows for documented changes within the project to be considered in an integrated manner while addressing overall project risk, which often arises from changes made without consideration of the overall project objectives or plans.

This process is performed throughout the project. The inputs, tools and techniques, and outputs are shown in Figure 7-3. Figure 7-4 presents the data flow diagram for this process.

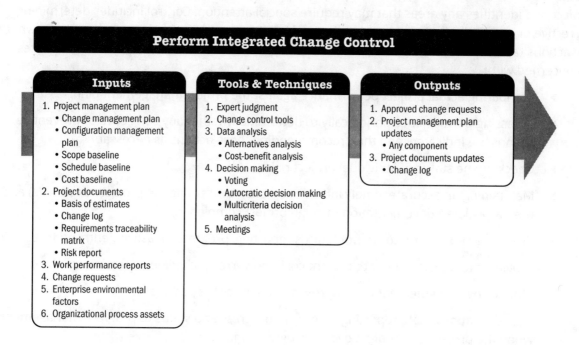

Note: This figure provides the inputs, tools and techniques, and outputs that may be used for this process. Descriptions for inputs and outputs appear in Section 9. Descriptions for tools and techniques appear in Section 10.

Figure 7-3. Perform Integrated Change Control: Inputs, Tools & Techniques, and Outputs

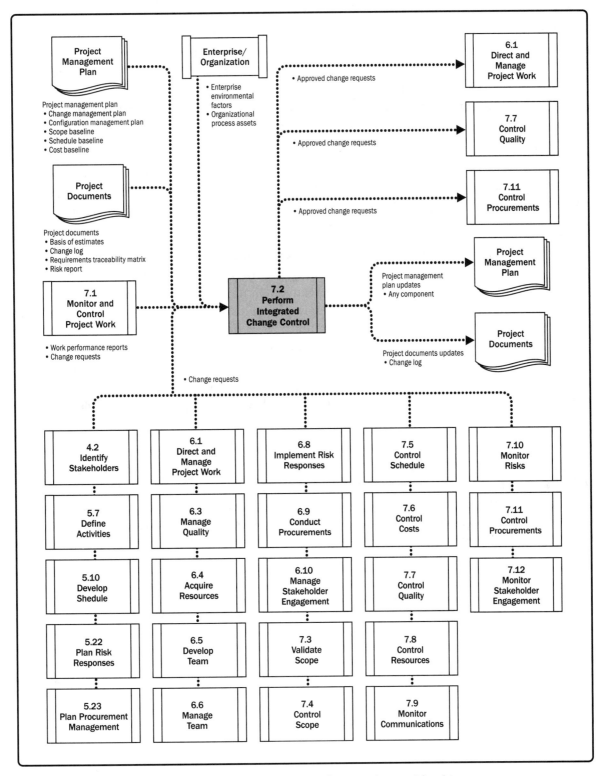

Note: This figure provides the inputs and outputs that may be used for this process. Descriptions for inputs and outputs appear in Section 9.

Figure 7-4. Perform Integrated Change Control: Data Flow Diagram

The Perform Integrated Change Control process is conducted from project start through completion and is the ultimate responsibility of the project manager. Change requests can impact the project scope and the product scope, as well as any project management plan component or any project document. Changes may be requested by any stakeholder involved with the project and may occur at any time throughout the project life cycle. The applied level of change control is dependent upon the application area, complexity of the specific project, contract requirements, and the context and environment in which the project is performed.

Before the baselines are established, changes are not required to be formally controlled by the Perform Integrated Change Control process. Once the project is baselined, change requests go through this process. As a general rule, each project's configuration management plan should define which project artifacts need to be placed under configuration control. Any change in a configuration element should be formally controlled and will require a change request.

Although changes may be initiated verbally, they should be recorded in written form and entered into the change management and/or configuration management system. Change requests may require information on estimated schedule impacts and estimated cost impacts prior to approval. Whenever a change request may impact any of the project baselines, a formal integrated change control process is always required. Every documented change request needs to be either approved, deferred, or rejected by a responsible individual, usually the project sponsor or project manager. The responsible individual will be identified in the project management plan or by organizational procedures. When required, the Perform Integrated Change Control process includes a change control board (CCB), which is a formally chartered group responsible for reviewing, evaluating, approving, deferring, or rejecting changes to the project and for recording and communicating such decisions.

Approved change requests can require new or revised cost estimates, activity sequences, schedule dates, resource requirements, and/or analysis of risk response alternatives. These changes can require adjustments to the project management plan and other project documents. Customer or sponsor approval may be required for certain change requests after CCB approval, unless they are part of the CCB.

7.3 VALIDATE SCOPE

Validate Scope is the process of formalizing acceptance of the completed project deliverables. The key benefit of this process is that it brings objectivity to the acceptance process and increases the probability of final product, service, or result acceptance by validating each deliverable.

This process is performed periodically throughout the project as needed. The inputs, tools and techniques, and outputs are shown in Figure 7-5. Figure 7-6 presents the data flow diagram for this process.

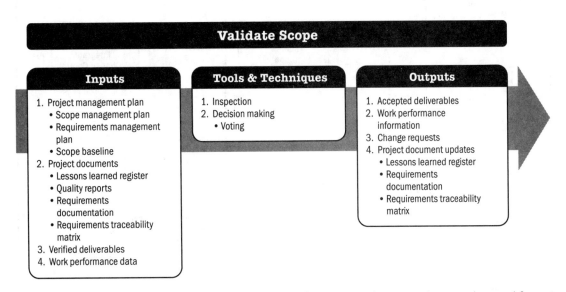

Note: This figure provides the inputs, tools and techniques, and outputs that may be used for this process. Descriptions for inputs and outputs appear in Section 9. Descriptions for tools and techniques appear in Section 10.

Figure 7-5. Validate Scope: Inputs, Tools & Techniques, and Outputs

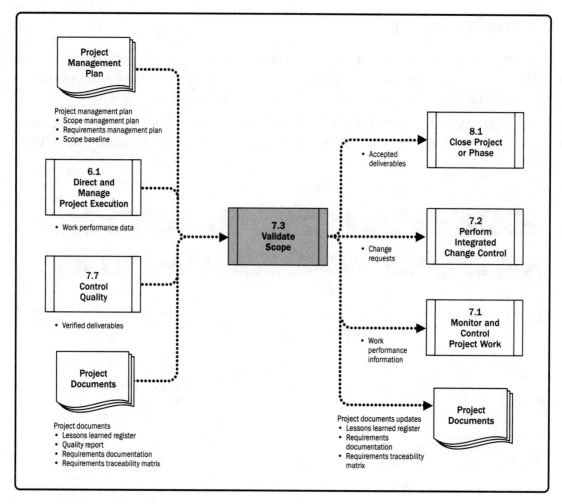

Note: This figure provides the inputs and outputs that may be used for this process. Descriptions for inputs and outputs appear in Section 9.

Figure 7-6. Validate Scope: Data Flow Diagram

The verified deliverables obtained from the Control Quality process are reviewed with the customer or sponsor to ensure they are completed satisfactorily and have received formal acceptance of the deliverables by the customer or sponsor. In this process, the outputs obtained as a result of the Planning processes for scope, such as the requirements documentation or the scope baseline, as well as the work performance data obtained from the Executing processes, are the basis for performing the validation and for final acceptance.

The Validate Scope process is primarily concerned with acceptance of the deliverables while the Control Quality process is primarily concerned with correctness of the deliverables and meeting the quality requirements specified for the deliverables. Control Quality is generally performed before Validate Scope, although the two processes may be performed in parallel.

7.4 CONTROL SCOPE

Control Scope is the process of monitoring the status of the project and product scope and managing changes to the scope baseline. The key benefit of this process is that the scope baseline is maintained throughout the project.

This process is performed throughout the project. The inputs, tools and techniques, and outputs are shown in Figure 7-7. Figure 7-8 presents the data flow diagram for this process.

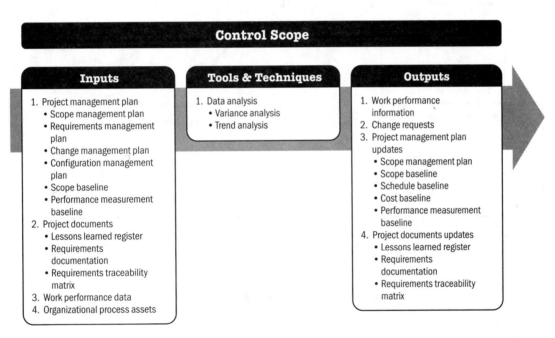

Note: This figure provides the inputs, tools and techniques, and outputs that may be used for this process. Descriptions for inputs and outputs appear in Section 9. Descriptions for tools and techniques appear in Section 10.

Figure 7-7. Control Scope: Inputs, Tools & Techniques, and Outputs

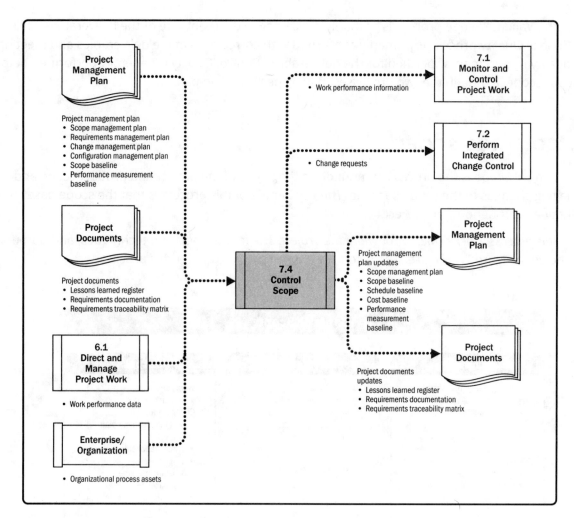

Note: This figure provides the inputs and outputs that may be used for this process. Descriptions for inputs and outputs appear in Section 9.

Figure 7-8. Control Scope: Data Flow Diagram

Controlling the project scope ensures all requested changes and recommended corrective or preventive actions are processed through the Perform Integrated Change Control process (see Section 7.2). Control Scope is also used to manage the actual changes when they occur and is integrated with the other control processes. The uncontrolled expansion to product or project scope without adjustments to time, cost, and resources is referred to as scope creep. Change is inevitable; therefore, some type of change control process is mandatory for every project.

7.5 CONTROL SCHEDULE

Control Schedule is the process of monitoring the status of the project to update the project schedule and managing changes to the schedule baseline. The key benefit of this process is that the schedule baseline is maintained throughout the project.

This process is performed throughout the project. The inputs, tools and techniques, and outputs are shown in Figure 7-9. Figure 7-10 presents the data flow diagram for this process.

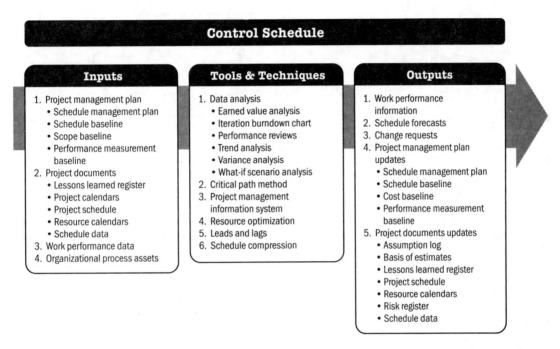

Control Schedule

Inputs	Tools & Techniques	Outputs

1. Project management plan
  • Schedule management plan
  • Schedule baseline
  • Scope baseline
  • Performance measurement baseline
2. Project documents
  • Lessons learned register
  • Project calendars
  • Project schedule
  • Resource calendars
  • Schedule data
3. Work performance data
4. Organizational process assets
	1. Data analysis
	  • Earned value analysis
	  • Iteration burndown chart
	  • Performance reviews
	  • Trend analysis
	  • Variance analysis
	  • What-if scenario analysis
	2. Critical path method
	3. Project management information system
	4. Resource optimization
	5. Leads and lags
	6. Schedule compression
		1. Work performance information
		2. Schedule forecasts
		3. Change requests
		4. Project management plan updates
		  • Schedule management plan
		  • Schedule baseline
		  • Cost baseline
		  • Performance measurement baseline
		5. Project documents updates
		  • Assumption log
		  • Basis of estimates
		  • Lessons learned register
		  • Project schedule
		  • Resource calendars
		  • Risk register
		  • Schedule data

Note: This figure provides the inputs, tools and techniques, and outputs that may be used for this process. Descriptions for inputs and outputs appear in Section 9. Descriptions for tools and techniques appear in Section 10.

Figure 7-9. Control Schedule: Inputs, Tools & Techniques, and Outputs

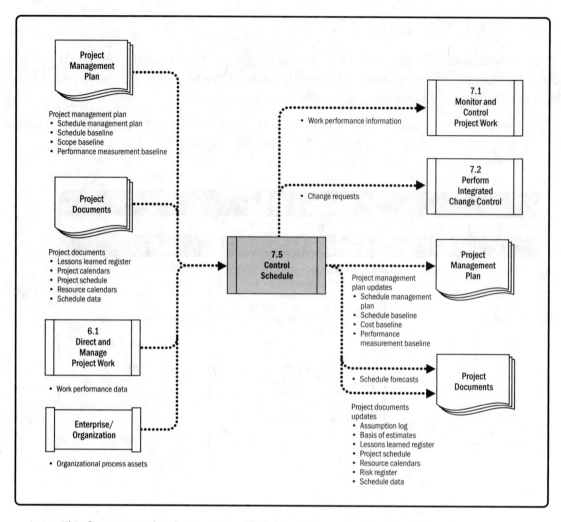

Note: This figure provides the inputs and outputs that may be used for this process. Descriptions for inputs and outputs appear in Section 9.

Figure 7-10. Control Schedule: Data Flow Diagram

Updating the schedule model requires knowing the actual performance to date. Any change to the schedule baseline can only be approved through the Perform Integrated Change Control process (Section 7.2). Control Schedule, as a component of the Perform Integrated Change Control process, is concerned with:

▶ Determining the current status of the project schedule,

▶ Influencing the factors that create schedule changes,

▶ Reconsidering necessary schedule reserves,

▶ Determining if the project schedule has changed, and

▶ Managing the actual changes as they occur.

When an agile approach is used, Control Schedule is concerned with:

▶ Determining the current status of the project schedule by comparing the total amount of work delivered and accepted against the estimates of work completed for the elapsed time cycle;

▶ Conducting retrospectives (scheduled reviews to record lessons learned) for correcting processes and improving, if required;

▶ Reprioritizing the remaining work plan (backlog);

▶ Determining the rate at which the deliverables are produced, validated, and accepted (velocity) in the given time per iteration (agreed-upon work cycle duration, typically 2 weeks or 1 month);

▶ Determining that the project schedule has changed; and

▶ Managing the actual changes as they occur.

When work is being contracted, regular and milestone status updates from contractors and suppliers are a means of ensuring the work is progressing as agreed upon to ensure the schedule is under control. Scheduled status reviews and walkthroughs should be done to ensure the contractor reports are accurate and complete.

7.6 CONTROL COSTS

Control Costs is the process of monitoring the status of the project to update the project costs and managing changes to the cost baseline. The key benefit of this process is that the cost baseline is maintained throughout the project.

This process is performed throughout the project. The inputs, tools and techniques, and outputs are shown in Figure 7-11. Figure 7-12 presents the data flow diagram for this process.

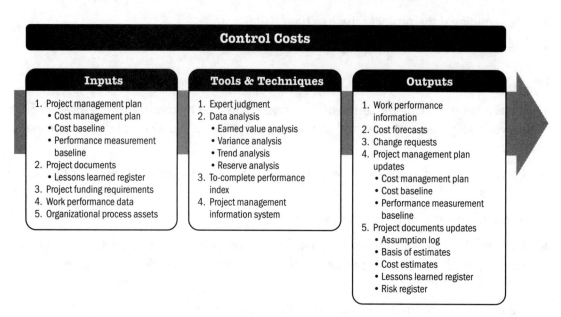

Note: This figure provides the inputs, tools and techniques, and outputs that may be used for this process. Descriptions for inputs and outputs appear in Section 9. Descriptions for tools and techniques appear in Section 10.

Figure 7-11. Control Costs: Inputs, Tools & Techniques, and Outputs

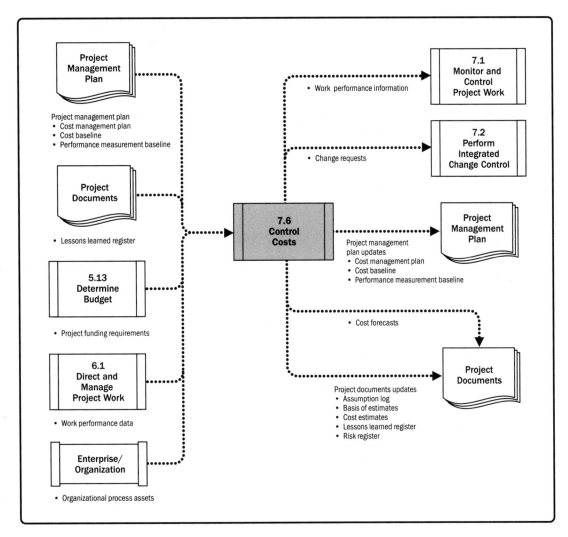

Note: This figure provides the inputs and outputs that may be used for this process. Descriptions for inputs and outputs appear in Section 9.

Figure 7-12. Control Costs: Data Flow Diagram

Updating the budget requires knowledge of the actual costs spent to date. Any increase to the authorized budget can only be approved through the Perform Integrated Change Control process (Section 7.2). Monitoring the expenditure of funds without regard to the value of work being accomplished for such expenditures has little value to the project, other than to track the outflow of funds. Much of the effort of cost control involves analyzing the relationship between the consumption of project funds and the work being accomplished for such expenditures. The key to effective cost control is the management of the approved cost baseline.

Project cost control includes:

▶ Influencing the factors that create changes to the authorized cost baseline;

▶ Ensuring that all change requests are acted on in a timely manner;

▶ Managing the actual changes when and as they occur;

▶ Ensuring that cost expenditures do not exceed the authorized funding by period, by WBS component, by activity, and in total for the project;

▶ Monitoring cost performance to isolate and understand variances from the approved cost baseline;

▶ Monitoring work performance against funds expended;

▶ Preventing unapproved changes from being included in the reported cost or resource usage;

▶ Informing appropriate stakeholders of all approved changes and associated cost; and

▶ Bringing expected cost overruns within acceptable limits.

7.7 CONTROL QUALITY

Control Quality is the process of monitoring and recording results of executing the quality management activities in order to assess performance and ensure the project outputs are complete, correct, and meet customer expectations. The key benefit of this process is verifying that project deliverables and work meet the requirements specified by key stakeholders for final acceptance. The Control Quality process determines if the project outputs do what they were intended to do. Those outputs need to comply with all applicable standards, requirements, regulations, and specifications.

This process is performed throughout the project. The inputs, tools and techniques, and outputs are shown in Figure 7-13. Figure 7-14 presents the data flow diagram for this process.

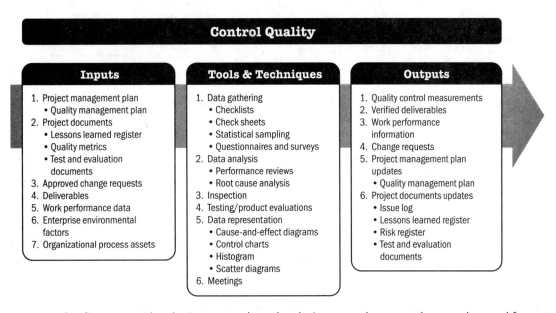

Control Quality

Inputs	Tools & Techniques	Outputs

1. Project management plan
  • Quality management plan
2. Project documents
  • Lessons learned register
  • Quality metrics
  • Test and evaluation documents
3. Approved change requests
4. Deliverables
5. Work performance data
6. Enterprise environmental factors
7. Organizational process assets
	1. Data gathering
	  • Checklists
	  • Check sheets
	  • Statistical sampling
	  • Questionnaires and surveys
	2. Data analysis
	  • Performance reviews
	  • Root cause analysis
	3. Inspection
	4. Testing/product evaluations
	5. Data representation
	  • Cause-and-effect diagrams
	  • Control charts
	  • Histogram
	  • Scatter diagrams
	6. Meetings
		1. Quality control measurements
		2. Verified deliverables
		3. Work performance information
		4. Change requests
		5. Project management plan updates
		  • Quality management plan
		6. Project documents updates
		  • Issue log
		  • Lessons learned register
		  • Risk register
		  • Test and evaluation documents

Note: This figure provides the inputs, tools and techniques, and outputs that may be used for this process. Descriptions for inputs and outputs appear in Section 9. Descriptions for tools and techniques appear in Section 10.

Figure 7-13. Control Quality: Inputs, Tools & Techniques, and Outputs

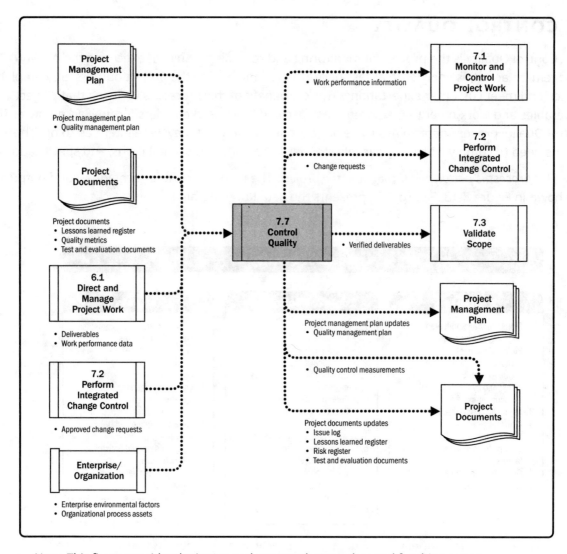

Note: This figure provides the inputs and outputs that may be used for this process. Descriptions for inputs and outputs appear in Section 9.

Figure 7-14. Control Quality: Data Flow Diagram

The Control Quality process is performed to measure the completeness, compliance, and fitness for use of a product or service prior to user acceptance and final delivery. This is done by measuring all steps, attributes, and variables used to verify conformance or compliance to the specifications stated during the planning stage.

Quality control should be performed throughout the project to formally demonstrate, with reliable data, that the sponsor's and/or customer's acceptance criteria have been met.

The level of effort to control quality and the degree of implementation may differ between industries and project management styles. For example, in the pharmaceutical, health, transportation, and nuclear industries, there may be stricter quality control procedures compared to other industries, and the effort needed to meet the standards may be extensive. In agile projects, the Control Quality activities may be performed by all team members throughout the project life cycle. In predictive (waterfall) model-based projects, the quality control activities are performed at specific times toward the end of the project or phase by specified team members.

7.8 CONTROL RESOURCES

Control Resources is the process of ensuring that the physical resources assigned and allocated to the project are available as planned, as well as monitoring the planned versus actual utilization of resources and taking corrective action as necessary. The key benefit of this process is ensuring that the assigned resources are available to the project at the right time and in the right place and are released when no longer needed.

This process is performed throughout the project. The inputs, tools and techniques, and outputs are shown in Figure 7-15. Figure 7-16 presents the data flow diagram for this process.

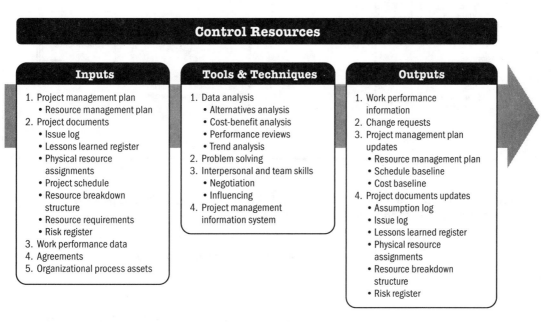

Note: This figure provides the inputs, tools and techniques, and outputs that may be used for this process. Descriptions for inputs and outputs appear in Section 9. Descriptions for tools and techniques appear in Section 10.

Figure 7-15. Control Resources: Inputs, Tools & Techniques, and Outputs

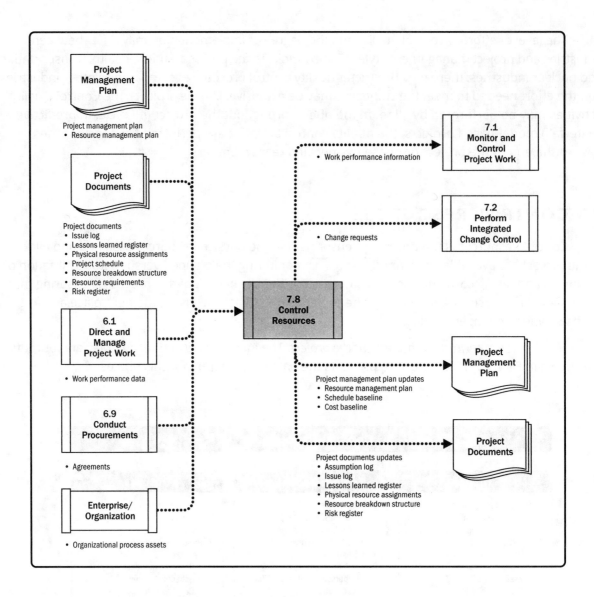

Note: This figure provides the inputs and outputs that may be used for this process. Descriptions for inputs and outputs appear in Section 9.

Figure 7-16. Control Resources: Data Flow Diagram

The Control Resources process should be performed continuously in all project phases and throughout the project life cycle. The resources needed for the project should be assigned and released at the right time, right place, and in the right amount for the project to continue without delays. The Control Resources process is concerned with physical resources such as equipment, materials, facilities, and infrastructure. Team members are addressed in the Manage Team process.

Updating resource allocation requires knowing what actual resources have been used to date and what is still needed. This is done mainly by reviewing the performance usage to date. Control Resources is concerned with:

- ▶ Monitoring resource expenditures,

- ▶ Identifying and dealing with resource shortage/surplus in a timely manner,

- ▶ Ensuring that resources are used and released according to the plan and project needs,

- ▶ Informing appropriate stakeholders if any issues arise with relevant resources,

- ▶ Influencing the factors that can create resource utilization changes, and

- ▶ Managing the actual changes as they occur.

Any changes needed to the schedule or cost baselines can be approved only through the Perform Integrated Change Control process (Section 7.2).

The Control Resources techniques discussed here are those used most frequently on projects. There are many others that may be useful on certain projects or in some application areas.

7.9 MONITOR COMMUNICATIONS

Monitor Communications is the process of ensuring the information needs of the project and its stakeholders are met. The key benefit of this process is the optimal information flow as defined in the communications management plan and the stakeholder engagement plan.

This process is performed throughout the project. The inputs, tools and techniques, and outputs are shown in Figure 7-17. Figure 7-18 presents the data flow diagram for this process.

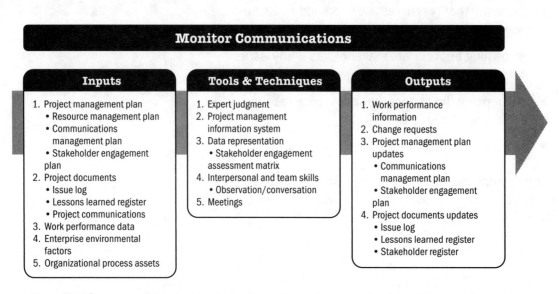

Monitor Communications		
Inputs	**Tools & Techniques**	**Outputs**

1. Project management plan
  • Resource management plan
  • Communications management plan
  • Stakeholder engagement plan
2. Project documents
  • Issue log
  • Lessons learned register
  • Project communications
3. Work performance data
4. Enterprise environmental factors
5. Organizational process assets
	1. Expert judgment
	2. Project management information system
	3. Data representation
	  • Stakeholder engagement assessment matrix
	4. Interpersonal and team skills
	  • Observation/conversation
	5. Meetings
		1. Work performance information
		2. Change requests
		3. Project management plan updates
		  • Communications management plan
		  • Stakeholder engagement plan
		4. Project documents updates
		  • Issue log
		  • Lessons learned register
		  • Stakeholder register

Note: This figure provides the inputs, tools and techniques, and outputs that may be used for this process. Descriptions for inputs and outputs appear in Section 9. Descriptions for tools and techniques appear in Section 10.

Figure 7-17. Monitor Communications: Inputs, Tools & Techniques, and Outputs

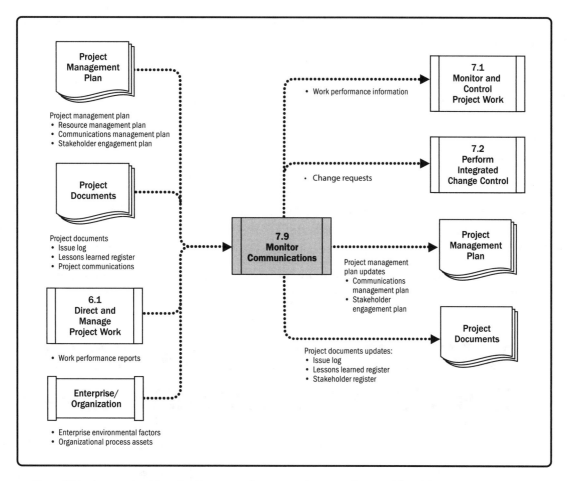

Note: This figure provides the inputs and outputs that may be used for this process. Descriptions for inputs and outputs appear in Section 9.

Figure 7-18. Monitor Communications: Data Flow Diagram

Monitor Communications determines if the planned communications artifacts and activities have had the desired effect of increasing or maintaining stakeholders' support for the project's deliverables and expected outcomes. The impact and consequences of project communications should be carefully evaluated and monitored to ensure that the right message with the right content (the same meaning for sender and receiver) is delivered to the right audience, through the right channel, and at the right time. Monitor Communications may require a variety of methods, such as customer satisfaction surveys, collecting lessons learned, observations of the team, reviewing data from the issue log, or evaluating changes in the stakeholder engagement assessment matrix (refer to data representation in Section 10, Figure 10-22).

The Monitor Communications process can trigger an iteration of the Plan Communications Management and/or Manage Communications processes to improve the effectiveness of communication through additional and possibly amended communications plans and activities. Such iterations illustrate the continuous nature of the communications management processes. Issues or key performance indicators, risks, or conflicts may trigger an immediate revision.

7.10 MONITOR RISKS

Monitor Risks is the process of monitoring the implementation of agreed-upon risk response plans, tracking identified risks, identifying and analyzing new risks, and evaluating risk process effectiveness throughout the project. The key benefit of this process is that it enables project decisions to be based on current information about overall project risk exposure and individual project risks.

This process is performed throughout the project. The inputs, tools and techniques, and outputs are shown in Figure 7-19. Figure 7-20 presents the data flow diagram for this process.

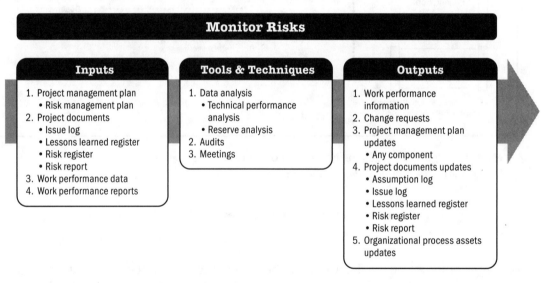

Monitor Risks

Inputs	Tools & Techniques	Outputs

1. Project management plan
  • Risk management plan
2. Project documents
  • Issue log
  • Lessons learned register
  • Risk register
  • Risk report
3. Work performance data
4. Work performance reports
	1. Data analysis
	  • Technical performance analysis
	  • Reserve analysis
	2. Audits
	3. Meetings
		1. Work performance information
		2. Change requests
		3. Project management plan updates
		  • Any component
		4. Project documents updates
		  • Assumption log
		  • Issue log
		  • Lessons learned register
		  • Risk register
		  • Risk report
		5. Organizational process assets updates

Note: This figure provides the inputs, tools and techniques, and outputs that may be used for this process. Descriptions for inputs and outputs appear in Section 9. Descriptions for tools and techniques appear in Section 10.

Figure 7-19. Monitor Risks: Inputs, Tools & Techniques, and Outputs

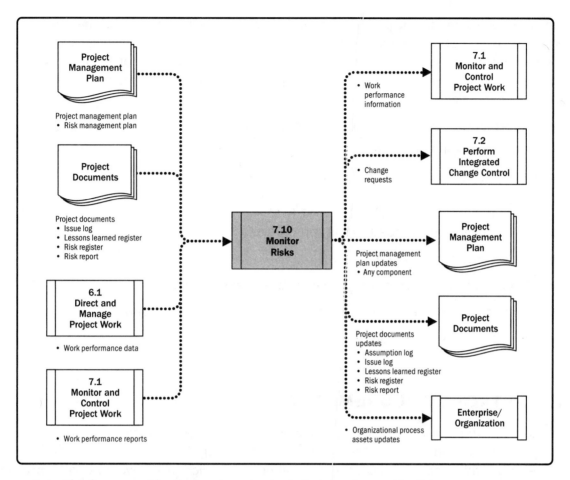

Note: This figure provides the inputs and outputs that may be used for this process. Descriptions for inputs and outputs appear in Section 9.

Figure 7-20. Monitor Risks: Data Flow Diagram

In order to ensure that the project team and key stakeholders are aware of the current level of risk exposure, project work should be continuously monitored for new, changing, and outdated individual project risks and for changes in the level of overall project risk by applying the Monitor Risks process. The Monitor Risks process uses the performance information generated during project execution to determine if:

▶ Implemented risk responses are effective,

▶ Level of overall project risk has changed,

▶ Status of identified individual project risks has changed,

▶ New individual project risks have arisen,

▶ Risk management approach is still appropriate,

▶ Project assumptions are still valid,

▶ Risk management policies and procedures are being followed,

▶ Contingency reserves for cost or schedule require modification, and

▶ Project strategy is still valid.

7.11 CONTROL PROCUREMENTS

Control Procurements is the process of managing procurement relationships, monitoring contract performance and making changes and corrections as appropriate, and closing out contracts. The key benefit of this process is that it ensures that both the seller's and buyer's performance meet the project's requirements according to the terms of the legal agreement.

This process is performed throughout the project as needed. The inputs, tools and techniques, and outputs are shown in Figure 7-21. Figure 7-22 presents the data flow diagram for this process.

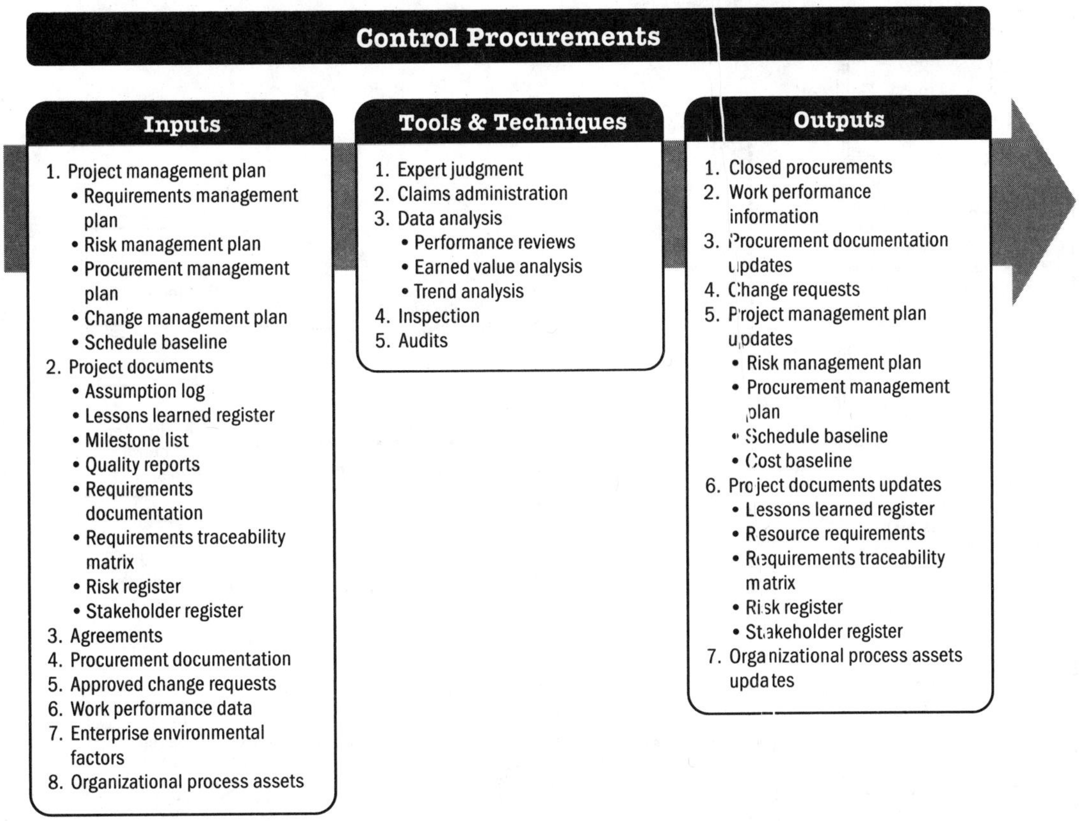

Control Procurements

Inputs	Tools & Techniques	Outputs

1. Project management plan
  • Requirements management plan
  • Risk management plan
  • Procurement management plan
  • Change management plan
  • Schedule baseline
2. Project documents
  • Assumption log
  • Lessons learned register
  • Milestone list
  • Quality reports
  • Requirements documentation
  • Requirements traceability matrix
  • Risk register
  • Stakeholder register
3. Agreements
4. Procurement documentation
5. Approved change requests
6. Work performance data
7. Enterprise environmental factors
8. Organizational process assets
	1. Expert judgment
	2. Claims administration
	3. Data analysis
	  • Performance reviews
	  • Earned value analysis
	  • Trend analysis
	4. Inspection
	5. Audits
		1. Closed procurements
		2. Work performance information
		3. Procurement documentation updates
		4. Change requests
		5. Project management plan updates
		  • Risk management plan
		  • Procurement management plan
		  • Schedule baseline
		  • Cost baseline
		6. Project documents updates
		  • Lessons learned register
		  • Resource requirements
		  • Requirements traceability matrix
		  • Risk register
		  • Stakeholder register
		7. Organizational process assets updates

Note: This figure provides the inputs, tools and techniques, and outputs that may be used for this process. Descriptions for inputs and outputs appear in Section 9. Descriptions for tools and techniques appear in Section 10.

Figure 7-21. Control Procurements: Inputs, Tools & Techniques, and Outputs

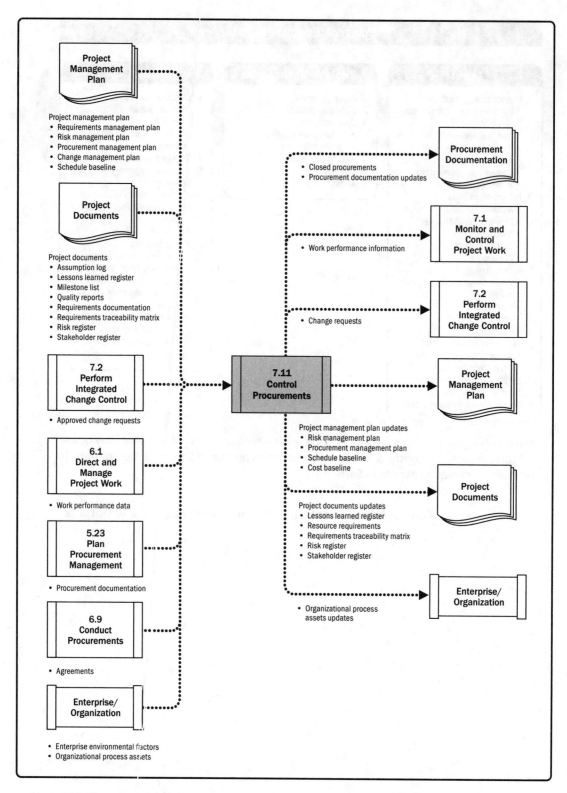

Note: This figure provides the inputs and outputs that may be used for this process.
Descriptions for inputs and outputs appear in Section 9.

Figure 7-22. Control Procurements: Data Flow Diagram

Both the buyer and the seller administer the procurement contract for similar purposes. Each is required to ensure that both parties meet their contractual obligations and that their own legal rights are protected. The legal nature of the relationship makes it imperative that the project management team is aware of the implications of actions taken when controlling any procurement. On larger projects with multiple providers, a key aspect of contract administration is managing communication among the various providers.

Because of the legal aspect, many organizations treat contract administration as an organizational function that is separate from the project. While a procurement administrator may be on the project team, this individual typically reports to a supervisor from a different department.

Control Procurements includes application of the appropriate project management processes to the contractual relationship(s) and integration of the outputs from these processes into the overall management of the project. This integration often occurs at multiple levels when there are multiple sellers and multiple products, services, or results involved.

Examples of Procurement Administrative Activities

Activities may include:

▶ Collection of data and management of project records, including maintenance of detailed records of physical and financial performance and establishment of measurable procurement performance indicators;

▶ Refinement of procurement plans and schedules;

▶ Setup for gathering, analyzing, and reporting procurement-related project data and preparation of periodic reports to the organization;

▶ Monitoring the procurement environment so that implementation can be facilitated or adjustments made; and

▶ Payment of invoices.

The quality of the controls, including the independence and credibility of procurement audits, is critical to the reliability of the procurement system. The organization's code of ethics, its legal counsel, and external legal advisory arrangements, including any ongoing anti-corruption initiatives, can contribute to proper procurement controls.

Control Procurements has a financial management component that involves monitoring payments to the seller. This ensures that payment terms defined within the contract are met and that compensation is linked to the seller's progress as defined in the contract. A principal concern when making payments is to ensure there is a close relationship of payments made to the work accomplished. A contract that requires payments linked to project outputs and deliverables, rather than inputs such as labor hours, has better controls.

Agreements can be amended at any time prior to contract closure by mutual consent in accordance with the change control terms of the agreement. Such amendments are typically captured in writing.

7.12 MONITOR STAKEHOLDER ENGAGEMENT

Monitor Stakeholder Engagement is the process of monitoring project stakeholder relationships and tailoring strategies for engaging stakeholders through the modification of engagement strategies and plans. The key benefit of this process is that it maintains or increases the efficiency and effectiveness of stakeholder engagement activities as the project evolves and its environment changes.

This process is performed throughout the project. The inputs, tools and techniques, and outputs are shown in Figure 7-23. Figure 7-24 presents the data flow diagram for this process.

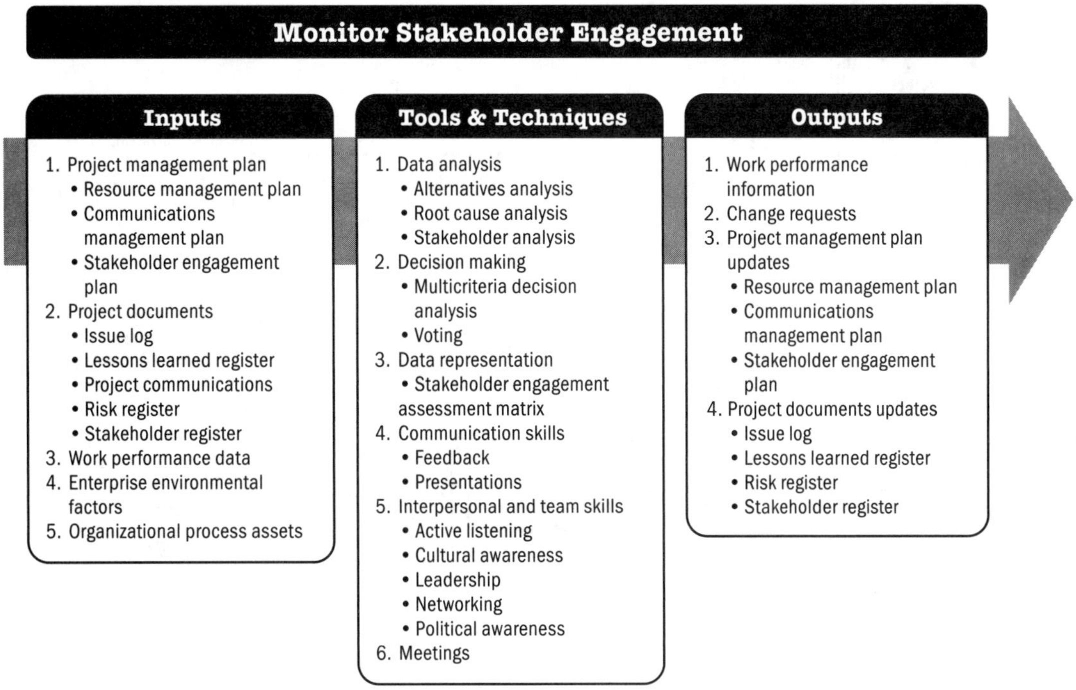

Monitor Stakeholder Engagement

Inputs	Tools & Techniques	Outputs

1. Project management plan
  • Resource management plan
  • Communications management plan
  • Stakeholder engagement plan
2. Project documents
  • Issue log
  • Lessons learned register
  • Project communications
  • Risk register
  • Stakeholder register
3. Work performance data
4. Enterprise environmental factors
5. Organizational process assets
	1. Data analysis
	  • Alternatives analysis
	  • Root cause analysis
	  • Stakeholder analysis
	2. Decision making
	  • Multicriteria decision analysis
	  • Voting
	3. Data representation
	  • Stakeholder engagement assessment matrix
	4. Communication skills
	  • Feedback
	  • Presentations
	5. Interpersonal and team skills
	  • Active listening
	  • Cultural awareness
	  • Leadership
	  • Networking
	  • Political awareness
	6. Meetings
		1. Work performance information
		2. Change requests
		3. Project management plan updates
		  • Resource management plan
		  • Communications management plan
		  • Stakeholder engagement plan
		4. Project documents updates
		  • Issue log
		  • Lessons learned register
		  • Risk register
		  • Stakeholder register

Note: This figure provides the inputs, tools and techniques, and outputs that may be used for this process. Descriptions for inputs and outputs appear in Section 9. Descriptions for tools and techniques appear in Section 10.

Figure 7-23. Monitor Stakeholder Engagement: Inputs, Tools & Techniques, and Outputs

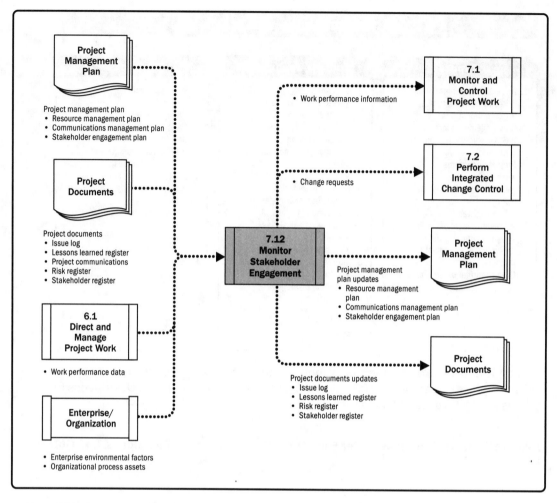

Note: This figure provides the inputs and outputs that may be used for this process. Descriptions for inputs and outputs appear in Section 9.

Figure 7-24. Monitor Stakeholder Engagement: Data Flow Diagram

Closing Process Group

The process in the Closing Process Group is shown in Table 8-1.

Table 8-1. Closing Process Group Process

Closing Processes
8.1 Close Project or Phase

The Closing Process Group consists of the process(es) performed to formally complete or close a project, phase, or contract. This Process Group verifies that the defined processes are completed within all Process Groups to close the project or phase, as appropriate, and formally establishes that the project or project phase is complete. The key benefit of this Process Group is that phases, projects, and contracts are closed out appropriately. While there is only one process in this Process Group, organizations may have their own processes associated with project, phase, or contract closure. Therefore, the term Process Group is maintained.

This Process Group may also address the early closure of the project, for example, aborted projects or canceled projects.

8.1 CLOSE PROJECT OR PHASE

Close Project or Phase is the process of finalizing all activities for the project, phase, or contract. The key benefits of this process are the project or phase information is archived, the planned work is completed, and organizational team resources are released to pursue new endeavors.

This process is performed once or at predefined points in the project. The inputs, tools and techniques, and outputs are shown in Figure 8-1. Figure 8-2 presents the data flow diagram for the process.

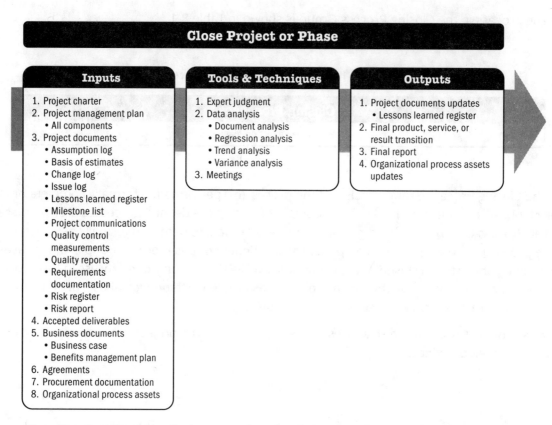

Close Project or Phase

Inputs	Tools & Techniques	Outputs

1. Project charter
2. Project management plan
  • All components
3. Project documents
  • Assumption log
  • Basis of estimates
  • Change log
  • Issue log
  • Lessons learned register
  • Milestone list
  • Project communications
  • Quality control measurements
  • Quality reports
  • Requirements documentation
  • Risk register
  • Risk report
4. Accepted deliverables
5. Business documents
  • Business case
  • Benefits management plan
6. Agreements
7. Procurement documentation
8. Organizational process assets
	1. Expert judgment
	2. Data analysis
	  • Document analysis
	  • Regression analysis
	  • Trend analysis
	  • Variance analysis
	3. Meetings
		1. Project documents updates
		  • Lessons learned register
		2. Final product, service, or result transition
		3. Final report
		4. Organizational process assets updates

Note: This figure provides the inputs, tools and techniques, and outputs that may be used for this process. Descriptions for inputs and outputs appear in Section 9. Descriptions for tools and techniques appear in Section 10.

Figure 8-1. Close Project or Phase: Inputs, Tools & Techniques, and Outputs

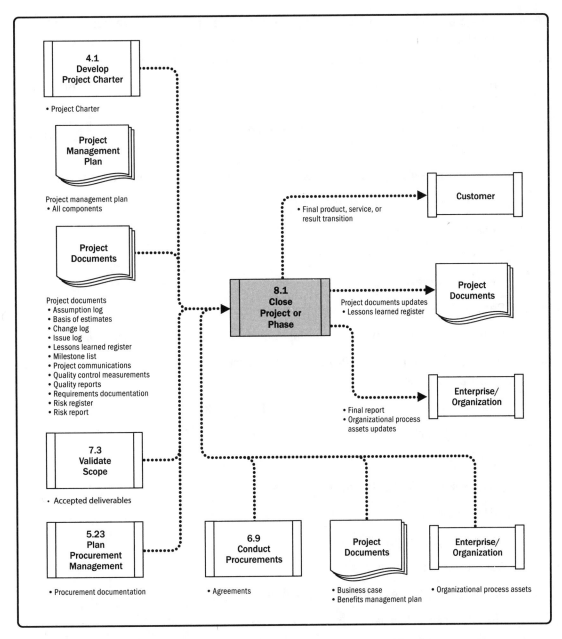

Note: This figure provides the inputs and outputs that may be used for this process. Descriptions for inputs and outputs appear in Section 9.

Figure 8-2. Close Project or Phase: Data Flow Diagram

When closing a project, the project manager reviews the project management plan to ensure that all project work is completed and that the project has met its objectives. The activities necessary for the administrative closure of the project or phase include, but are not limited to:

- Actions and activities necessary to satisfy completion or exit criteria for the phase or project, such as:

  ▷ Make certain that all documents and deliverables are up to date and that all issues are resolved.

  ▷ Confirm the delivery and formal acceptance of deliverables by the customer.

  ▷ Ensure that all costs are charged to the project.

  ▷ Close project accounts.

  ▷ Reassign personnel.

  ▷ Deal with the excess project material.

  ▷ Reallocate project facilities, equipment, and other resources.

  ▷ Elaborate the final project reports as required by organizational policies.

- Activities related to the completion of the contractual agreements applicable to the project or project phase, such as:

  ▷ Confirm the formal acceptance of the seller's work.

  ▷ Finalize open claims.

  ▷ Update records to reflect final results.

  ▷ Archive such information for future use.

- Activities needed to:

  ▷ Collect project or phase records.

  ▷ Audit project success or failure.

  ▷ Manage knowledge sharing and transfer.

  ▷ Identify lessons learned.

  ▷ Archive project information for future use by the organization.

- ▶ Actions and activities necessary to transfer the project's products, services, or results to the next phase or to production and/or operations.

- ▶ Collection of suggestions for improving or updating the policies and procedures of the organization and sending them to the appropriate organizational unit.

- ▶ Actions and activities to measure stakeholder satisfaction.

The Close Project or Phase process also establishes the procedures to investigate and document the reasons for actions taken when a project is terminated before completion. To successfully achieve this, the project manager needs to engage all of the proper stakeholders in the process.

9

Inputs and Outputs

All of the inputs and outputs in this section appear in alphabetical order; therefore, no sections numbers are assigned.

Accepted deliverables. Products, results, or capabilities produced by a project and validated by the project customer or sponsors as meeting their specified acceptance criteria.

The authorized stakeholder who signs off and approves the deliverables should get involved early on in the process and provide feedback regarding the quality of the deliverables so that the team can assess quality, performance, and recommend necessary changes.

Activity attributes. Activity attributes are multiple attributes associated with each schedule activity that can be included within the activity list. Activity attributes include activity codes, predecessor activities, successor activities, logical relationships, leads and lags, resource requirements, imposed dates, constraints, and assumptions.

Activity attributes extend the description of the activity by identifying multiple components associated with each activity. The components for each activity evolve over time. During the initial stages of the project, they include the unique activity identifier (ID), WBS ID, and activity label or name. When completed, they may include activity descriptions, predecessor activities, successor activities, logical relationships, leads and lags, resource requirements, imposed dates, constraints, and assumptions. Activity attributes can be used to identify the place where the work needs to be performed, the project calendar the activity is assigned to, and the type of effort involved. Activity attributes are used for schedule development and for selecting, ordering, and sorting the planned schedule activities in various ways within reports.

Activity list. A documented tabulation of schedule activities that shows the activity description, activity identifier, and a sufficiently detailed scope of work description so project team members understand what work is to be performed.

Agreements. Any document or communication that defines the initial intentions of a project. This can take the form of a contract, service-level agreement, memorandum of understanding (MOU), letters of agreement, verbal agreement, purchase order, email, etc.

Agreements can be simple or complex. A complex project may involve multiple contracts simultaneously or in sequence. Agreements must comply with local, national, and international laws regarding contracts.

All components (of the project management plan). All components of the project management plan are an input to this process. These components can be found in Table 1-6 of this practice guide.

Any component (of the project management plan). Any component of the project management plan is an input to this process. These components can be found in Table 1-6 of this practice guide.

Approved change requests. Change requests processed according to the change management plan by the project manager, change control board, or other designated person are either approved, deferred, or rejected.

Approved change requests are implemented via the Direct and Manage Project Work process. Deferred or rejected change requests are communicated to the person or group requesting the change.

The dispositions of all change requests are recorded in the change log as a project document update. See also *change requests*.

Assumption log. A project document used to record all assumptions and constraints throughout the project life cycle. New assumptions and constraints may be added, and the status of existing assumptions and constraints may be updated or closed out.

High-level (strategic and operational) constraints are normally identified in the business case before the project is initiated and then flow into the project charter. Lower-level activity and task assumptions are generated throughout the project, such as defining technical specifications, estimates, schedule activities, risks, etc. The assumption log is used to record all assumptions and constraints throughout the project life cycle.

Basis of estimates. Supporting documentation outlining the details used in establishing project estimates such as assumptions, constraints, level of detail, ranges, and confidence levels.

Regardless of the level of detail, the basis of estimates should provide a clear and complete understanding of how an estimate was derived. Documentation may include how the basis of estimate was developed, assumptions made, known constraints, range of possible estimates (e.g., ±10%), confidence level of the final estimate, and individual project risks influencing this estimate.

Benefits management plan. The documented explanation defining the processes for creating, maximizing, and sustaining the benefits provided by a project or program.

The benefits management plan is the document that describes how and when the benefits of the project will be delivered and the mechanisms that should be in place to measure those benefits. A project benefit is an outcome of actions, behaviors, products, services, or results that provides value to the sponsoring organization as well as to the project's intended beneficiaries. Development of the plan begins early in the project life cycle with the definition of the target benefits. The plan describes key elements of the benefits and may include the following:

- **Target benefits.** The expected tangible and intangible value to be gained by the implementation of the project; financial value is expressed as net present value (NPV).

- **Strategic alignment.** The alignment of the project to the business strategies of the organization.

- **Time frame for realizing benefits.** The length of time to realize benefits, for example, short-term, long-term, ongoing, or by phase.

- **Benefits owner.** The person accountable for monitoring, recording, and reporting realized benefits throughout the time frame established in the plan.

- **Metrics.** The direct and indirect measures used to determine benefits realized.

- **Assumptions.** The factors expected to be in place or to be in evidence.

- **Risks.** Those risks pertaining to realization of benefit.

The data and information that are documented in the business case and needs assessment are used to develop the benefits management plan. The benefits management plan and the project management plan include a description of how the business value resulting from the project becomes part of the organization's ongoing operations, including the metrics to be used. The metrics provide verification of the business value and validation of the project's success.

Development and maintenance of the benefits management plan is an iterative activity. It complements the business case, project charter, and project management plan. The project manager works with the sponsor to ensure that the project charter, project management plan, and benefits management plan remain in alignment throughout the life cycle of the project.

Both the business case and the benefits management plan are developed prior to the project being initiated. Additionally, both documents are referenced after the project has been completed. Therefore, they are considered business documents rather than project documents or components of the project management plan. As appropriate, these business documents may be inputs to some of the processes involved in managing the project, such as developing the project charter.

Bid documents. Bid documents are used to solicit proposals from prospective sellers. Terms such as bid, tender, or quotation are generally used when the seller selection decision is based on price (as when buying commercial or standard items), while a term such as proposal is generally used when other considerations such as technical capability or technical approach are the most important. Specific procurement terminology used may vary by industry and location of the procurement.

Depending on the goods or services needed, the bidding documents can include a request for information, request for quotation, request for proposal, or other appropriate documents. The conditions involving their use are presented below:

▸ **Request for information (RFI).** An RFI is used when more information on the goods and services to be acquired is needed from the sellers. It will typically be followed by an RFQ or RFP.

▸ **Request for quotation (RFQ).** An RFQ is commonly used when more information is needed on how vendors would satisfy the requirements and/or how much it will cost.

▸ **Request for proposal (RFP).** An RFP is used when there is a problem in the project and the solution is not easy to determine. This is the most formal of the "request for" documents and has strict procurement rules for content, time line, and seller responses.

The buyer structures bid documents to facilitate both an accurate and complete response from each prospective seller and an easy evaluation of the responses. These documents include a description of the desired form of the response, the relevant procurement statement of work (SOW), and any required contractual provisions.

The complexity and level of detail of the bid documents should be consistent with the value of, and risks associated with, the planned procurement. Bid documents are required to be sufficiently detailed to ensure consistent, appropriate responses, but flexible enough to allow consideration of any seller suggestions for better ways to satisfy the same requirements.

Business case. A documented economic feasibility study used to establish the validity of the benefits of a selected component lacking sufficient definition and that is used as a basis for the authorization of further project management activities.

The business case lists the objectives and reasons for project initiation. It helps measure the project success at the end of the project against the project objectives. The business case is a project business document that is used throughout the project life cycle. The business case may be used before project initiation and may result in a go/no-go decision for the project.

Both the business case and the benefits management plan are developed prior to the project being initiated. Additionally, both documents are referenced after the project has been completed. Therefore, they are considered business documents rather than project documents or components of the project management plan. As appropriate, these business documents may be inputs to some of the processes involved in managing the project, such as developing the project charter.

Business documents. The business case and benefits management plan contain information about the project's objectives and how the project will contribute to the business goals. Although both documents are developed prior to the project, they are reviewed periodically.

In some organizations, the business case and benefits management plan are maintained at the program level. The project sponsor is generally accountable for the development and maintenance of the project business case document. The project manager is responsible for providing recommendations and oversight to keep the project business case, project management plan, project charter, and project benefits management plan success measures in alignment with one another and with the goals and objectives of the organization.

Change log. A comprehensive list of changes submitted during the project, which includes the current status. The disposition of all change requests is recorded in the change log as a project document update.

Change management plan. A component of the project management plan that establishes the change control board (CCB), documents the extent of its authority, and describes how the change control system will be implemented.

The change management plan provides the direction for managing the change control process and documents the roles and responsibilities of the CCB.

Change requests. A change request is a formal proposal to modify any document, deliverable, or baseline. Change requests may be initiated internally or externally to the project.

When issues are found while project work is being performed, change requests are submitted to modify project policies or procedures, project or product scope, project cost or budget, project schedule, or the quality of the project or product results. Change requests may include corrective action, preventive action, defect repair, or updates that reflect modified or additional ideas or content.

Other change requests cover the needed preventive or corrective actions to eliminate or minimize a negative impact later in the project.

Any stakeholder may request a change. Change requests are processed for review and disposition through the Perform Integrated Change Control process.

Closed procurements. The buyer, usually through its authorized procurement administrator, provides the seller with formal written notice that the contract has been completed. Requirements for formal procurement closure are usually defined in the terms and conditions of the contract and are included in the procurement management plan. Typically, all deliverables should have been provided on time and meet technical and quality requirements, there should be no outstanding claims or invoices, and all final payments should have been made. The project management team should have approved all deliverables prior to closure.

Communications management plan. The communications management plan is a component of the project management plan and describes how project communications will be planned, structured, implemented, and monitored for effectiveness. The plan contains the following information:

▶ Stakeholder communication requirements;

▶ Information to be communicated, including language, format, content, and level of detail;

▶ Escalation processes;

▶ Reason for the distribution of that information;

▶ Time frame and frequency for the distribution of required information and receipt of acknowledgment or response, if applicable;

▶ Person responsible for communicating the information;

▶ Person responsible for authorizing release of confidential information;

▶ Person or groups who will receive the information, including information about their needs, requirements, and expectations;

- Methods or technologies used to convey the information, such as memos, email, press releases, or social media;

- Resources allocated for communication activities, including time and budget;

- Method for updating and refining the communications management plan as the project progresses and develops, such as when the stakeholder community changes as the project moves through different phases;

- Glossary of common terminology;

- Flowcharts of the information flow in the project, workflows with possible sequence of authorization, list of reports, meeting plans, etc.; and

- Constraints derived from specific legislation or regulation, technology, organizational policies, etc.

The communications management plan can include guidelines and templates for project status meetings, project team meetings, virtual meetings, and email messages. The use of a project website and project management software can be included if these are to be used in the project.

Configuration management plan. A component of the project management plan that describes how to identify and account for project artifacts under configuration control, and how to record and report changes to them.

The plan describes how information will be recorded and updated so that the product, service, or result remains consistent and/or operative. As a general rule, each project's configuration management plan should define which project artifacts need to be placed under configuration control. Any change in a configuration element should be formally controlled and will require a change request.

Cost baseline. The approved version of the time-phased project budget, excluding any management reserves, which can be changed only through formal change control procedures and is used as a basis for comparison to actual results.

Cost estimates. A cost estimate is a quantitative assessment of the likely costs for resources required to complete the activity. It is a prediction that is based on the information known at a given point in time. Cost estimates include the identification and consideration of costing alternatives to initiate and complete the project. Cost trade-offs and risks should be considered, such as make versus buy, buy versus lease, and the sharing of resources in order to achieve optimal costs for the project.

Cost estimates are generally expressed in units of some currency (i.e., dollars, euros, yen, etc.). In some instances, other units of measure, such as staff hours or staff days, may be used to facilitate comparisons by eliminating the effects of currency fluctuations.

Cost estimates should be reviewed and refined during the course of the project to reflect additional details as they become available and assumptions are tested. The accuracy of a project estimate will increase as the project progresses through the project life cycle.

Costs are estimated for all resources that will be charged to the project. This includes but is not limited to labor, materials, equipment, services, and facilities, as well as special categories such as an inflation allowance, cost of financing, or contingency costs. Cost estimates may be presented at the activity level or in summary form.

Cost forecasts. Based on the project's past performance, cost forecasts are used to determine if the project is within defined tolerance ranges for budget and to identify any necessary change requests. Either a calculated estimate at completion (EAC) value or a bottom-up EAC value is documented and communicated to stakeholders.

Cost management plan. A component of a project or program management plan that describes how costs will be planned, structured, and controlled. The cost management processes and their associated tools and techniques are documented in the cost management plan.

For example, the cost management plan can establish the following:

▶ **Units of measure.** Each unit used in measurements (such as staff hours, staff days, or weeks for time measures; meters, liters, tons, kilometers, or cubic yards for quantity measures; or lump sum in currency form) is defined for each of the resources.

▶ **Level of precision.** This is the degree to which cost estimates will be rounded up or down (e.g., US$995.59 to US$1,000), based on the scope of the activities and magnitude of the project.

▶ **Level of accuracy.** The acceptable range (e.g., ±10%) used in determining realistic cost estimates is specified and may include an amount for contingencies.

▶ **Organizational procedures links.** The work breakdown structure (WBS) (Section 5.5) provides the framework for the cost management plan, allowing for consistency with the estimates, budgets, and control of costs. The WBS component used for project cost accounting is called the control account. Each control account is assigned a unique code or account number(s) that links directly to the performing organization's accounting system.

- **Control thresholds.** Variance thresholds for monitoring cost performance may be specified to indicate an agreed-upon amount of variation to be allowed before some action needs to be taken. Thresholds are typically expressed as percentage deviations from the baseline plan.

- **Rules of performance measurement.** Earned value management (EVM) rules of performance measurement are set. For example, the cost management plan may:
  - Define the points in the WBS at which measurement of control accounts will be performed;
  - Establish the EVM techniques (e.g., weighted milestones, fixed-formula, percent complete, etc.) to be employed; and
  - Specify tracking methodologies and the EVM computation equations for calculating projected estimate at completion (EAC) forecasts to provide a validity check on the bottom-up EAC.

- **Reporting formats.** The formats and frequency for the various cost reports are defined.

- **Additional details.** Additional details about cost management activities include but are not limited to:
  - Description of strategic funding choices,
  - Procedure to account for fluctuations in currency exchange rates, and
  - Procedure for project cost recording.

For more specific information regarding earned value management, refer to *The Standard for Earned Value Management* [9].

Deliverables. Unique and verifiable products, results, or capabilities to perform a service that is required to be produced to complete a process, phase, or project.

Projects are undertaken to fulfill objectives by producing deliverables. Deliverables may be tangible or intangible.

Development approach. The development approach defines whether a predictive (waterfall), iterative, adaptive, agile, or hybrid development approach will be used.

Duration estimates. Duration estimates are quantitative assessments of the likely number of time periods that are required to complete an activity, phase, or project. Duration estimates do not include any lags. Duration estimates may include some indication of the range of possible results. For example:

- A range of 2 weeks ± 2 days, which indicates that the activity will take at least 8 days and not more than 12 (assuming a 5-day work week); or

- A 15% probability of exceeding 3 weeks, which indicates a high probability—85%—that the activity will take 3 weeks or less.

Enterprise environmental factors (EEFs). Conditions, not under the immediate control of the team, that influence, constrain, or direct the project, program, or portfolio. These conditions can be internal and/or external to the organization. EEFs are considered as inputs to many project management processes, specifically for most planning processes. These factors may enhance or constrain project management options. In addition, these factors may have a positive or negative influence on the outcome.

- EEFs internal to the organization:

  - *Organizational culture, structure, and governance.* Examples include vision, mission, values, beliefs, cultural norms, leadership style, hierarchy and authority relationships, organizational style, ethics, code of conduct, policies, and procedures.

  - *Geographic distribution of facilities and resources.* Examples include factory locations and virtual teams.

  - *Infrastructure.* Examples include existing facilities, equipment, organizational telecommunications channels, information technology hardware, availability, and capacity.

  - *Information technology software.* Examples include scheduling software tools, configuration management systems, web interfaces to other online automated systems, and work authorization systems.

  - *Resource availability.* Examples include contracting and purchasing constraints, approved providers and subcontractors, and collaboration agreements.

  - *Employee capability.* Examples include existing human resources expertise, skills, competencies, and specialized knowledge.

- ▶ EEFs external to the organization:
  - ▷ *Marketplace conditions.* Examples include competitors, market share brand recognition, and trademarks.
  - ▷ *Social and cultural influences and issues.* Examples include political climate, codes of conduct, ethics, and perceptions.
  - ▷ *Legal restrictions.* Examples include country or local laws and regulations related to security, data protection, business conduct, employment, and procurement.
  - ▷ *Commercial databases.* Examples include benchmarking results, standardized cost estimating data, industry risk study information, and risk databases.
  - ▷ *Academic research.* Examples include industry studies, publications, and benchmarking results.
  - ▷ *Government or industry standards.* Examples include regulatory agency regulations and standards related to products, production, environment, quality, and workmanship.
  - ▷ *Financial considerations.* Examples include currency exchange rates, interest rates, inflation rates, tariffs, and geographic location.
  - ▷ *Physical environmental elements.* Examples include working conditions, weather, and constraints.

Final product, service, or result transition. A product, service, or result, once delivered by the project, may be handed over to a different group or organization that will operate, maintain, and support it throughout its life cycle.

This output refers to this transition of the final product, service, or result that the project was authorized to produce (or in the case of phase closure, the intermediate product, service, or result of that phase) from one team to another.

Final report. A summary of project performance, which can include information such as:

- ▶ Summary-level description of the project or phase.
- ▶ Scope objectives, the criteria used to evaluate the scope, and evidence that the completion criteria were met.
- ▶ Quality objectives, the criteria used to evaluate the project and product quality, the verification and actual milestone delivery dates, and reasons for variances.

- Cost objectives, including the acceptable cost range, actual costs, and reasons for any variances.

- Summary of the validation information for the final product, service, or result.

- Schedule objectives, including whether results achieved the benefits that the project was undertaken to address. If the benefits are not met at the close of the project, indicate the degree to which they were achieved and estimate for future benefits realization.

- Summary of how the final product, service, or result achieved the business needs identified in the business plan. If the business needs are not met at the close of the project, indicate the degree to which they were achieved and estimate for when the business needs will be met in the future.

- Summary of any risks or issues encountered on the project and how they were addressed.

Independent cost estimates. For large procurements, a procuring organization may elect to either prepare its own independent estimate or have a cost estimate prepared by an outside professional estimator to serve as a benchmark on proposed responses. Significant differences in cost estimates can be an indication that the procurement statement of work (SOW) was deficient or ambiguous, or that the prospective sellers either misunderstood or failed to respond fully to the procurement SOW.

Issue log. A project document where information about issues is recorded and monitored.

Lessons learned register. A project document used to record knowledge gained during a project so that it can be used in the current project and entered into the lessons learned repository.

The lessons learned register can include the category and description of the situation. It may also include the impact, recommendations, and proposed actions associated with the situation. The lessons learned register records challenges, problems, realized risks and opportunities, or other content as appropriate.

The lessons learned register is created as an output of the Manage Project Knowledge process early in the project. Thereafter it is used as an input and updated as an output in many processes throughout the project. The persons or teams involved in the work are also involved in capturing the lessons learned. Knowledge can be documented using videos, pictures, audios, or other suitable means that ensure the efficiency of the lessons captured.

At the end of a project or phase, the information is transferred to an organizational process asset called a lessons learned repository.

Make-or-buy decisions. Make-or-buy decisions are made regarding the external purchase or internal manufacture of a product. A make-or-buy analysis results in a decision as to whether particular work can best be accomplished by the project team or needs to be purchased from outside sources.

Milestone list. A milestone list identifies all project milestones and indicates whether the milestone is mandatory, such as those required by contract, or optional, such as those based on historical information. Milestones have zero duration because they represent a significant point or event in a project.

Organizational process assets (OPAs). The plans, processes, documents, templates, and knowledge repositories specific to and used by the performing organization. These assets influence the management of the project.

OPAs include any artifact, practice, or knowledge from any or all of the performing organizations involved in the project that can be used to execute or govern the project. The OPAs also include the organization's lessons learned from previous projects and historical information. OPAs may include completed schedules, risk data, and earned value data. OPAs are inputs to many project management processes. Since OPAs are internal to the organization, the project team members may be able to update and add to the organizational process assets as necessary throughout the project. They may be grouped into two categories:

- ▶ **Processes, documents, and templates.** Generally, assets in this category are not updated as part of the project work. Processes, documents, and templates are usually established by the project management office (PMO) or another function outside of the project. These can be updated only by following the appropriate organizational policies associated with updating these assets. Some organizations encourage the team to tailor templates, life cycles, and checklists for the project. In these instances, the project management team should tailor those assets to meet the needs of the project.

- ▶ **Organizational knowledge repositories.** Assets in this category are updated throughout the project with project information. For example, information on financial performance, lessons learned, performance metrics and issues, and defects are continually updated throughout the project.

Organizational process assets updates. Any organizational process asset can be updated as a result of a process. Updates include plans, processes, and knowledge repositories specific to and used by the performing organization.

Outputs from other processes. Outputs from other processes are integrated to create the project management plan. Subsidiary plans and baselines that are an output from other processes are inputs to this process. In addition, changes to these documents may necessitate updates to the project management plan.

Performance measurement baseline (PMB). An integrated scope, schedule, and cost plan for the project work used for comparison to manage, measure, and control project performance.

Physical resource assignments. This documentation records the material, equipment, supplies, locations, and other physical resources that will be used during the project. It describes the expected resource utilization and whether the resource is internal to the organization or outsourced. Physical resource assignments are dynamic and subject to change due to availability, the project, organization, environment, or other factors.

Pre-assignment. When physical or team resources for a project are determined in advance, they are considered pre-assigned. This situation can occur if the project is the result of specific resources being identified as part of a competitive proposal or if the project is dependent upon the expertise of particular persons. Pre-assignment might also include the team members who have already been assigned in Develop Project Charter Process or other processes before the initial resource management plan has been completed.

Probability and impact matrix. A probability and impact matrix is a grid for mapping the probability of each risk occurrence and its impact on project objectives if that risk occurs. This matrix specifies combinations of probability and impact that allow individual project risks to be divided into priority groups (see Figure 9-1). Risks can be prioritized for further analysis and planning of risk responses based on their probability and impacts. The probability of occurrence for each individual project risk is assessed as well as its impact on one or more project objectives if it does occur, using definitions of probability and impact for the project as specified in the risk management plan. Individual project risks are assigned to a priority level based on the combination of their assessed probability and impact, using a probability and impact matrix.

An organization can assess a risk separately for each objective (e.g., cost, time, and scope) by having a separate probability and impact matrix for each. Alternatively, it may develop ways to determine one overall priority level for each risk, either by combining assessments for different objectives, or by taking the highest priority level regardless of which objective is affected.

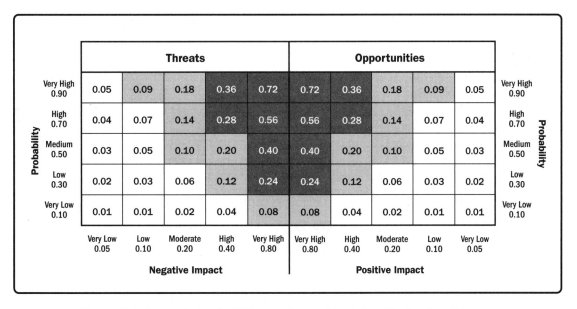

	Threats					Opportunities				
Very High 0.90	0.05	0.09	0.18	0.36	0.72	0.72	0.36	0.18	0.09	0.05
High 0.70	0.04	0.07	0.14	0.28	0.56	0.56	0.28	0.14	0.07	0.04
Medium 0.50	0.03	0.05	0.10	0.20	0.40	0.40	0.20	0.10	0.05	0.03
Low 0.30	0.02	0.03	0.06	0.12	0.24	0.24	0.12	0.06	0.03	0.02
Very Low 0.10	0.01	0.01	0.02	0.04	0.08	0.08	0.04	0.02	0.01	0.01
	Very Low 0.05	Low 0.10	Moderate 0.20	High 0.40	Very High 0.80	Very High 0.80	High 0.40	Moderate 0.20	Low 0.10	Very Low 0.05
	Negative Impact					Positive Impact				

Probability (left axis): Very High 0.90, High 0.70, Medium 0.50, Low 0.30, Very Low 0.10
Probability (right axis): Very High 0.90, High 0.70, Medium 0.50, Low 0.30, Very Low 0.10

Figure 9-1. Example Probability and Impact Matrix with Scoring Scheme

Procurement documentation. All documents used in signing, executing, and closing an agreement. Procurement documentation may include documents predating the project. Procurement documentation contains complete supporting records for administration of the procurement processes. Procurement documentation includes the statement of work, payment information, contractor work performance information, plans, drawings, and other correspondence.

Procurement documentation updates. Procurement documentation that may be updated includes the contract with all supporting schedules, requested unapproved contract changes, and approved change requests. Procurement documentation also includes any seller-developed technical documentation and other work performance information such as deliverables, seller performance reports and warranties, financial documents including invoices and payment records, and the results of contract-related inspections.

Procurement management plan. A component of the project or program management plan that describes how a project team will acquire goods and services from outside of the performing organization.

The procurement management plan contains the activities to be undertaken during the procurement process. It should document whether international competitive bidding, national competitive bidding, local bidding, etc., should be done. If the project is financed externally, the sources and availability of funding should be aligned with the procurement management plan and the project schedule.

The procurement management plan can include guidance for:

- How procurement will be coordinated with other project aspects, such as project schedule development and control processes;

- Timetable of key procurement activities;

- Procurement metrics to be used to manage contracts;

- Stakeholder roles and responsibilities related to procurement, including authority and constraints of the project team when the performing organization has a procurement department;

- Constraints and assumptions that could affect planned procurements;

- Legal jurisdiction and the currency in which payments will be made;

- Determination of whether independent estimates will be used and whether they are needed as evaluation criteria;

- Risk management issues including identifying requirements for performance bonds or insurance contracts to mitigate some forms of project risk; and

- Prequalified sellers, if any, to be used.

A procurement management plan can be formal or informal, can be highly detailed or broadly framed, and is based upon the needs of each project.

Procurement statement of work. The statement of work (SOW) for each procurement is developed from the project scope baseline and defines only that portion of the project scope that is to be included within the related contract. The SOW describes the procurement item in sufficient detail to allow prospective sellers to determine if they are capable of providing the products, services, or results. Sufficient detail can vary based on the nature of the item, the needs of the buyer, or the expected contract form. Information included in a SOW can include specifications, quantity desired, quality levels, performance data, period of performance, work location, and other requirements.

The procurement SOW should be clear, complete, and concise. It includes a description of any collateral services required, such as performance reporting or post-project operational support for the procured item. The SOW can be revised as required as it moves through the procurement process until incorporated into a signed agreement.

The phrase *terms of reference (TOR)* is sometimes used when contracting for services. Similar to the procurement SOW, a TOR typically includes these elements:

▶ Tasks the contractor is required to perform as well as specified coordination requirements;

▶ Standards the contractor will fulfill that are applicable to the project;

▶ Data that need to be submitted for approval;

▶ Detailed list of all data and services that will be provided to the contractor by the buyer for use in performing the contract, if applicable; and

▶ Definition of the schedule for initial submission and the review/approval time required.

Procurement strategy. Once the make-or-buy analysis is complete and the decision is made to acquire from outside the project, a procurement strategy should be identified. The objective of the procurement strategy is to determine the project delivery method, the type of legally binding agreement(s), and how the procurement will advance through the procurement phases.

▶ **Delivery methods.** Delivery methods are different for professional services versus construction projects.

  ▷ *For professional services*, delivery methods include: buyer/services provider with no subcontracting, buyer/services provider with subcontracting allowed, joint venture between buyer and services provider, and buyer/services provider acts as the representative.

  ▷ *For industrial or commercial construction*, project delivery methods include but are not limited to: turnkey, design build (DB), design bid build (DBB), design build operate (DBO), build own operate transfer (BOOT), and others.

▶ **Contract payment types.** Contract payment types are separate from the project delivery methods and are coordinated with the buying organization's internal financial systems. They include but are not limited to these contract types plus variations: lump sum, firm fixed price, cost plus fixed fee, cost plus award fees, cost plus incentive fees, time and materials, target cost, and others.

▷ Fixed-price contracts are suitable when the type of work is predictable and the requirements are well defined and not likely to change.

▷ Cost plus contracts are suitable when the work is evolving, likely to change, or not well defined.

▷ Incentives and awards may be used to align the objectives of buyer and seller.

▶ **Procurement phases.** The procurement strategy can also include information on procurement phases. Information may include:

▷ Sequencing or phasing of the procurement, a description of each phase and the specific objectives of each phase;

▷ Procurement performance indicators and milestones to be used in monitoring;

▷ Criteria for moving from phase to phase;

▷ Monitoring and evaluation plan for tracking progress; and

▷ Process for knowledge transfer for use in subsequent phases.

Project calendars. A project calendar identifies working days and shifts that are available for scheduled activities. It distinguishes time periods in days or parts of days that are available to complete scheduled activities from time periods that are not available for work. A schedule model may require more than one project calendar to allow for different work periods for some activities to calculate the project schedule. Project calendars may be updated.

Project charter. A document issued by the project initiator or sponsor that formally authorizes the existence of a project and provides the project manager with the authority to apply organizational resources to project activities.

Project communications. Project communications artifacts may include but are not limited to: performance reports, deliverable status, schedule progress, cost incurred, presentations, and other information required by stakeholders.

Project documents. The documentation created throughout the five Process Groups to initiate, plan, execute, manage and control, close, and deliver the project. There are 33 project documents listed in Table 1-6 of this practice guide. Examples include change log, issue log, project schedule, project scope statement, requirements documentation, risk register, and stakeholder register.

Project documents updates. The documentation that is updated throughout the five Process Groups to initiate, plan, execute, manage and control, close, and deliver the project. There are 33 project documents listed in Table 1-6 of this practice guide. Examples include change log, issue log, project schedule, project scope statement, requirements documentation, risk register, and stakeholder register.

Project funding requirements. Total funding requirements and periodic funding requirements (e.g., quarterly, annually) are derived from the cost baseline. The cost baseline includes projected expenditures plus anticipated liabilities. Funding often occurs in incremental amounts, and may not be evenly distributed, which appear as steps in Figure 9-2. The total funds required are those included in the cost baseline plus management reserves, if any. Funding requirements may include the source(s) of the funding. The budget at completion (BAC) is the sum of all budgets established for the work to be performed.

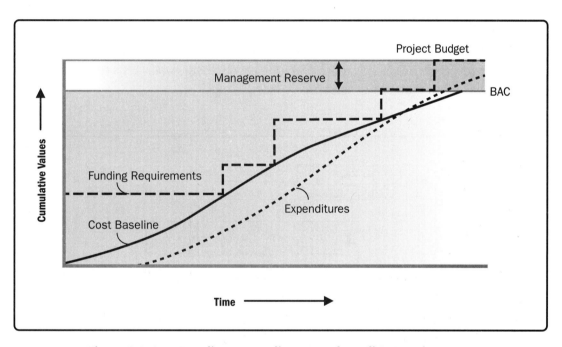

Figure 9-2. Cost Baseline, Expenditures, and Funding Requirements

Project life cycle description. The project life cycle determines the series of phases that a project passes through from its inception to the end of the project.

Project management plan. The document that describes how the project will be executed, monitored and controlled, and closed.

Project management plan updates. Updates to the document that describes how the project is being executed, monitored and controlled, and closed.

Project schedule. A schedule model output that presents linked activities with planned dates, durations, milestones, and resources. The detailed project schedule should be flexible throughout the project to adjust for the knowledge gained, increased understanding of the risks, and value-added activities.

Project schedule network diagrams. A project schedule network diagram is a graphical representation of the logical relationships, also referred to as dependencies, among the project schedule activities. Figure 9-3 illustrates a project schedule network diagram. A project schedule network diagram is produced manually or by using project management software. It can include full project details or have one or more summary activities. A summary narrative can accompany the diagram and describe the basic approach used to sequence the activities. Any unusual activity sequences within the network should be fully described within the narrative.

Activities that have multiple predecessor activities indicate a path convergence. Activities that have multiple successor activities indicate a path divergence. Activities with divergence and convergence are at greater risk as they are affected by multiple activities or can affect multiple activities. Activity I is called a path convergence, as it has more than one predecessor, while activity K is called a path divergence, as it has more than one successor.

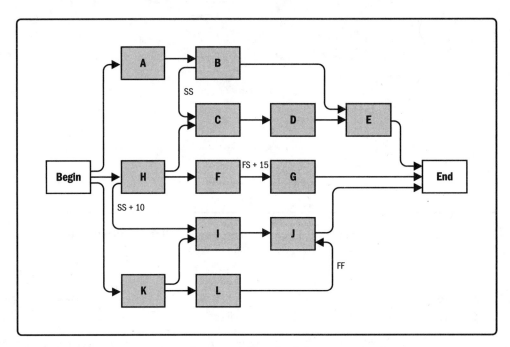

Figure 9-3. Example of Project Schedule Network Diagram

Project scope statement. The project scope statement includes the description of the project scope, major deliverables, and exclusions. The project scope statement documents the entire scope, including project and product scope. It describes the project's deliverables in detail. It also provides a common understanding of the project scope among project stakeholders. It may contain explicit scope exclusions that can assist in managing stakeholder expectations. It enables the project team to perform more detailed planning, guides the project team's work during execution, and provides the baseline for evaluating whether requests for changes or additional work are contained within or outside the project's boundaries.

The degree and level of detail to which the project scope statement defines the work that will be performed and the work that is excluded, can help determine how well the project management team can control the overall project scope. The detailed project scope statement, either directly or by reference to other documents, includes the following:

- ▶ **Product scope description.** Progressively elaborates the characteristics of the product, service, or result described in the project charter and requirements documentation.

- ▶ **Deliverables.** Any unique and verifiable product, result, or capability to perform a service that is required to be produced to complete a process, phase, or project. Deliverables also include ancillary results, such as project management reports and documentation. These deliverables may be described at a summary level or in great detail.

- ▶ **Acceptance criteria.** A set of conditions that is required to be met before deliverables are accepted.

- ▶ **Project exclusions.** Identifies what is excluded from the project. Explicitly stating what is out of scope for the project helps manage stakeholders' expectations and can reduce scope creep.

Although the project charter and the project scope statement are sometimes perceived as containing a certain degree of redundancy, they are different in the level of detail contained in each. The project charter contains high-level information, while the project scope statement contains a detailed description of the scope components. These components are progressively elaborated throughout the project. Table 9-1 describes some of the key elements for each document.

Table 9-1. Elements of the Project Charter and Project Scope Statement

Project Charter	Project Scope Statement
Project purpose	Project scope description (progressively elaborated)
Measurable project objectives and related success criteria	Project deliverables
High-level requirements	Acceptance criteria
High-level project description, boundaries, and key deliverables	Project exclusions
Overall project risk	
Summary milestone schedule	
Preapproved financial resources	
Key stakeholder list	
Project approval requirements (i.e., what constitutes success, who decides the project is successful, who signs off on the project)	
Project exit criteria (i.e., what are the conditions to be met in order to close or to cancel the project or phase)	
Assigned project manager, responsibility, and authority level	
Name and authority of the sponsor or other person(s) authorizing the project	

Project team assignments. A document containing a record of the team members and their roles and responsibilities for the project. This documentation can include a project team directory and names inserted into the project management plan, such as the project organization charts and schedules.

Quality control measurements. The documented results of the Control Quality process activities. The measurements should be captured in the format specified in the quality management plan.

Quality management plan. The quality management plan is a component of the project management plan and describes how applicable policies, procedures, and guidelines will be implemented to achieve the quality objectives. It describes the activities and resources necessary for the project management team to achieve the quality objectives set for the project. The quality management plan may be formal or informal, detailed or broadly framed. The style and detail of the quality management plan are determined by the requirements of the project. It should be reviewed early in the project to ensure that decisions are based on accurate information. The benefits of this review can include a sharper focus on the project's value proposition, reductions in costs, and less frequent schedule overruns that are caused by rework.

The quality management plan may include but is not limited to the following components:

- ▶ Quality standards that will be used by the project,
- ▶ Quality objectives of the project,
- ▶ Quality roles and responsibilities,
- ▶ Project deliverables and processes subject to quality review,
- ▶ Quality control and quality management activities planned for the project,
- ▶ Quality tools that will be used for the project, and
- ▶ Major procedures relevant for the project, such as dealing with nonconformance, corrective actions procedures, and continuous improvement procedures.

Quality metrics. A quality metric specifically describes a project or product attribute and how the Control Quality process will verify compliance to it. Some examples of quality metrics include percentage of tasks completed on time, cost performance measured by a cost performance index (CPI), failure rate, number of defects identified per day, total downtime per month, errors found per line of code, customer satisfaction scores, and percentage of requirements covered by the test plan as a measure of test coverage.

Quality report. A project document that includes quality management issues, recommendations for corrective actions, and a summary of findings from quality control activities. It may include recommendations for process, project, and product improvements.

Quality reports can be graphical, numerical, or qualitative. The information provided can be used by other processes and departments to take corrective actions in order to achieve the expected quality. Information presented in the quality reports may include all quality management issues escalated by the team; recommendations for process, project, and product improvements; corrective actions recommendations (including rework, defect/bugs repair, 100% inspection, and more); and the summary of findings from the Control Quality process.

Requirements documentation. A description of how individual requirements meet the business need for the project.

Requirements may start out at a high level and become progressively more detailed as more information about the requirements becomes known. Before being baselined, requirements need to be unambiguous (measurable and testable), traceable, complete, consistent, and acceptable to key stakeholders. The format of the requirements document may range from a simple document listing all of the requirements categorized by stakeholder and priority, to more elaborate forms containing an executive summary, detailed descriptions, and attachments.

Many organizations categorize requirements into different types, such as business and technical solutions. Business solutions refer to stakeholder needs and technical solutions determine how those needs will be implemented. Requirements can be grouped into classifications allowing for further refinement and detail as the requirements are elaborated. These classifications include:

▶ **Business requirements.** These describe the higher-level needs of the organization as a whole, such as business issues or opportunities, and reasons why a project has been undertaken.

▶ **Stakeholder requirements.** These describe the needs of a stakeholder or stakeholder group.

▶ **Solution requirements.** These describe features, functions, and characteristics of the product, service, or result that will meet the business and stakeholder requirements. Solution requirements are further grouped into functional and nonfunctional requirements:

> *Functional requirements.* Functional requirements describe the behaviors of the product. Examples include actions, processes, data, and interactions that the product should execute.

> *Nonfunctional requirements.* Nonfunctional requirements supplement functional requirements and describe the environmental conditions or qualities required for the product to be effective. Examples include reliability, security, performance, safety, level of service, supportability, retention/purge, etc.

▶ **Transition and readiness requirements.** These describe temporary capabilities, such as data conversion and training requirements, needed to transition from the current as-is state to the desired future state.

▶ **Project requirements.** These describe the actions, processes, or other conditions the project needs to meet. Examples include milestone dates, contractual obligations, constraints, etc.

▶ **Quality requirements.** These capture any condition or criteria needed to validate the successful completion of a project deliverable or fulfillment of other project requirements. Examples include tests, certifications, validations, etc.

Requirements management plan. The requirements management plan is a component of the project management plan and describes how project and product requirements will be analyzed, documented, and managed. According to *Business Analysis for Practitioners: A Practice Guide* [3], some organizations refer to it as a business analysis plan. Components of the requirements management plan can include but are not limited to:

▶ How requirements activities will be planned, tracked, and reported;

▶ Configuration management activities, such as:

> How changes will be initiated;

> How impacts will be analyzed;

> How changes will be traced, tracked, and reported; and

> Authorization levels required to approve these changes.

▶ Requirements prioritization process;

▶ Metrics that will be used and the rationale for using them; and

▶ Traceability structure that reflects the requirement attributes captured on the traceability matrix.

Requirements traceability matrix. The requirements traceability matrix is a grid that links product requirements from their origin to the deliverables that satisfy them. The implementation of a requirements traceability matrix helps to ensure that each requirement adds business value by linking it to the business and project objectives. It provides a means to track requirements throughout the project life cycle, helping to ensure that requirements approved in the requirements documentation are delivered at the end of the project. Finally, it provides a structure for managing changes to the product scope.

Tracing requirements includes but is not limited to:

▶ Business needs, opportunities, goals, and objectives;

▶ Project objectives;

▶ Project scope and WBS deliverables;

▶ Product design;

▶ Product development;

▶ Test strategy and test scenarios; and

▶ High-level requirements to more detailed requirements.

Attributes associated with each requirement can be recorded in the requirements traceability matrix. These attributes help to define key information about the requirement. Typical attributes used in the requirements traceability matrix may include: a unique identifier, a textual description of the requirement, the rationale for inclusion, owner, source, priority, version, current status (e.g., active, cancelled, deferred, added, approved, assigned, completed), and status date. Additional attributes to ensure that the requirement has met stakeholders' satisfaction may include stability, complexity, and acceptance criteria. Figure 9-4 provides an example of a requirements traceability matrix with its associated attributes.

Resource breakdown structure. A hierarchical representation of resources by category and type. Examples of resource categories include but are not limited to labor, material, equipment, and supplies. Resource types may include the skill level, grade level, required certifications, or other information as appropriate to the project. See Figure 9-5 for an example.

Requirements Traceability Matrix

ID	Associate ID	Requirements Description	Business Needs, Opportunities, Goals, Objectives	Project Objectives	WBS Deliverables	Product Design	Product Development	Test Cases
Project Name:								
Cost Center:								
Project Description:								
001	1.0							
	1.1							
	1.2							
	1.2.1							
002	2.0							
	2.1							
	2.1.1							
003	3.0							
	3.1							
	3.2							
004	4.0							
005	5.0							

Figure 9-4. Example of a Requirements Traceability Matrix

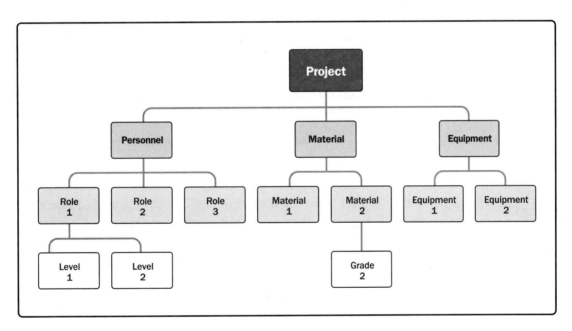

Figure 9-5. Sample Resource Breakdown Structure

Resource calendars. A resource calendar identifies the working days, shifts, start and end of normal business hours, weekends, and public holidays when each specific resource is available. Information on which resources (such as team resource, equipment, and material) are potentially available during a planned activity period is used for estimating resource utilization. Resource calendars also specify when, and for how long, identified team and physical resources will be available during the project. This information may be at the activity or project level. This includes consideration of attributes such as resource experience and/or skill level, as well as various geographical locations.

Resource management plan. The resource management plan is a component of the project management plan that provides guidance on how project resources should be categorized, allocated, managed, and released. It may be divided between the team management plan and physical resource management plan according to the specifics of the project. The resource management plan may include but is not limited to:

▶ **Identification of resources.** Methods for identifying and quantifying team and physical resources needed.

▶ **Acquiring resources.** Guidance on how to acquire team and physical resources for the project.

▶ **Roles and responsibilities:**

  ▷ *Role.* The function assumed by, or assigned to, a person in the project. Examples of project roles are civil engineer, business analyst, and testing coordinator.

  ▷ *Authority.* The right to apply project resources, make decisions, sign approvals, accept deliverables, and influence others to carry out the work of the project. Examples of decisions that need clear authority include the selection of a method for completing an activity, quality acceptance criteria, and how to respond to project variances. Team members operate best when their individual levels of authority match their individual responsibilities.

  ▷ *Responsibility.* The assigned duties and work that a project team member is expected to perform in order to complete the project's activities.

  ▷ *Competence.* The skill and capacity required to complete assigned activities within the project constraints. If project team members do not possess required competencies, performance can be jeopardized. When such mismatches are identified, proactive responses such as training, hiring, schedule changes, or scope changes are initiated.

- **Project organization charts.** A project organization chart is a graphic display of project team members and their reporting relationships. It can be formal or informal, highly detailed or broadly framed, based on the needs of the project. For example, the project organization chart for a 3,000-person disaster response team will have greater detail than a project organization chart for an internal, 20-person project.

- **Project team resource management.** Guidance on how project team resources should be defined, staffed, managed, and eventually released.

- **Training.** Training strategies for team members.

- **Team development.** Methods for developing the project team.

- **Resource control.** Methods for ensuring adequate physical resources are available as needed and that the acquisition of physical resources is optimized for project needs. Includes information on managing inventory, equipment, and supplies throughout the project life cycle.

- **Recognition plan.** Which recognition and rewards will be given to team members, and when they will be given.

Resource requirements. Resource requirements identify the types and quantities of resources required for each work package or activity in a work package and can be aggregated to determine the estimated resources for each work package, each WBS branch, and the entire project. The amount of detail and the level of specificity of the resource requirement descriptions can vary by application area. The resource requirements' documentation can include assumptions that were made in determining which types of resources are applied, their availability, and what quantities are needed.

Risk register. A repository in which outputs of risk processes are recorded. The risk register captures details of identified individual project risks. Record the results of the following processes in the risk register as these processes are conducted throughout the project:

- Perform Qualitative Risk Analysis,

- Plan Risk Responses,

- Implement Risk Responses, and

- Monitor Risks.

The risk register may contain limited or extensive risk information depending on project variables such as size and complexity.

When the Identify Risks process is performed, the content of the risk register may include but is not limited to:

- ▶ **List of identified risks.** Each individual project risk is given a unique identifier in the risk register. Identified risks are described in as much detail as required to ensure unambiguous understanding. A structured risk statement may be used to distinguish risks from their cause(s) and their effect(s).

- ▶ **Potential risk owners.** Where a potential risk owner has been identified during the Identify Risks process, the risk owner is recorded in the risk register. This will be confirmed during the Perform Qualitative Risk Analysis process.

- ▶ **List of potential risk responses.** Where a potential risk response has been identified during the Identify Risks process, it is recorded in the risk register. This will be confirmed during the Plan Risk Responses process.

Additional data may be recorded for each identified risk, depending on the risk register format specified in the risk management plan. This may include:

- ▶ Short risk title,

- ▶ Risk category,

- ▶ Current risk status,

- ▶ One or more causes,

- ▶ One or more effects on objectives,

- ▶ Risk triggers (events or conditions that indicate that a risk is about to occur),

- ▶ WBS reference of affected activities, and

- ▶ Timing information (when risk was identified, when risk might occur, when risk may no longer be relevant, and the deadline for taking action).

Risk management plan. The risk management plan is a component of the project management plan and describes how risk management activities will be structured and performed. The risk management plan may include some or all of the following elements:

- ▶ **Risk strategy.** Describes the general approach to managing risk on this project.

- ▶ **Methodology.** Defines the specific approaches, tools, and data sources that will be used to perform risk management on the project.

- ▶ **Roles and responsibilities.** Defines the lead, support, and risk management team members for each type of activity described in the risk management plan and clarifies their responsibilities.

- ▶ **Funding.** Identifies the funds needed to perform activities related to the management of risk. Establishes protocols for the application of contingency and management reserves.

- ▶ **Timing.** Defines when and how often the risk processes will be performed throughout the project life cycle and establishes risk management activities for inclusion into the project schedule.

- ▶ **Risk categories.** Provide a means for grouping individual project risks. A common way to structure risk categories is with a risk breakdown structure (RBS), which is a hierarchical representation of potential sources of risk (see example in Figure 9-6). An RBS helps the project team consider the full range of sources from which individual project risks may arise. This can be useful when identifying risks or when categorizing identified risks. The organization may have a generic RBS to be used for all projects, or there may be several RBS frameworks for different types of projects, or the project may develop a tailored RBS. Where an RBS is not used, an organization may use a custom risk categorization framework, which may take the form of a simple list of categories or a structure based on project objectives.

RBS LEVEL 0	RBS LEVEL 1	RBS LEVEL 2
0. ALL SOURCES OF PROJECT RISK	1. TECHNICAL RISK	1.1 Scope definition
		1.2 Requirements definition
		1.3 Estimates, assumptions, and constraints
		1.4 Technical processes
		1.5 Technology
		1.6 Technical interfaces
		Etc.
	2. MANAGEMENT RISK	2.1 Project management
		2.2 Program/portfolio management
		2.3 Operations management
		2.4 Organization
		2.5 Resourcing
		2.6 Communication
		Etc.
	3. COMMERCIAL RISK	3.1 Contractual terms and conditions
		3.2 Internal procurement
		3.3 Suppliers and vendors
		3.4 Subcontracts
		3.5 Client/customer stability
		3.6 Partnerships and joint ventures
		Etc.
	4. EXTERNAL RISK	4.1 Legislation
		4.2 Exchange rates
		4.3 Site/facilities
		4.4 Environmental/weather
		4.5 Competition
		4.6 Regulatory
		Etc.

Figure 9-6. Excerpt from Sample Risk Breakdown Structure (RBS)

▶ **Stakeholder risk appetite.** The risk appetites of key stakeholders on the project are recorded in the risk management plan, as they inform the details of the Plan Risk Management process. Stakeholder risk appetite should be expressed as measurable risk thresholds around each project objective. These thresholds will determine the acceptable level of overall project risk exposure, and they are also used to inform the definitions of probability and impacts to be used when assessing and prioritizing individual project risks.

▶ **Definitions of risk probability and impacts.** Definitions of risk probability and impact levels are specific to the project context and reflect the risk appetite and thresholds of the organization and key stakeholders. The project may generate specific definitions of probability and impact levels, or it may start with general definitions provided by the organization. The number of levels reflects the degree of detail required for the risk process, with more levels used for a more detailed risk approach (typically five levels), and fewer for a simple process (usually three). Table 9-2 provides an example of definitions of probability and impacts against three project objectives. These scales can be used to evaluate both threats and opportunities by interpreting the impact definitions as negative for threats (delay, additional cost, and performance shortfall) and positive for opportunities (reduced time or cost, and performance enhancement).

Table 9-2. Example of Definitions for Probability and Impacts

SCALE	PROBABILITY	+/− IMPACT ON PROJECT OBJECTIVES		
		TIME	COST	QUALITY
Very High	>70%	>6 months	>$5M	Very significant impact on overall functionality
High	51-70%	3-6 months	$1M-$5M	Significant impact on overall functionality
Medium	31-50%	1-3 months	$501K-$1M	Some impact in key functional areas
Low	11-30%	1-4 weeks	$100K-$500K	Minor impact on overall functionality
Very Low	1-10%	1 week	<$100K	Minor impact on secondary functions
Nil	<1%	No change	No change	No change in functionality

Risk report. The risk report presents information on sources of overall project risk, together with summary information on identified individual project risks. The risk report is developed progressively throughout the risk processes. Include the results of the following processes in the risk report as these processes are completed:

▶ Perform Qualitative Risk Analysis,

▶ Perform Quantitative Risk Analysis,

▶ Plan Risk Responses,

▶ Implement Risk Responses, and

▶ Monitor Risks.

When the Identify Risks process is completed, information in the risk report may include but is not limited to:

▶ Sources of overall project risk, indicating which are the most important drivers of overall project risk exposure; and

▶ Summary information on identified individual project risks, such as number of identified threats and opportunities, distribution of risks across risk categories, metrics and trends, etc.

Additional information may be included in the risk report, depending on the reporting requirements specified in the risk management plan.

Schedule baseline. The approved version of a schedule model that can be changed only through formal change control procedures and is used as the basis for comparison to actual results. It is accepted and approved by the appropriate stakeholders as the schedule baseline with baseline start dates and baseline finish dates. During monitoring and controlling, the approved baseline dates are compared to the actual start and finish dates to determine if variances have occurred. The schedule baseline is a component of the project management plan.

Schedule data. The schedule data for the project schedule model is the collection of information for describing and controlling the schedule. The schedule data includes, at a minimum, the schedule milestones, schedule activities, activity attributes, and documentation of all identified assumptions and constraints. The amount of additional data varies by application area. Information frequently supplied as supporting detail includes but is not limited to:

- ▶ Resource requirements by time period, often in the form of a resource histogram;

- ▶ Alternative schedules, such as best case or worst case, not resource-leveled or resource-leveled, or with or without imposed dates; and

- ▶ Applied schedule reserves.

Schedule data could also include such items as resource histograms, cashflow projections, order and delivery schedules, or other relevant information.

Schedule forecasts. Estimates or predictions of conditions and events in the project's future based on information and knowledge available at the time the schedule is calculated. Forecasts are updated and reissued based on work performance information provided as the project is executed. The information is based on the project's past performance and expected future performance based on corrective or preventive actions. This can include earned value performance indicators, as well as schedule reserve information that could impact the project in the future.

Schedule management plan. A component of the project or program management plan that establishes the criteria and the activities for developing, monitoring, and controlling the schedule. The schedule management plan may be formal or informal, highly detailed or broadly framed based on the needs of the project, and it includes appropriate control thresholds.

The schedule management plan can establish the following:

- ▶ **Project schedule model development.** The scheduling methodology and the scheduling tool to be used in the development of the project schedule model are specified.

- ▶ **Release and iteration length.** When using an adaptive life cycle, the timeboxed periods for releases, waves, and iterations are specified. Timeboxed periods are durations during which the team works steadily toward completion of a goal. Timeboxing helps to minimize scope creep as it forces the teams to process essential features first, then other features when time permits.

- ▶ **Level of accuracy.** The level of accuracy specifies the acceptable range used in determining realistic activity duration estimates and may include an amount for contingencies.

- ▶ **Units of measure.** Each unit of measurement (such as staff hours, staff days, or weeks for time measures, or meters, liters, tons, kilometers, or cubic yards for quantity measures) is defined for each of the resources.

- **Organizational procedures links.** The work breakdown structure (WBS) provides the framework for the schedule management plan, allowing for consistency with the estimates and resulting schedules.

- **Project schedule model maintenance.** The process used to update the status and record progress of the project in the schedule model during the execution of the project is defined.

- **Control thresholds.** Variance thresholds for monitoring schedule performance may be specified to indicate an agreed-upon amount of variation to be allowed before some action needs to be taken. Thresholds are typically expressed as percentage deviations from the parameters established in the baseline plan.

- **Rules of performance measurement.** Earned value management (EVM) rules or other physical measurement rules of performance measurement are set. For example, the schedule management plan may specify:

  ▷ Rules for establishing percent complete,

  ▷ EVM techniques (e.g., baselines, fixed-formula, percent complete, etc.) to be employed (for more specific information, refer to the *Standard for Earned Value Management* [9]), and

  ▷ Schedule performance measurements, such as schedule variance (SV) and schedule performance index (SPI), used to assess the magnitude of variation to the original schedule baseline.

- **Reporting formats.** The formats and frequency for the various schedule reports are defined.

Scope baseline. The approved version of a scope statement, work breakdown structure (WBS), and its associated WBS dictionary, which can be changed using formal change control procedures and is used as a basis for comparison to actual results. It is a component of the project management plan. Components of the scope baseline include:

- **Project scope statement.** The project scope statement includes the description of the project scope, major deliverables, and exclusions.

- **WBS.** The WBS is a hierarchical decomposition of the total scope of work to be carried out by the project team to accomplish the project objectives and create the required deliverables. Each descending level of the WBS represents an increasingly detailed definition of the project work.

▷ *Work package.* The lowest level of the WBS is a work package with a unique identifier. These identifiers provide a structure for hierarchical summation of costs, schedule, and resource information and form a code of accounts. Each work package is part of a control account. A control account is a management control point where the scope, budget, and schedule are integrated and compared to the earned value for performance measurement. A control account has two or more work packages, though each work package is associated with a single control account.

▷ *Planning package.* A control account may include one or more planning packages. A planning package is a WBS component below the control account and above the work package with known work content but without detailed schedule activities.

▶ **WBS dictionary.** The WBS dictionary is a document that provides detailed deliverable, activity, and scheduling information about each component in the WBS. The WBS dictionary is a document that supports the WBS. Most of the information included in the WBS dictionary is created by other processes and added to this document at a later stage. Information in the WBS dictionary may include but is not limited to:

▷ Code of account identifier,

▷ Description of work,

▷ Assumptions and constraints,

▷ Responsible organization,

▷ Schedule milestones,

▷ Associated schedule activities,

▷ Resources required,

▷ Cost estimates,

▷ Quality requirements,

▷ Acceptance criteria,

▷ Technical references, and

▷ Agreement information.

Scope management plan. The scope management plan is a component of the project management plan and describes how the scope will be defined, developed, monitored, controlled, and validated. The components of a scope management plan include:

- Process for preparing a project scope statement,

- Process that enables the creation of the work breakdown structure (WBS) from the detailed project scope statement,

- Process that establishes how the scope baseline will be approved and maintained, and

- Process that specifies how formal acceptance of the completed project deliverables will be obtained.

The scope management plan can be formal or informal, broadly framed or highly detailed, based on the needs of the project.

Selected sellers. The selected sellers are those who have been judged to be in a competitive range based on the outcome of the proposal or bid evaluation. Final approval of complex, high-value, high-risk procurements will generally require organizational senior management approval prior to award.

Seller proposals. Seller proposals are prepared in response to a bid document package and form the basic information that will be used by an evaluation body to select one or more successful bidders (sellers). If the seller is going to submit a price proposal, good practice is to require that it be separate from the technical proposal. The evaluation body reviews each submitted proposal according to the source selection criteria and selects the seller that can best satisfy the buying organization's requirements.

Source selection criteria. In choosing evaluation criteria, the buyer seeks to ensure that the proposal selected will offer the best quality for the services required. The source selection criteria may include but are not limited to:

- Capability and capacity;

- Product cost and life cycle cost;

- Delivery dates;

- Technical expertise and approach;

- Specific relevant experience;

- ▶ Adequacy of the proposed approach and work plan in responding to the SOW;

- ▶ Key staff's qualifications, availability, and competence;

- ▶ Financial stability of the firm;

- ▶ Management experience; and

- ▶ Suitability of the knowledge transfer program, including training.

For international projects, evaluation criteria may include "local content" requirements, for example, participation by nationals among proposed key staff.

The specific criteria may be a numerical score, color-code, or a written description of how well the seller satisfies the buying organization's needs. The criteria will be part of a weighting system that can be used to select a single seller that will be asked to sign a contract and establish a negotiating sequence by ranking all of the proposals by the weighted evaluation scores assigned to each proposal.

Stakeholder engagement plan. The stakeholder engagement plan is a component of the project management plan that identifies the strategies and actions required to promote productive involvement of stakeholders in decision making and execution. It can be formal or informal and highly detailed or broadly framed, based on the needs of the project and the expectations of stakeholders.

The stakeholder engagement plan may include but is not limited to specific strategies or approaches for engaging with individuals or groups of stakeholders.

Stakeholder register. A project document including the identification, assessment, and classification of project stakeholders. This document contains information about identified stakeholders that includes but is not limited to:

- ▶ **Identification information.** Name, organizational position, location and contact details, and role on the project.

- ▶ **Assessment information.** Major requirements, expectations, potential for influencing project outcomes, and the phase of the project life cycle where the stakeholder has the most influence or impact.

- ▶ **Stakeholder classification.** Internal/external, impact/influence/power/interest, upward/downward/outward/sideward, or any other classification model chosen by the project manager.

Team charter. The team charter is a document that establishes the team values, agreements, and operating guidelines for the team. The team charter may include but is not limited to:

- Team values,
- Communication guidelines,
- Decision-making criteria and process,
- Conflict resolution process,
- Meeting guidelines, and
- Team agreements.

The team charter establishes clear expectations regarding acceptable behavior by project team members. Early commitment to clear guidelines decreases misunderstandings and increases productivity. Discussing areas such as codes of conduct, communication, decision making, and meeting etiquette allows team members to discover values that are important to one another. The team charter works best when the team develops it, or at least has an opportunity to contribute to it. All project team members share responsibility for ensuring the rules documented in the team charter are followed. The team charter can be reviewed and updated periodically to ensure a continued understanding of the team ground rules and to orient and integrate new team members.

Team performance assessments. As project team development efforts such as training, team building, and colocation are implemented, the project management team makes formal or informal assessments of the project team's effectiveness. Effective team development strategies and activities are expected to increase the team's performance, which increases the likelihood of meeting project objectives.

The evaluation of a team's effectiveness may include indicators such as:

- Improvements in skills that allow individuals to perform assignments more effectively,
- Improvements in competencies that help team members perform better as a team,
- Reduced staff turnover rate, and
- Increased team cohesiveness where team members share information and experiences openly and help each other to improve the overall project performance.

As a result of conducting an evaluation of the team's overall performance, the project management team can identify the specific training, coaching, mentoring, assistance, or changes required to improve the team's performance. This should also include identifying the appropriate or required resources necessary to achieve and implement the improvements identified in the assessment.

Test and evaluation documents. Project documents that describe the activities used to determine if the product meets the quality objectives stated in the quality management plan. Test and evaluation documents can be created based on industry needs and the organization's templates. They are used to evaluate the achievement of the quality objectives. These documents may include dedicated checklists and detailed requirements traceability matrices as part of the document.

Verified deliverables. Completed project deliverables that have been checked and confirmed for correctness through the Control Quality process. A goal of the Control Quality process is to determine the correctness of deliverables. The results of performing the Control Quality process are verified deliverables that become an input to the Validate Scope process for formalized acceptance. If there were any change requests or improvements related to the deliverables, they may be changed, inspected, and reverified.

Virtual teams. Groups of people with a shared goal who fulfill their roles with little or no time spent meeting face to face.

The use of virtual teams creates new possibilities when acquiring project team members. Virtual teams can be defined as groups of people with a shared goal who fulfill their roles with little or no time spent meeting face to face. The availability of communication technology such as email, audio conferencing, social media, web-based meetings, and videoconferencing has made virtual teams feasible. The virtual team model makes it possible to:

- ▶ Form teams of people from the same organization who live in widespread geographic areas;
- ▶ Add special expertise to a project team even though the expert is not in the same geographic area;
- ▶ Incorporate employees who work from home offices;
- ▶ Form teams of people who work different shifts, hours, or days;

- ▶ Include people with mobility limitations or disabilities;
- ▶ Move forward with projects that would have been held or canceled due to travel expenses; and
- ▶ Save the expense of offices and all physical equipment needed for employees.

The use of virtual teams can bring benefits such as the use of more skilled resources, reduced costs, less travel and relocation expenses, and the proximity of team members to suppliers, customers, or other key stakeholders. Virtual teams can use technology to create an online team environment where the team can store files, use conversations threads to discuss issues, and keep a team calendar.

Communication planning becomes increasingly important in a virtual team environment. Additional time may be needed to set clear expectations, facilitate communications, develop protocols for resolving conflicts, include people in decision making, understand cultural differences, and share credit in successes.

Work performance data. The raw observations and measurements identified during activities being performed to carry out the project work. Data are often viewed as the lowest level of detail from which information is derived by other processes. Data are gathered through work execution and passed to the controlling processes for further analysis.

Examples of work performance data include work completed, key performance indicators (KPIs), technical performance measures, actual start and finish dates of schedule activities, story points completed, deliverables status, schedule progress, number of change requests, number of defects, actual costs incurred, actual durations, etc.

Work performance information. The performance data collected from controlling processes, analyzed in comparison with project management plan components, project documents, and other work performance information.

To become work performance information, the work performance data are compared with the project management plan components, project documents, and other project variables. This comparison helps to indicate how the project is performing.

Specific work performance metrics for scope, schedule, budget, and quality are defined at the start of the project as part of the project management plan. Performance data are collected during the project and compared to the plan and other variables to provide a context for work performance.

For example, work performance data on cost may include funds that have been expended. However, to be useful, that data should be compared to the budget, the work that was performed, the resources used to accomplish the work, and the funding schedule. This additional information provides the context to determine if the project is on budget or if there is a variance. It also indicates the degree of variance from the plan, and by comparing it to the variance thresholds in the project management plan it can indicate if preventive or corrective action is required. Interpreting work performance data and the additional information provides a sound foundation for making project decisions.

Work performance reports. The physical or electronic representation of work performance information compiled in project documents, which is intended to generate decisions, actions, or awareness. They are circulated to project stakeholders through the communication processes as defined in the project communications management plan.

Examples of work performance reports include status reports and progress reports. Work performance reports may contain earned value graphs and information, trend lines and forecasts, reserve burndown charts, defect histograms, contract performance information, and risk summaries. They can be presented as dashboards, heat reports, stoplight charts, or other representations useful for creating awareness and generating decisions and actions.

10

Tools and Techniques

All of the tools and techniques in this section appear in alphabetical order; therefore, no sections numbers are assigned.

Active listening. Techniques that involve acknowledging, clarifying and confirming, understanding, and removing barriers that adversely affect comprehension. Active listening is used to reduce misunderstandings and other miscommunications.

Advertising. Communications with users or potential users of a product, service, or result. Existing lists of potential sellers often can be expanded by placing advertisements in general circulation publications such as selected newspapers or in specialty trade publications. Most government jurisdictions require public advertising or online posting of pending government contracts.

Affinity diagrams. A technique that allows large numbers of ideas to be classified into groups for review and analysis. Affinity diagrams can also organize potential causes of defects into groups showing the areas that should be focused on the most.

Agile release planning. Agile release planning provides a high-level summary time line of the release schedule (typically 3 to 6 months) based on the product roadmap and the product vision for the product's evolution. Agile release planning determines the number of iterations or sprints in the release. It also allows the product owner and team to decide how much needs to be developed and how long it will take to have a releasable product based on business goals, dependencies, and impediments.

Since features represent value to the customer, the time line provides a more easily understood project schedule as it defines which features will be available at the end of each iteration, which is exactly the depth of information the customer is looking for.

Figure 10-1 shows the relationship among product vision, product roadmap, release planning, and iteration planning.

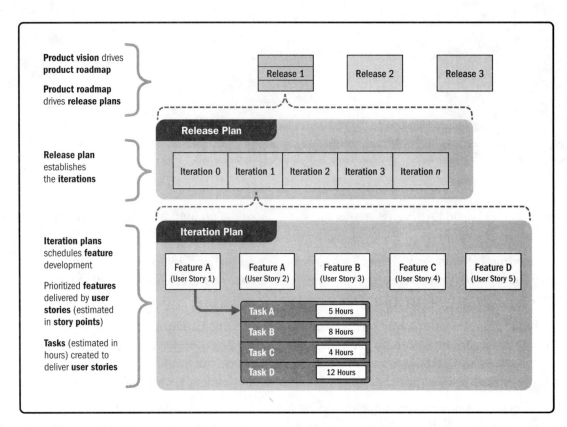

Figure 10-1. Relationship between Product Vision, Release Planning, and Iteration Planning

Alternatives analysis. Used to evaluate identified options in order to select the options or approaches to use to execute and perform project work. Alternatives analysis assists in providing the best solution to perform project activities, within the defined constraints.

Analogous estimating. Analogous estimating is a technique for estimating the duration or cost of an activity or a project using historical data from a similar activity or project. Analogous estimating uses parameters from a previous, similar project, such as duration, budget, size, weight, and complexity, as the basis for estimating the same parameter or measure for a future project. When estimating durations, this technique relies on the actual duration of previous, similar projects as the basis for estimating the duration of the current project. It is a gross value estimating approach, sometimes adjusted for known differences in project complexity. Analogous duration estimating is frequently used to estimate project duration when there is a limited amount of detailed information about the project.

Analogous estimating is generally less costly and less time-consuming than other techniques, but it is also less accurate. Analogous duration estimates can be applied to a total project or to segments of a project and may be used in conjunction with other estimating methods. Analogous estimating is most reliable when the previous activities are similar in fact and not just in appearance, and the project team members preparing the estimates have the needed expertise.

Assessment of other risk parameters. A project team may consider other characteristics of risk (in addition to probability and impact) when prioritizing individual project risks for further analysis and action. These characteristics may include but are not limited to:

- ▶ **Urgency.** The period of time within which a response to the risk is to be implemented in order to be effective. A short period indicates high urgency.

- ▶ **Proximity.** The period of time before the risk might have an impact on one or more project objectives. A short period indicates high proximity.

- ▶ **Dormancy.** The period of time that may elapse after a risk has occurred before its impact is discovered. A short period indicates low dormancy.

- ▶ **Manageability.** The ease with which the risk owner (or owning organization) can manage the occurrence or impact of a risk. Where management is easy, manageability is high.

- ▶ **Controllability.** The degree to which the risk owner (or owning organization) is able to control the risk's outcome. Where the outcome can be easily controlled, controllability is high.

- ▶ **Detectability.** The ease with which the results of the risk occurring, or being about to occur, can be detected and recognized. Where the risk occurrence can be detected easily, detectability is high.

- ▶ **Connectivity.** The extent to which the risk is related to other individual project risks. Where a risk is connected to many other risks, connectivity is high.

- ▶ **Strategic impact.** The potential for the risk to have a positive or negative effect on the organization's strategic goals. Where the risk has a major effect on strategic goals, strategic impact is high.

- ▶ **Propinquity.** The degree to which a risk is perceived to matter by one or more stakeholders. Where a risk is perceived as very significant, propinquity is high.

The consideration of some of these characteristics can provide a more robust prioritization of risks than is possible by only assessing probability and impact.

Assumption and constraint analysis. Every project and its project management plan are conceived and developed based on a set of assumptions and within a series of constraints. These are often already incorporated in the scope baseline and project estimates. Assumption and constraint analysis explores the validity of assumptions and constraints to determine which pose a risk to the project. Threats may be identified from the inaccuracy, instability, inconsistency, or incompleteness of assumptions. Constraints may give rise to opportunities through removing or relaxing a limiting factor that affects the execution of a project or process.

Audits. An audit is a structured, independent process used to determine if project activities comply with organizational and project policies, processes, and procedures.

▶ **Procurement audits.** Audits are a structured review of the procurement process, which includes the review of contracts and contracting processes for completeness, accuracy, and effectiveness. Rights and obligations related to audits should be described in the procurement contract. Resulting audit observations should be brought to the attention of the buyer's project manager and the seller's project manager for adjustments to the project, when necessary.

▶ **Quality audits.** A quality audit is usually conducted by a team external to the project, such as the organization's internal audit department, project management office (PMO), or by an auditor external to the organization. Quality audit objectives may include but are not limited to:

▷ Identifying all good and best practices being implemented;

▷ Identifying all nonconformities, gaps, and shortcomings;

▷ Sharing good practices introduced or implemented in similar projects in the organization and/or industry;

▷ Proactively offering assistance in a positive manner to improve the implementation of processes to help raise team productivity;

▷ Highlighting contributions of each audit in the lessons learned repository of the organization;

▷ Subsequent efforts to correct any deficiencies should result in a reduced cost of quality and an increase in sponsor or customer acceptance of the project's product.

▷ Quality audits may be scheduled or random, and may be conducted by internal or external auditors; and

▷ Quality audits can confirm the implementation of approved change requests including updates, corrective actions, defect repairs, and preventive actions.

▶ **Risk audits.** Risk audits are a type of audit that may be used to consider the effectiveness of the risk management process. The project manager is responsible for ensuring that risk audits are performed at an appropriate frequency, as defined in the project's risk management plan. Risk audits may be included during routine project review meetings or may form part of a risk review meeting, or the team may choose to hold separate risk audit meetings. The format for the risk audit and its objectives should be clearly defined before the audit is conducted.

Autocratic decision making. In this decision-making technique, one individual takes responsibility for making the decision for the entire group.

Benchmarking. Benchmarking involves comparing actual or planned project practices or the project's quality standards to those of comparable projects to identify best practices, generate ideas for improvement, and provide a basis for measuring performance. Benchmarked projects may exist within the performing organization or outside of it; or can be within the same application area or other application area. Benchmarking allows analogies to be made for projects in different application areas or different industries.

Bidder conferences. Bidder conferences (also called contractor conferences, vendor conferences, and pre-bid conferences) are meetings between the buyer and prospective sellers prior to proposal submittal. They are used to ensure that all prospective bidders have a clear and common understanding of the procurement and no bidders receive preferential treatment.

Bottom-up estimating. Bottom-up estimating is a method of estimating project duration or cost by aggregating the estimates of the lower-level components of the work breakdown structure (WBS). When an activity's duration cannot be estimated with a reasonable degree of confidence, the work within the activity is decomposed into more detail. The detail durations are estimated. These estimates are then aggregated into a total quantity for each of the activity's durations. Activities may or may not have dependencies between them that can affect the application and use of resources. If there are dependencies, this pattern of resource usage is reflected and documented in the estimated requirements of the activity.

Brainstorming. This technique is used to identify a list of ideas in a short period of time. It is conducted in a group environment and is led by a facilitator. Brainstorming comprises two parts: idea generation and analysis. Brainstorming can be used to gather data and solutions or ideas from stakeholders, subject matter experts, and team members.

Cause-and-effect diagrams. Cause-and-effect diagrams are also known as fishbone diagrams, why-why diagrams, or Ishikawa diagrams. This type of diagram breaks down the causes of the problem statement identified into discrete branches, helping to identify the main or root cause of the problem. Figure 10-2 is an example of a cause-and-effect diagram.

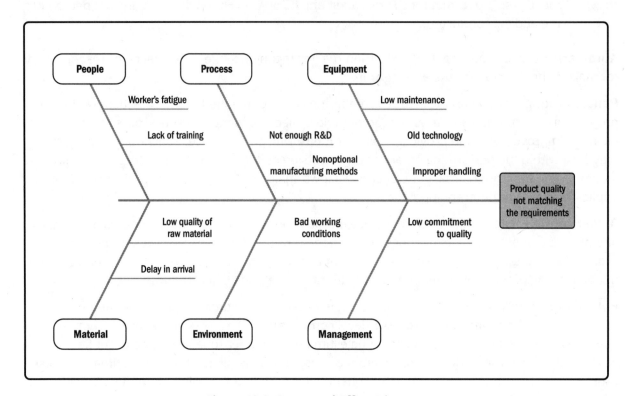

Figure 10-2. Cause-and-Effect Diagram

Change control tools. Manual or automated tools to assist with change and/or configuration management. At a minimum, the tools should support the activities of the change control board (CCB).

In order to facilitate configuration and change management, manual or automated tools may be used. Configuration control is focused on the specification of both the deliverables and the processes, while change control is focused on identifying, documenting, and approving or rejecting changes to the project documents, deliverables, or baselines. Tool selection should be based on the needs of the project stakeholders, including organizational and environmental considerations and/or constraints.

Checklists. A checklist is a list of items, actions, or points to be considered. It is often used as a reminder. Checklists are developed based on historical information and knowledge that has been accumulated from similar projects and from other sources of information. They are an effective way to capture lessons learned from similar completed projects, listing specific individual project risks that have occurred previously and that may be relevant to this project. The organization may maintain checklists based on its own completed projects or may use generic checklists from the industry. While a checklist may be quick and simple to use, it is impossible to build an exhaustive one. The project team should also explore items that do not appear on the checklist. Additionally, the checklist should be reviewed from time to time to update new information as well as remove or archive obsolete information.

Check sheets. Check sheets are also known as tally sheets. They are used to organize facts in a way that facilitates the effective collection of useful data about a potential quality problem. They are especially useful for gathering attributes data while performing inspections to identify defects; for example, data about the frequencies or consequences of defects collected. See Figure 10-3.

Defects/Date	Date 1	Date 2	Date 3	Date 4	Total
Small scratch	1	2	2	2	7
Large scratch	0	1	0	0	1
Bent	3	3	1	2	9
Missing component	5	0	2	1	8
Wrong color	2	0	1	3	6
Labeling error	1	2	1	2	6

Figure 10-3. Check Sheets

Tools and Techniques

Claims administration. Claims administration is the process of processing, adjudicating, and communicating contract claims. Contested changes and potential constructive changes are those requested changes where the buyer and seller cannot reach an agreement on compensation for the change or cannot agree that a change has occurred. These contested changes are called claims. When they cannot be resolved, they become disputes and, finally, appeals. Claims are documented, processed, monitored, and managed throughout the contract life cycle, usually in accordance with the terms of the contract. If the parties themselves do not resolve a claim, it may have to be handled in accordance with alternative dispute resolution (ADR) typically following procedures established in the contract. Settlement of all claims and disputes through negotiation is the preferred method.

Colocation. An organizational placement strategy where the project team members are physically located close to one another in order to improve communication, working relationships, and productivity.

Colocation involves placing many or all of the most active project team members in the same physical location to enhance their ability to perform as a team. Colocation can be temporary, such as at strategically important times during the project, or can continue for the entire project. Colocation strategies can include a team meeting room, common places to post schedules, and other conveniences that enhance communication and a sense of community.

Communication competence. A combination of tailored communication skills that considers factors such as clarity of purpose in key messages, effective relationships and information sharing, and leadership behaviors.

Communication methods. A systematic procedure, technique, or process used to transfer information among project stakeholders.

There are several communication methods that are used to share information among project stakeholders. These methods are broadly classified as follows:

> ▶ **Interactive communication.** Interactive communication takes place between two or more parties who are performing a multidirectional exchange of information in real time. It employs communications artifacts such as meetings, phone calls, instant messaging, some forms of social media, and videoconferencing.

- ▶ **Push communication.** Push communications are sent or distributed directly to specific recipients who need to receive the information. This ensures that the information is distributed but does not ensure that it reached or was understood by the intended audience. Push communication artifacts include letters, memos, reports, emails, faxes, voice mails, blogs, and press releases.

- ▶ **Pull communication.** A pull communication is used for large complex information sets or for large audiences, and requires the recipients to access content at their own discretion subject to security procedures. These methods include web portals, intranet sites, eLearning, lessons learned databases, or knowledge repositories.

Different approaches should be applied to meet the needs of the major forms of communication defined in the communications management plan:

- ▶ **Interpersonal communication.** Information that is exchanged between individuals, typically face to face.

- ▶ **Small group communication.** Communications that occur within groups of three to six people.

- ▶ **Public communication.** A public communication occurs when a single speaker is addressing a group of people.

- ▶ **Mass communication.** Mass communication is an approach with a minimal connection between the person or group sending the message and the large, sometimes anonymous, groups for whom the information is intended.

- ▶ **Networks and social computing communication.** This type of approach supports emerging communication trends of many-to-many supported by social computing technology and media.

Possible communications artifacts and methods include but are not limited to:

- ▶ Notice boards,

- ▶ Newsletters/in-house magazines/e-magazines,

- ▶ Letters to staff/volunteers,

- ▶ Press releases,

- ▶ Annual reports,

- ► Emails and intranets,

- ► Web portals and other information repositories (for pull communication),

- ► Phone conversations,

- ► Presentations,

- ► Team briefings/group meetings,

- ► Focus groups,

- ► Face-to-face formal or informal meetings between various stakeholders,

- ► Consultation groups or staff forums, and

- ► Social computing technology and media.

Communication models. A description, analogy, or schematic used to represent how the communication process will be performed for the project.

Communication models can represent the communication process in its most basic linear form (sender and receiver), in a more interactive form that encompasses the additional element of feedback (sender, receiver, and feedback), or in a more complex model that incorporates the human elements of the sender(s) or receiver(s) and attempts to show the complexity of any communication that involves people.

- ► **Sample basic sender/receiver communication model.** This model describes communication as a process and consists of two parties, defined as the sender and receiver. This model is concerned with ensuring that the message is delivered rather than understood. The sequence of steps in a basic communication model is:

  - ▷ *Encode.* The message is coded into symbols, such as text, sound, or some other medium, for transmission (sending).

  - ▷ *Transmit message.* The message is sent via a communication channel. The transmission of this message may be compromised by various physical factors such as unfamiliar technology or inadequate infrastructure. Noise and other factors may be present and contribute to loss of information in transmission and/or reception of the message.

  - ▷ *Decode.* The data received is translated by the receiver back into a form useful to the receiver.

- **Sample interactive communication model.** This model also describes communication as a process consisting of two parties, the sender and receiver, but recognizes the need to ensure that the message has been understood. In this model, noise includes any interference or barriers that might compromise the understanding of the message, such as the distraction of the receiver, variations in the perceptions of receivers, or lack of appropriate knowledge or interest. The additional steps in an interactive communication model are:

  ▷ *Acknowledge.* Upon receipt of a message, the receiver may signal (acknowledge) receipt of the message, but this does not necessarily mean agreement with or comprehension of the message—merely that it has been received.

  ▷ *Feedback/response.* When the received message has been decoded and understood, the receiver encodes thoughts and ideas into a message and then transmits this message to the original sender. If the sender perceives that the feedback matches the original message, the communication has been successful. In communication between people, feedback can be achieved through active listening.

  As part of the communication process, the sender is responsible for the transmission of the message, ensuring the information being communicated is clear and complete, and confirming the message is correctly interpreted. The receiver is responsible for ensuring that the information is received in its entirety, interpreted correctly, and acknowledged or responded to appropriately. These components take place in an environment where there will likely be noise and other barriers to effective communication.

Cross-cultural communication presents challenges to ensuring that the meaning of the message has been understood. Differences in communication styles can arise from differences in working methods, age, nationality, professional discipline, ethnicity, race, or gender. People from different cultures communicate using different languages (e.g., technical design documents, different styles) and expect different processes and protocols.

The communication model shown in Figure 10-4 incorporates the idea that the message itself, and how it is transmitted, is influenced by the sender's current emotional state, knowledge, background, personality, culture, and biases. Similarly, the receiver's emotional state, knowledge, background, personality, culture, and biases will influence how the message is received and interpreted, and will contribute to the barriers or noise.

This communication model and its enhancements can assist in developing communication strategies and plans for person-to-person or even small-group-to-small-group communications. It is not useful for other communications artifacts such as emails, broadcast messages, or social media.

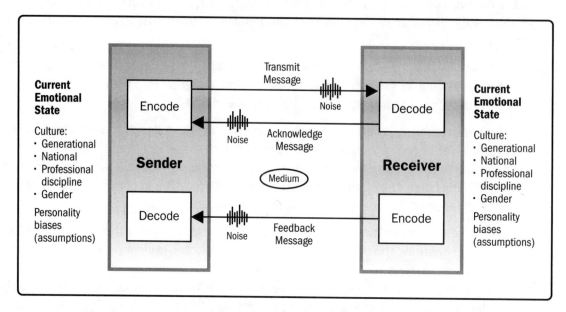

Figure 10-4. Communication Model for Cross-Cultural Communication

Communication requirements analysis. An analytical technique to determine the information needs of the project stakeholders through interviews, workshops, study of lessons learned from previous projects, etc. Analysis of communication requirements determines the information needs of the project stakeholders. These requirements are defined by combining the type and format of information needed with an analysis of the value of that information.

Sources of information typically used to identify and define project communication requirements include but are not limited to:

▶ Stakeholder information and communication requirements from within the stakeholder register and stakeholder engagement plan;

▶ Number of potential communication channels or paths, including one-to-one, one-to-many, and many-to-many communications;

- ▶ Organizational charts;

- ▶ Project organization and stakeholder responsibilities, relationships, and interdependencies;

- ▶ Development approach;

- ▶ Disciplines, departments, and specialties involved in the project;

- ▶ Logistics of how many persons will be involved with the project and at which locations;

- ▶ Internal information needs (e.g., when communicating within organizations);

- ▶ External information needs (e.g., when communicating with the media, public, or contractors); and

- ▶ Legal requirements.

Communication styles assessment. A technique used to assess communication styles and identify the preferred communication method, format, and content for planned communication activities. Often used with unsupportive stakeholders, this assessment may follow a stakeholder engagement assessment to identify gaps in stakeholder engagement that require additional tailored communication activities and artifacts.

Communication technology. Specific tools, systems, computer programs, etc., used to transfer information among project stakeholders.

The methods used to transfer information among project stakeholders may vary significantly. Common methods used for information exchange and collaboration include conversations, meetings, written documents, databases, social media, and websites.

Factors that can affect the choice of communication technology include:

- ▶ **Urgency of the need for information.** The urgency, frequency, and format of the information to be communicated may vary from project to project and within different phases of a project.

- ▶ **Availability and reliability of technology.** The technology that is required for distribution of project communications artifacts should be compatible, available, and accessible for all stakeholders throughout the project.

- ▶ **Ease of use.** The choice of communication technologies should be suitable for project participants and proper training events should be planned, where appropriate.

- **Project environment.** Factors to consider are:
  - ▷ Will the team meet and operate on a face-to-face basis or in a virtual environment?
  - ▷ Will the team be located in one or multiple time zones?
  - ▷ Will the team use multiple languages for communication?
  - ▷ Are there any other project environmental factors, such as various aspects of culture, which may constrain the efficiency of the communication?
- **Sensitivity and confidentiality of the information.** Some aspects to consider are:
  - ▷ Will the information to be communicated be sensitive or confidential? If so, additional security measures may be required.
  - ▷ Does the organization have social media policies for employees to ensure appropriate behavior, security, and the protection of proprietary information?

Conflict management. Conflict is inevitable in a project environment. Sources of conflict include scarce resources, scheduling priorities, and personal work styles. Team ground rules, group norms, and solid project management practices, such as communication planning and role definition, reduce the amount of conflict.

Successful conflict management results in greater productivity and positive working relationships. When managed properly, differences of opinion can lead to increased creativity and better decision making. If the differences become a negative factor, project team members are initially responsible for their resolution. If conflict escalates, the project manager should help facilitate a satisfactory resolution. Conflict should be addressed early and usually in private, using a direct, collaborative approach. If disruptive conflict continues, formal procedures may be used, including disciplinary actions.

The success of project managers in managing their project teams often depends on their ability to resolve conflict. Different project managers may use different conflict resolution methods. Factors that influence conflict resolution methods include:

- ▶ Importance and intensity of the conflict,
- ▶ Time pressure for resolving the conflict,
- ▶ Relative power of the people involved in the conflict,
- ▶ Importance of maintaining a good relationship, and
- ▶ Motivation to resolve conflict on a long-term or short-term basis.

There are five general techniques for resolving conflict. Each technique has its place and use:

▶ **Withdraw/avoid.** Retreating from an actual or potential conflict situation; postponing the issue to be better prepared or to be resolved by others.

▶ **Smooth/accommodate.** Emphasizing areas of agreement rather than areas of difference; conceding one's position to the needs of others to maintain harmony and relationships.

▶ **Compromise/reconcile.** Searching for solutions that bring some degree of satisfaction to all parties in order to temporarily or partially resolve the conflict. This approach occasionally results in a lose-lose situation.

▶ **Force/direct.** Pushing one's viewpoint at the expense of others; offering only win-lose solutions, usually enforced through a power position to resolve an emergency. This approach often results in a win-lose situation.

▶ **Collaborate/problem solve.** Incorporating multiple viewpoints and insights from differing perspectives; requires a cooperative attitude and open dialogue that typically leads to consensus and commitment. This approach can result in a win-win situation.

Context diagram. A visual depiction of the product scope showing a business system (process, equipment, computer system, etc.), and how people and other systems (actors) interact with it. The context diagram is an example of a scope model. Context diagrams show inputs to the business system, the actor(s) providing the input, the outputs from the business system, and the actor(s) receiving the output.

Contingent response strategies. There are five alternative strategies that may be considered for dealing with opportunities, as follows:

▶ **Escalate.** This risk response strategy is appropriate when the project team or the project sponsor agrees that an opportunity is outside the scope of the project or that the proposed response would exceed the project manager's authority. Escalated opportunities are managed at the program level, portfolio level, or other relevant part of the organization, but not on the project level. The project manager determines who should be notified about the opportunity and communicates the details to that person or part of the organization. It is important that ownership of escalated opportunities is accepted by the relevant party in the organization. Opportunities are usually escalated to the level that matches the objectives that would be affected if the opportunity occurred. Escalated opportunities are not monitored further by the project team after escalation, although they may be recorded in the risk register for information.

- ▶ **Exploit.** The exploit strategy may be selected for high-priority opportunities where the organization wants to ensure that the opportunity is realized. This strategy seeks to capture the benefit associated with a particular opportunity by ensuring that it definitely happens, increasing the probability of occurrence to 100%. Examples of exploiting responses may include assigning an organization's most talented resources to the project to reduce the time to completion or using new technologies or technology upgrades to reduce cost and duration.

- ▶ **Share.** Sharing involves transferring ownership of an opportunity to a third party so that it shares some of the benefit if the opportunity occurs. It is important to select the new owner of a shared opportunity carefully, so they are best able to capture the opportunity for the benefit of the project. Risk sharing often involves payment of a risk premium to the party taking on the opportunity. Examples of sharing actions include forming risk-sharing partnerships, teams, special-purpose companies, or joint ventures.

- ▶ **Enhance.** The enhance strategy is used to increase the probability and/or impact of an opportunity. Early enhancement action is often more effective than trying to improve the benefit after the opportunity has occurred. The probability of occurrence of an opportunity may be increased by focusing attention on its causes. Where it is not possible to increase probability, an enhancement response might increase the impact by targeting factors that drive the size of the potential benefit. Examples of enhancing opportunities include adding more resources to an activity to finish early.

- ▶ **Accept.** Accepting an opportunity acknowledges its existence but no proactive action is taken. This strategy may be appropriate for low-priority opportunities, and it may also be adopted where it is not possible or cost-effective to address an opportunity in any other way. Acceptance can be either active or passive. The most common active acceptance strategy is to establish a contingency reserve, including amounts of time, money, or resources to take advantage of the opportunity if it occurs. Passive acceptance involves no proactive action apart from periodic review of the opportunity to ensure that it does not change significantly.

Control charts. Control charts are used to determine whether or not a process is stable or has predictable performance. Upper and lower specification limits are based on the requirements and reflect the maximum and minimum values allowed. Upper and lower control limits are different from specification limits. The control limits are determined using standard statistical calculations and principles to ultimately establish the natural capability for a stable process. The project manager and appropriate stakeholders may use the statistically calculated control limits to identify the points at which corrective action will be taken to prevent performance that remains outside the control limits. Control charts can be used to monitor various types of output variables. Although used most frequently to track repetitive activities required for producing manufactured lots, control charts may also be used to monitor cost and schedule variances, volume, frequency of scope changes, or other management results to help determine if the project management processes are in control.

Cost aggregation. Cost estimates are aggregated by work packages in accordance with the work breakdown structure (WBS). The work package cost estimates are then aggregated for the higher component levels of the WBS (such as control accounts) and, ultimately, for the entire project.

Cost-benefit analysis. A financial analysis tool used to determine the benefits provided by a project against its costs. A cost-benefit analysis is used to estimate the strengths and weaknesses of alternatives in order to determine the best alternative in terms of benefits provided. A cost-benefit analysis will help the project manager determine if project activities are cost effective. A cost-benefit analysis compares the cost of an activity to the expected benefit.

Cost of quality. The cost of quality (COQ) associated with a project consists of one or more of the following costs (Figure 10-5 lists examples for each cost group):

▶ **Prevention costs.** Costs related to the prevention of poor quality in products, deliverables, or services of the specific project.

▶ **Appraisal costs.** Costs related to evaluating, measuring, auditing, and testing products, deliverables, or services of a specific project.

▶ **Failure costs (internal/external).** Costs related to nonconformance of products, deliverables, or services based on the needs or expectations of the stakeholders.

The optimal COQ is one that reflects the appropriate balance for investing in the cost of prevention and appraisal to avoid failure costs. Models show that there is an optimal quality cost for projects, where investing in additional prevention/appraisal costs is neither beneficial nor cost effective.

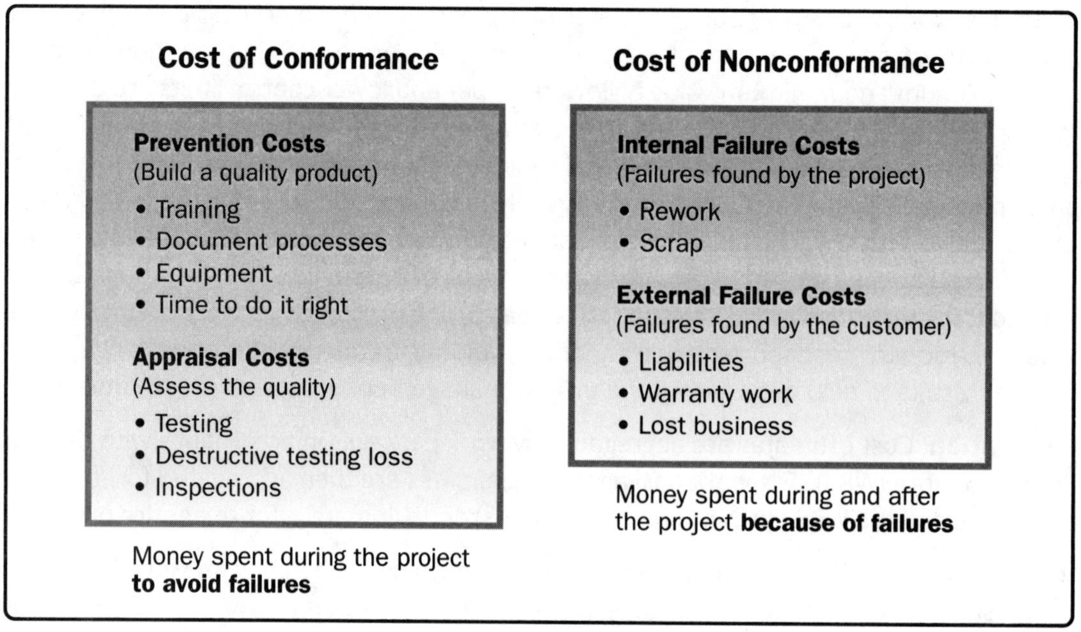

Cost of Conformance

Prevention Costs
(Build a quality product)
- Training
- Document processes
- Equipment
- Time to do it right

Appraisal Costs
(Assess the quality)
- Testing
- Destructive testing loss
- Inspections

Money spent during the project
to avoid failures

Cost of Nonconformance

Internal Failure Costs
(Failures found by the project)
- Rework
- Scrap

External Failure Costs
(Failures found by the customer)
- Liabilities
- Warranty work
- Lost business

Money spent during and after
the project **because of failures**

Figure 10-5. Cost of Quality

Critical path method. The critical path method is used to estimate the minimum project duration and determine the amount of schedule flexibility on the logical network paths within the schedule model. This schedule network analysis technique calculates the early start, early finish, late start, and late finish dates for all activities without regard for any resource limitations by performing a forward and backward pass analysis through the schedule network, as shown in Figure 10-6. In this example, the longest path includes activities A, C, and D, and therefore, the sequence of A-C-D is the critical path. The critical path is the sequence of activities that represents the longest path through a project, which determines the shortest possible project duration. The longest path has the least total float—usually zero. The resulting early and late start and finish dates are not necessarily the project schedule; rather they indicate the time periods within which the activity could be executed, using the parameters entered in the schedule model for activity durations, logical relationships, leads, lags, and other known constraints. The critical path method is used to calculate the critical path(s) and the amount of total and free float or schedule flexibility on the logical network paths within the schedule model.

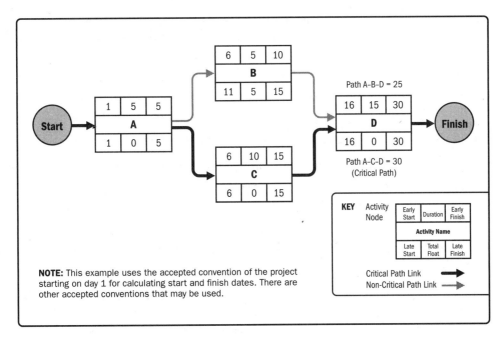

Figure 10-6. Example of Critical Path Method

On any network path, the total float or schedule flexibility is measured by the amount of time that a schedule activity can be delayed or extended from its early start date without delaying the project finish date or violating a schedule constraint. A critical path is normally characterized by zero total float on the critical path. As implemented with the precedence diagramming method sequencing, critical paths may have positive, zero, or negative total float depending on the constraints applied. Positive total float is caused when the backward pass is calculated from a schedule constraint that is later than the early finish date that has been calculated during forward pass calculation. Negative total float is caused when a constraint on the late dates is violated by duration and logic. Negative float analysis is a technique that helps to find possible accelerated ways of bringing a delayed schedule back on track. Schedule networks may have multiple near-critical paths. Many software packages allow the user to define the parameters used to determine the critical path(s). Adjustments to activity durations (when more resources or less scope can be arranged), logical relationships (when the relationships were discretionary to begin with), leads and lags, or other schedule constraints may be necessary to produce network paths with a zero or positive total float. Once the total float and the free float have been calculated, the free float is the amount of time that a schedule activity can be delayed without delaying the early start date of any successor or violating a schedule constraint. For example, the free float for Activity B, in Figure 10-6, is 5 days.

Tools and Techniques

Cultural awareness. Cultural awareness is an understanding of the differences between individuals, groups, and organizations and adapting the project's communication strategy in the context of these differences. This awareness and any consequent actions minimize misunderstandings and miscommunication that may result from cultural differences within the project's stakeholder community. Cultural awareness and cultural sensitivity help the project manager to plan communications based on the cultural differences and requirements of stakeholders and team members.

Decision making. Decision-making techniques include but are not limited to:

- ▶ **Voting.** Voting is a collective decision-making technique and an assessment process having multiple alternatives with an expected outcome in the form of future actions. These techniques can be used to generate, classify, and prioritize product requirements. Examples of voting techniques include:

  - ▷ *Unanimity.* A decision that is reached whereby everyone agrees on a single course of action.

  - ▷ *Majority.* A decision that is reached with support obtained from more than 50% of the members of the group. Having a group size with an uneven number of participants can ensure that a decision will be reached rather than resulting in a tie.

  - ▷ *Plurality.* A decision that is reached whereby the largest block in a group decides, even if a majority is not achieved. This method is generally used when the number of options nominated is more than two.

- ▶ **Autocratic decision making.** In this method, one individual takes responsibility for making the decision for the group.

- ▶ **Multicriteria decision analysis.** A technique that uses a decision matrix to provide a systematic analytical approach for establishing criteria, such as risk levels, uncertainty, and valuation, to evaluate and rank many ideas.

Decision Tree Analysis. Decision tree analysis is a diagramming and calculation technique for evaluating the implications of a chain of multiple options in the presence of uncertainty. Decision trees are used to support selection of the best of several alternative courses of action. Alternative paths through the project are shown in the decision tree using branches representing different decisions or events, each of which can have associated costs and related individual project risks (including both threats and opportunities). The end points of branches in the decision tree represent the outcome from following that particular path, which can be negative or positive.

A decision tree is evaluated by calculating the expected monetary value of each branch, allowing the optimal path to be selected. An example of a decision tree is shown in Figure 10-7.

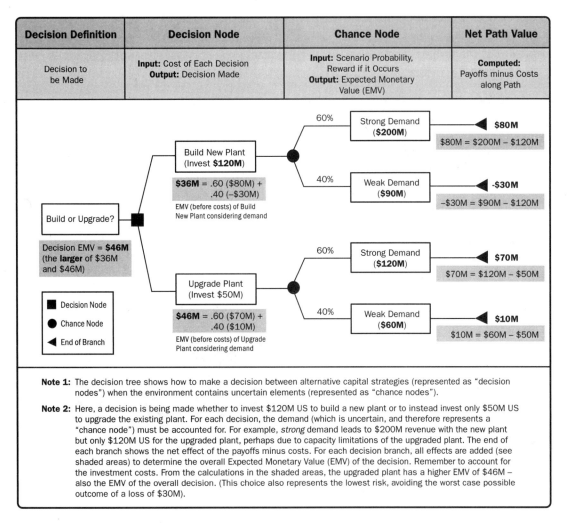

Decision Definition	Decision Node	Chance Node	Net Path Value
Decision to be Made	**Input:** Cost of Each Decision **Output:** Decision Made	**Input:** Scenario Probability, Reward if it Occurs **Output:** Expected Monetary Value (EMV)	**Computed:** Payoffs minus Costs along Path

Build or Upgrade?

Decision EMV = **$46M** (the **larger** of $36M and $46M)

■ Decision Node
● Chance Node
◀ End of Branch

Build New Plant (Invest **$120M**)

$36M = .60 ($80M) + .40 (–$30M)

EMV (before costs) of Build New Plant considering demand

60% Strong Demand ($200M) ◀ **$80M**
$80M = $200M – $120M

40% Weak Demand ($90M) ◀ -$30M
–$30M = $90M – $120M

Upgrade Plant (Invest $50M)

$46M = .60 ($70M) + .40 ($10M)

EMV (before costs) of Upgrade Plant considering demand

60% Strong Demand ($120M) ◀ **$70M**
$70M = $120M – $50M

40% Weak Demand ($60M) ◀ **$10M**
$10M = $60M – $50M

Note 1: The decision tree shows how to make a decision between alternative capital strategies (represented as "decision nodes") when the environment contains uncertain elements (represented as "chance nodes").

Note 2: Here, a decision is being made whether to invest $120M US to build a new plant or to instead invest only $50M US to upgrade the existing plant. For each decision, the demand (which is uncertain, and therefore represents a "chance node") must be accounted for. For example, *strong* demand leads to $200M revenue with the new plant but only $120M US for the upgraded plant, perhaps due to capacity limitations of the upgraded plant. The end of each branch shows the net effect of the payoffs minus costs. For each decision branch, all effects are added (see shaded areas) to determine the overall Expected Monetary Value (EMV) of the decision. Remember to account for the investment costs. From the calculations in the shaded areas, the upgraded plant has a higher EMV of $46M – also the EMV of the overall decision. (This choice also represents the lowest risk, avoiding the worst case possible outcome of a loss of $30M).

Figure 10-7. Example Decision Tree

Decomposition. A technique used for dividing and subdividing the project scope and project deliverables into smaller, more manageable parts. The work package is the work defined at the lowest level of the work breakdown structure (WBS) for which cost and duration can be estimated and managed. The level of decomposition is often guided by the degree of control needed to effectively manage the project. The level of detail for work packages varies depending on the size and complexity of the project. Decomposition of the total project work into work packages generally involves the following activities:

▶ Identifying and analyzing the deliverables and related work,

▶ Structuring and organizing the WBS,

▶ Decomposing the upper WBS levels into lower-level detailed components,

▶ Developing and assigning identification codes to the WBS components, and

▶ Verifying that the degree of decomposition of the deliverables is appropriate.

A portion of a WBS with some branches of the WBS decomposed down through the work package level is shown in Figure 10-8.

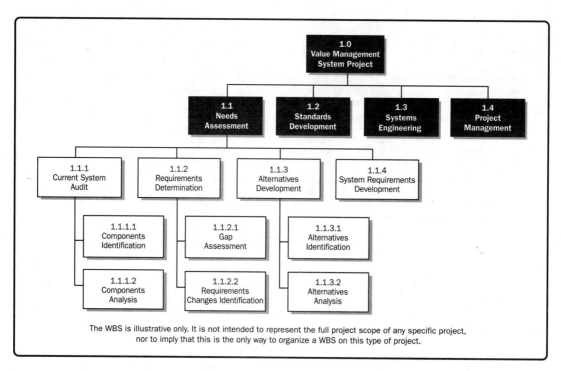

Figure 10-8. Sample WBS Decomposed Down through Work Packages

A WBS structure may be created through various approaches. Some of the popular methods include the top-down approach, the use of organization-specific guidelines, and the use of WBS templates. A bottom-up approach can be used to group subcomponents. The WBS structure can be represented in various forms, such as:

▶ Using phases of the project life cycle as the second level of decomposition, with the product and project deliverables inserted at the third level, as shown in Figure 10-9;

▶ Using major deliverables as the second level of decomposition, as shown in Figure 10-10; and

▶ Incorporating subcomponents that may be developed by organizations outside the project team, such as contracted work. The seller then develops the supporting contract WBS as part of the contracted work.

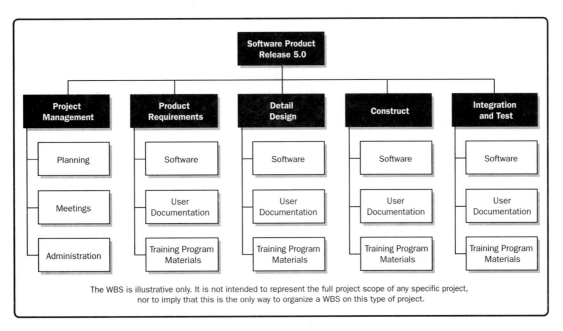

The WBS is illustrative only. It is not intended to represent the full project scope of any specific project, nor to imply that this is the only way to organize a WBS on this type of project.

Figure 10-9. Sample WBS Organized by Phase

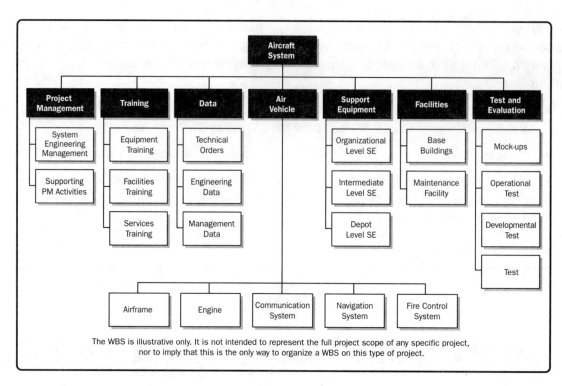

The WBS is illustrative only. It is not intended to represent the full project scope of any specific project, nor to imply that this is the only way to organize a WBS on this type of project.

Figure 10-10. Sample WBS with Major Deliverables

Decomposition of the upper-level WBS components requires subdividing the work for each of the deliverables or subcomponents into its most fundamental components, where the WBS components represent verifiable products, services, or results. If an agile approach is used, epics can be decomposed into user stories. The WBS may be structured as an outline, an organizational chart, or other method that identifies a hierarchical breakdown. Verifying the correctness of the decomposition requires determining that the lower-level WBS components are those that are necessary and sufficient for completion of the corresponding higher-level deliverables. Different deliverables can have different levels of decomposition. To arrive at a work package, the work for some deliverables needs to be decomposed only to the next level, while others need additional levels of decomposition. As the work is decomposed to greater levels of detail, the ability to plan, manage, and control the work is enhanced. However, excessive decomposition can lead to nonproductive management effort, inefficient use of resources, decreased efficiency in performing the work, and difficulty aggregating data over different levels of the WBS.

Decomposition may not be possible for a deliverable or subcomponent that will be accomplished far into the future. The project management team usually waits until the deliverable or subcomponent is agreed on, so the details of the WBS can be developed. This technique is sometimes referred to as rolling wave planning.

The WBS represents all product and project work, including the project management work. The total of the work at the lowest levels should roll up to the higher levels so that nothing is left out and no extra work is performed. This is sometimes called the 100 percent rule.

For specific information regarding the WBS, refer to the *Practice Standard for Work Breakdown Structures* – Second Edition [10]. This standard contains industry-specific examples of WBS templates that can be tailored to specific projects in a particular application area.

Dependency determination and integration. Dependencies may be characterized by the following attributes: mandatory or discretionary, internal or external (as described below). Dependency has four attributes, but two can be applicable at the same time in the following ways: mandatory external dependencies, mandatory internal dependencies, discretionary external dependencies, or discretionary internal dependencies.

▶ **Mandatory dependencies.** Mandatory dependencies are those that are legally or contractually required or inherent in the nature of the work. Mandatory dependencies often involve physical limitations, such as on a construction project, where it is impossible to erect the superstructure until after the foundation has been built, or on an electronics project, where a prototype has to be built before it can be tested. Mandatory dependencies are sometimes referred to as hard logic or hard dependencies. Technical dependencies may not be mandatory. The project team determines which dependencies are mandatory during the process of sequencing the activities. Mandatory dependencies should not be confused with assigning schedule constraints in the scheduling tool.

▶ **Discretionary dependencies.** Discretionary dependencies are sometimes referred to as preferred logic, preferential logic, or soft logic. Discretionary dependencies are established based on knowledge of best practices within a particular application area or some unusual aspect of the project where a specific sequence is desired, even though there may be other acceptable sequences. For example, generally accepted best practices recommend that during construction, the electrical work should start after finishing the plumbing work. This order is not mandatory and both activities may occur at the same time (in parallel); however, performing the activities in sequential order reduces the overall project risk.

Discretionary dependencies should be fully documented since they can create arbitrary total float values and can limit later scheduling options. When fast-tracking techniques are employed, these discretionary dependencies should be reviewed and considered for modification or removal. The project team determines which dependencies are discretionary during the process of sequencing the activities.

▶ **External dependencies.** External dependencies involve a relationship between project activities and non-project activities. These dependencies are usually outside of the project team's control. For example, the testing activity in a software project may be dependent on the delivery of hardware from an external source, or governmental environmental hearings may need to be held before site preparation can begin on a construction project. The project management team determines which dependencies are external during the process of sequencing the activities.

▶ **Internal dependencies.** Internal dependencies involve a precedence relationship between project activities and are generally inside the project team's control. For example, if the team cannot test a machine until they assemble it, there is an internal mandatory dependency. The project management team determines which dependencies are internal during the process of sequencing the activities

Design for X. Design for X (DfX) is a set of technical guidelines that may be applied during the design of a product for the optimization of a specific aspect of the design. DfX can control or even improve the product's final characteristics. The X in DfX can be different aspects of product development, such as reliability, deployment, assembly, manufacturing, cost, service, usability, safety, and quality. Using the DfX may result in cost reduction, quality improvement, better performance, and customer satisfaction.

Document analysis. Document analysis consists of reviewing and assessing any relevant documented information. There is a wide range of documents that may be analyzed. Examples of documents that may be analyzed include but are not limited to:

▶ Agreements and contracts;

▶ Business plans, processes, or interface documentation;

▶ Business rules repositories;

▶ Current process flows;

▶ Marketing literature;

▶ Plans, assumptions, constraints, historical files, and technical documentation;

- ▶ Problem/issue logs;

- ▶ Policies and procedures;

- ▶ Quality reports, test reports, performance reports, and variance analysis;

- ▶ Regulatory documentation such as laws, codes, or ordinances, etc.;

- ▶ Requests for proposal; and

- ▶ Use cases.

Earned value analysis. Earned value analysis compares the performance measurement baseline to the actual schedule and cost performance. EVM integrates the scope baseline with the cost baseline and schedule baseline to form the performance measurement baseline. EVM develops and monitors three key dimensions for each work package and control account:

- ▶ **Planned value.** Planned value (PV) is the authorized budget assigned to scheduled work. It is the authorized budget planned for the work to be accomplished for an activity or work breakdown structure (WBS) component, not including management reserve. This budget is allocated by phase over the life of the project, but at a given point in time, PV defines the physical work that should have been accomplished. The total of the PV is sometimes referred to as the performance measurement baseline (PMB). The total PV for the project is also known as budget at completion (BAC).

- ▶ **Earned value.** Earned value (EV) is a measure of work performed expressed in terms of the budget authorized for that work. It is the budget associated with the authorized work that has been completed. The EV being measured needs to be related to the PMB, and the EV measured cannot be greater than the authorized PV budget for a component. The EV is often used to calculate the percent complete of a project. Progress measurement criteria should be established for each WBS component to measure work in progress. Project managers monitor EV, both incrementally to determine current status and cumulatively to determine the long-term performance trends.

- ▶ **Actual cost.** Actual cost (AC) is the realized cost incurred for the work performed on an activity during a specific time period. It is the total cost incurred in accomplishing the work that the EV measured. The AC needs to correspond in definition to what was budgeted in the PV and measured in the EV (e.g., direct hours only, direct costs only, or all costs including indirect costs). The AC will have no upper limit; whatever is spent to achieve the EV will be measured.

Emotional intelligence (EI). The ability to identify, assess, and manage the personal emotions of oneself and other people, as well as the collective emotions of groups of people. A project team can use emotional intelligence to reduce tension and increase cooperation by identifying, assessing, and controlling the sentiments of project team members, anticipating their actions, acknowledging their concerns, and following up on their issues.

A project manager should invest in personal EI by improving inbound (e.g., self-management and self-awareness) and outbound (e.g., relationship management) competencies. Research suggests that project teams that succeed in developing team EI or become an emotionally competent group are more effective. Additionally, there is a reduction in staff turnover.

Expert judgment. Judgment provided based upon expertise in an application area, discipline, industry, etc., as appropriate for the activity being performed. Such expertise may be provided by any group or person with specialized education, knowledge, skill, experience, or training.

Facilitation. Facilitation is the ability to effectively guide a group event to a successful decision, solution, or conclusion. A facilitator ensures the following:

- ▶ There is effective participation.
- ▶ Participants achieve a mutual understanding.
- ▶ All contributions are considered.
- ▶ Conclusions or results have full buy-in according to the decision process established for the project.
- ▶ Actions and agreements that are achieved are appropriately dealt with afterward.

Feedback. Feedback is information about reactions to communications, a deliverable, or a situation. Feedback supports interactive communication between the project manager, project team, and all other project stakeholders. Examples include coaching, mentoring, and negotiating.

Financing. Financing entails acquiring funding for projects. It is common for long-term infrastructure, industrial, and public services projects to seek external sources of funds. If a project is funded externally, the funding entity may have certain requirements that are required to be met.

Flowcharts. Flowcharts are also referred to as process maps because they display the sequence of steps and the branching possibilities that exist for a process that transforms one or more inputs into one or more outputs. Flowcharts show the activities, decision points, branching loops, parallel paths, and the overall order of processing by mapping the operational details of procedures that exist within a horizontal value chain. One version of a value chain, known as a SIPOC (suppliers, inputs, process, outputs, and customers) model, is shown in Figure 10-11. Flowcharts may prove useful in understanding and estimating the cost of quality for a process. Information is obtained by using the workflow branching logic and associated relative frequencies to estimate the expected monetary value for the conformance and nonconformance work required to deliver the expected conforming output. When flowcharts are used to represent the steps in a process, they are sometimes called process flows or process flow diagrams and they can be used for process improvement as well as identifying where quality defects can occur or where to incorporate quality checks.

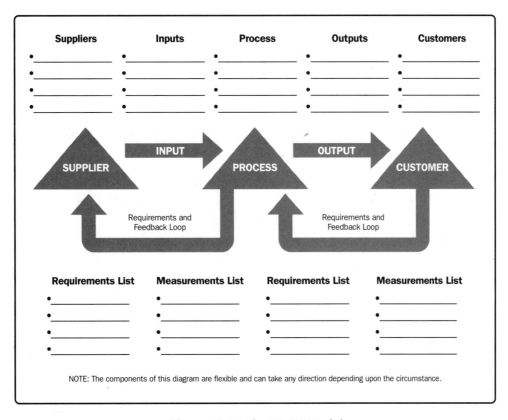

Figure 10-11. The SIPOC Model

Focus groups. An elicitation technique that brings together prequalified stakeholders and subject matter experts to learn about their expectations and attitudes about a proposed product, service, or result. A trained moderator guides the group through an interactive discussion designed to be more conversational than a one-on-one interview.

Funding limit reconciliation. The process of reconciling the expenditure of funds with any funding limits on the commitment of funds for the project. A variance between the funding limits and the planned expenditures will sometimes necessitate the rescheduling of work to level out the rate of expenditures. This is accomplished by placing imposed date constraints for work into the project schedule.

Ground rules. Defined in the team charter, ground rules set the expected behavior for project team members and other stakeholders with regard to stakeholder engagement.

Hierarchical charts. The traditional organizational chart structure can be used to show positions and relationships in a graphical, top-down format.

- **Work breakdown structures (WBS).** The WBS is designed to show how project deliverables are broken down into work packages and provide a way of showing high-level areas of responsibility.

- **Organizational breakdown structure (OBS).** While the WBS shows a breakdown of project deliverables, an OBS is arranged according to an organization's existing departments, units, or teams, with the project activities or work packages listed under each department. An operational department, such as information technology or purchasing, can see all of its project responsibilities by looking at its portion of the OBS.

- **Resource breakdown structure.** The resource breakdown structure is a hierarchical list of team and physical resources related by category and resource type that is used for planning, managing, and controlling project work. Each descending (lower) level represents an increasingly detailed description of the resource until the information is small enough to be used in conjunction with the WBS to allow the work to be planned, monitored, and controlled.

Histograms. Histograms show a graphical representation of numerical data. Histograms can show the number of defects per deliverable, a ranking of the cause of defects, the number of times each process is noncompliant, or other representations of project or product defects.

Historical information review. Reviewing historical information can assist in developing parametric estimates or analogous estimates. Historical information may include project characteristics (parameters) to develop mathematical models to predict total project costs. Such models may be simple (e.g., residential home construction is based on a certain cost per square foot of space) or complex (e.g., one model of software development costing uses multiple separate adjustment factors, each of which has numerous points within it).

Both the cost and accuracy of analogous and parametric models can vary widely. They are most likely to be reliable when:

- Historical information used to develop the model is accurate,

- Parameters used in the model are readily quantifiable, and

- Models are scalable, such that they work for large projects, small projects, and phases of a project.

Individual and team assessments. Individual and team assessment tools give the project manager and the project team insight into areas of strengths and weaknesses. These tools help project managers assess team members' preferences, aspirations, how they process and organize information, how they make decisions, and how they interact with people. Various tools are available such as attitudinal surveys, specific assessments, structured interviews, ability tests, and focus groups. These tools can provide improved understanding, trust, commitment, and communications among team members and facilitate more productive teams throughout the project.

Influence diagrams. Influence diagrams are graphical aids to decision making under uncertainty. An influence diagram represents a project or situation within the project as a set of entities, outcomes, and influences, together with the relationships and effects between them. Where an element in the influence diagram is uncertain as a result of the existence of individual project risks or other sources of uncertainty, this can be represented in the influence diagram using ranges or probability distributions. The influence diagram is then evaluated using a simulation technique, such as Monte Carlo analysis, to indicate which elements have the greatest influence on key outcomes. Outputs from an influence diagram are similar to other quantitative risk analysis methods, including S-curves and tornado diagrams.

Influencing. Because project managers often have little or no direct authority over team members in a matrix environment, their ability to influence stakeholders on a timely basis is critical to project success. Key influencing skills include:

▶ Ability to be persuasive,

▶ Clearly articulating points and positions,

▶ High levels of active and effective listening skills,

▶ Awareness of, and consideration for, the various perspectives in any situation, and

▶ Gathering relevant information to address issues and reach agreements while maintaining mutual trust.

Information management. Information management tools and techniques are used to create and connect people to information. They are effective for sharing simple, unambiguous, codified explicit knowledge. They include but are not limited to:

▶ Methods for codifying explicit knowledge; for example, for producing lessons learned entries for the lessons learned register;

▶ Lessons learned register;

▶ Library services;

▶ Information gathering, for example, web searches and reading published articles; and

▶ Project management information system (PMIS). Project management information systems often include document management systems.

Tools and techniques that connect people to information can be enhanced by adding an element of interaction, for example, include a "contact me" function so users can get in touch with the originators of the lessons and ask for advice specific to their project and context.

Knowledge and information management tools and techniques should be connected to project processes and process owners. Communities of practice and subject matter experts (SMEs), for example, may generate insights that lead to improved control processes. Having an internal sponsor can ensure improvements are implemented. Lessons learned register entries may be analyzed to identify common issues that can be addressed by changes to project procedures.

Inspection. An inspection is the examination of a work product to determine if it conforms to documented standards. The results of inspections generally include measurements and may be conducted at any level. The results of a single activity can be inspected, or the final product of the project can be inspected. Inspections may be called reviews, peer reviews, audits, or walkthroughs. In some application areas, these terms have narrow and specific meanings. Inspections also are used to verify defect repairs.

Interviews. A formal or informal approach to elicit information from stakeholders by talking to them directly. It is typically performed by asking prepared and spontaneous questions and recording the responses. Interviews are often conducted on an individual basis between an interviewer and an interviewee but may involve multiple interviewers and/or multiple interviewees. Interviewing experienced project participants, sponsors, other executives, and subject matter experts can aid in identifying and defining the features and functions of the desired product deliverables. Interviews are also useful for obtaining confidential information.

Iteration burndown chart. This chart tracks the work that remains to be completed in the iteration backlog. It is used to analyze the variance with respect to an ideal burndown based on the work committed from iteration planning. A forecast trend line can be used to predict the likely variance at iteration completion and take appropriate actions during the course of the iteration. A diagonal line representing the ideal burndown and daily actual remaining work is then plotted. A trend line is then calculated to forecast completion based on remaining work. Figure 10-12 is an example of an iteration burndown chart.

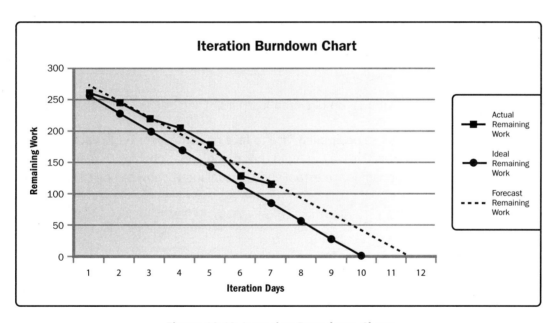

Figure 10-12. Iteration Burndown Chart

Knowledge management. Knowledge management tools and techniques connect people so they can work together to create new knowledge, share tacit knowledge, and integrate the knowledge of diverse team members. The tools and techniques appropriate in a project depend on the nature of the project, especially the degree of innovation involved, the project complexity, and the level of diversity (including diversity of disciplines) among team members.

Tools and techniques include but are not limited to:

▶ Networking, including informal social interaction and online social networking. Online forums where people can ask open questions ("What does anyone know about...?") are useful for starting knowledge-sharing conversations with specialists;

▶ Communities of practice (sometimes called communities of interest or just communities) and special interest groups;

▶ Meetings, including virtual meetings where participants can interact using communications technology;

▶ Work shadowing and reverse shadowing;

▶ Discussion forums such as focus groups;

▶ Knowledge-sharing events such as seminars and conferences;

▶ Workshops, including problem-solving sessions and learning reviews designed to identify lessons learned;

▶ Storytelling;

▶ Creativity and ideas management techniques;

▶ Knowledge fairs and cafés; and

▶ Training that involves interaction between learners.

All of these tools and techniques can be applied face to face or virtually, or both. Face-to-face interaction is usually the most effective way to build the trusting relationships that are needed to manage knowledge. Once relationships are established, virtual interaction can be used to maintain the relationship.

Leadership. The knowledge, skills, and behaviors needed to guide, motivate, and direct a team to help an organization achieve its business goals. These skills may include demonstrating essential capabilities such as negotiation, resilience, communication, problem solving, critical thinking, and interpersonal skills. Projects are becoming increasingly more complicated with more and more businesses executing their strategy through projects. Project management is more than just working with numbers, templates, charts, graphs, and computing systems. A common denominator in all projects is people. People can be counted, but they are not numbers.

Leads and lags. A lead is the amount of time a successor activity can be advanced with respect to a predecessor activity. For example, on a project to construct a new office building, the landscaping could be scheduled to start 2 weeks prior to the scheduled punch list completion. This would be shown as a finish-to-start with a 2-week lead as shown in Figure 10-13. A lead is often represented as a negative value for lag in scheduling software.

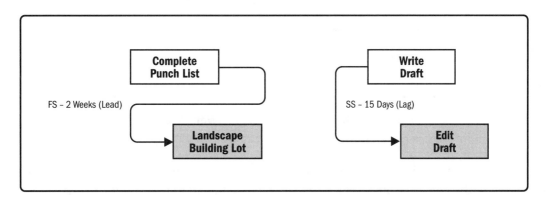

Figure 10-13. Examples of Lead and Lag

A lag is the amount of time a successor activity will be delayed with respect to a predecessor activity. For example, a technical writing team may begin editing the draft of a large document 15 days after they begin writing it. This can be shown as a start-to-start relationship with a 15-day lag as shown in Figure 10-13. Lag can also be represented in project schedule network diagrams, as shown in Figure 10-14, in the relationship between activities H and I (as indicated by the nomenclature SS+10 (start-to-start plus 10 days lag) even though the offset is not shown relative to a timescale).

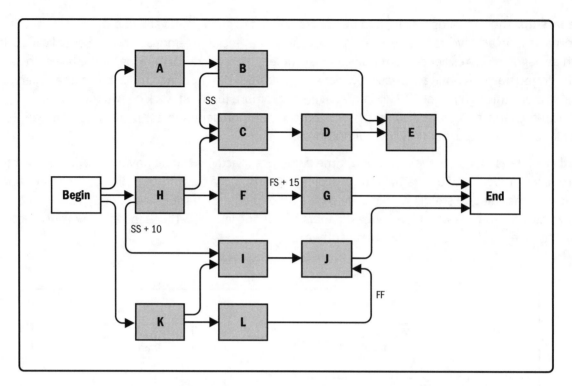

Figure 10-14. Project Schedule Network Diagram

The project management team determines the dependencies that may require a lead or a lag to accurately define the logical relationship. The use of leads and lags should not replace schedule logic. Also, duration estimates do not include any leads or lags. Activities and their related assumptions should be documented.

Logical data model. A logical data model is a visual representation of an organization's data, described in business language and independent of any specific technology. A logical data model can be used to identify where data integrity or other quality issues can arise.

Make-or-buy analysis. A make-or-buy analysis is used to determine whether work or deliverables can best be accomplished by the project team or should be purchased from outside sources. Factors to consider in the make-or-buy decision include the organization's current resource allocation and their skills and abilities, the need for specialized expertise, the desire to not expand permanent employment obligations, and the need for independent expertise. It also includes evaluating the risks involved with each make-or-buy decision.

A make-or-buy analysis may use payback period, return on investment (ROI), internal rate of return (IRR), discounted cash flow, net present value (NPV), benefit/cost analysis (BCA), or other techniques in order to decide whether to include something as part of the project or purchase it externally.

Market research. Market research is a data gathering technique that includes examination of industry and specific seller capabilities. Procurement teams may leverage information gained at conferences, online reviews, and a variety of sources to identify market capabilities. The team may also refine specific procurement objectives to leverage maturing technologies while balancing risks associated with the breadth of sellers who can provide the desired materials or services.

Matrix diagrams. Matrix diagrams help to find the strength of relationships among different factors, causes, and objectives that exist between the rows and columns that form the matrix. Depending on how many factors are compared, a project manager can use different shapes of matrix diagrams, for example, L, T, Y, X, C, and roof shaped. Matrix diagrams facilitate the identification of key quality metrics that are important for the success of the project.

Meeting management. An interpersonal and team skill used to ensure meetings meet their intended objectives effectively and efficiently. The following steps should be used for meeting planning:

- ▶ Prepare and distribute the agenda stating the objectives of the meeting.
- ▶ Ensure that the meeting starts and finishes at the published time.
- ▶ Ensure the appropriate participants are invited and attend.
- ▶ Stay on topic.
- ▶ Manage expectations, issues, and conflicts during the meeting.
- ▶ Record all actions along with the individual who has responsibility for completing the action.

Meetings. Project meetings can include virtual (e-meetings) or face-to-face meetings, and can be supported with document collaboration technologies, including email messages and project websites. Examples of meetings include but are not limited to the following:

- ▶ Decision making,
- ▶ Issue resolution,
- ▶ Lessons learned and retrospectives,
- ▶ Project kickoff,
- ▶ Sprint planning, and
- ▶ Status updates.

Mind mapping. Mind mapping consolidates ideas created through individual brainstorming sessions into a single map to reflect commonality and differences in understanding and to generate new ideas. Mind mapping is a diagrammatic method used to visually organize information.

Motivation. Motivation is providing a reason for someone to act. Teams are motivated by empowering them to participate in decision making and encouraging them to work independently.

Multicriteria decision analysis. This technique utilizes a decision matrix to provide a systematic analytical approach for establishing criteria, such as risk levels, uncertainty, and valuation, to evaluate and rank many ideas. Multicriteria decision analysis tools (e.g., prioritization matrix) can be used to identify the key issues and suitable alternatives to be prioritized as a set of decisions for implementation. Criteria are prioritized and weighted before being applied to all available alternatives to obtain a mathematical score for each alternative. The alternatives are then ranked by score.

Negotiation. Negotiation is a discussion aimed at reaching an agreement. Negotiation is used to achieve support or agreement that supports the work of the project or its outcomes and to resolve conflicts within the team or with other stakeholders. Negotiation among team members is used to reach consensus on project needs. Negotiation can build trust and harmony among team members.

Procurement negotiation clarifies the structure, rights, and obligations of the parties and other terms of the purchases so that mutual agreement can be reached prior to signing a contract. Final document language reflects all agreements reached. Negotiation concludes with a signed contract document or other formal agreement that can be executed by both buyer and seller.

The negotiation should be led by a member of the procurement team who has the authority to sign contracts. The project manager and other members of the project management team may be present during negotiation to provide assistance as needed.

Networking. The establishment of connections and relationships with other people from the same or other organizations for the purpose of exchanging information and developing contacts. Networks provide project managers and their teams with access to informal organizations to solve problems, influence actions of their stakeholders, and increase stakeholder support for the work and outcomes of the project, thus improving performance.

Nonverbal. Examples of nonverbal communication include appropriate body language to transmit meaning through gestures, tone of voice, and facial expressions. Mirroring and eye contact are also important techniques. The team members should be aware of how they are expressing themselves, both through what they say and what they don't say.

Nominal group technique. A technique that enhances brainstorming with a voting process used to rank the most useful ideas for further brainstorming or for prioritization. The nominal group technique is a structured form of brainstorming consisting of four steps:

▶ **Step 1.** A question or problem is posed to the group. Each person silently generates and writes down their ideas.

▶ **Step 2.** The moderator writes down the ideas on a flip chart until all ideas are recorded.

▶ **Step 3.** Each recorded idea is discussed until all group members have a clear understanding.

▶ **Step 4.** Individuals vote privately to prioritize the ideas, usually using a scale of 1 to 5, with 1 being the lowest and 5 being the highest. Voting may take place in many rounds to reduce and focus in on ideas. After each round, the moderator tallies the votes, and the highest scoring ideas are selected.

Observation/conversation. Observation and conversation provide a direct way of viewing individuals in their environment and to see how they perform their jobs or tasks and carry out processes. It is particularly helpful for detailed processes when the people who use the product have difficulty or are reluctant to articulate their requirements. Observation is also known as "job shadowing." It is usually done externally by an observer viewing a business expert performing a job. It can also be done by a "participant observer" who performs a process or procedure to experience how it is done to uncover hidden requirements.

Organizational theory. Organizational theory provides information regarding the way in which people, teams, and organizational units behave. Effective use of common techniques identified in organizational theory can shorten the amount of time, cost, and effort needed to create the Plan Resource Management process outputs and improve planning efficiency. Applicable organizational theories may recommend exercising a flexible leadership style that adapts to the changes in a team's maturity level throughout the project life cycle. It is important to recognize that the organization's structure and culture impact the project organizational structure.

Parametric estimating. Parametric estimating is an estimating technique in which an algorithm is used to calculate cost or duration based on historical data and project parameters. Parametric estimating uses a statistical relationship between historical data and other variables (e.g., square footage in construction) to calculate an estimate for activity parameters, such as cost, budget, and duration.

Durations can be quantitatively determined by multiplying the quantity of work to be performed by the number of labor hours per unit of work. For example, duration on a design project is estimated by the number of drawings multiplied by the number of labor hours per drawing, or on a cable installation, the meters of cable multiplied by the number of labor hours per meter. If the assigned resource is capable of installing 25 meters of cable per hour, the duration required to install 1,000 meters is 40 hours (1,000 meters divided by 25 meters per hour).

This technique can produce higher levels of accuracy depending on the sophistication and underlying data built into the model. Parametric schedule estimates can be applied to a total project or to segments of a project, in conjunction with other estimating methods.

Performance reviews. Performance reviews measure, compare, and analyze actual performance of work in progress on the project against the schedule baseline, such as actual start and finish dates, percent complete, and remaining duration for work in progress.

Political awareness. Political awareness helps the project manager to plan communications based on the project environment as well as the organization's political environment. Political awareness concerns the recognition of formal and informal power relationships and the willingness to operate within these structures. Aspects of political awareness include:

▶ Understanding the strategies of the organization,

▶ Knowing who wields power and influence in this arena, and

▶ Developing an ability to communicate with these stakeholders.

Precedence diagramming method (PDM). A technique used for constructing a schedule model in which activities are represented by nodes and are graphically linked by one or more logical relationships to show the sequence in which the activities are to be performed.

PDM includes four types of dependencies or logical relationships. A predecessor activity is an activity that logically comes before a dependent activity in a schedule. A successor activity is a dependent activity that logically comes after another activity in a schedule. These relationships are defined below and are illustrated in Figure 10-15:

▶ **Finish-to-start (FS).** A logical relationship in which a successor activity cannot start until a predecessor activity has finished. For example, installing the operating system on a PC (successor) cannot start until the PC hardware is assembled (predecessor).

▶ **Finish-to-finish (FF).** A logical relationship in which a successor activity cannot finish until a predecessor activity has finished. For example, writing a document (predecessor) is required to finish before editing the document (successor) can finish.

▶ **Start-to-start (SS).** A logical relationship in which a successor activity cannot start until a predecessor activity has started. For example, leveling concrete (successor) cannot begin until pouring the foundation (predecessor) begins.

▶ **Start-to-finish (SF).** A logical relationship in which a predecessor activity cannot finish until a successor activity has started. For example, a new accounts payable system (successor) has to start before the old accounts payable system can be shut down (predecessor).

In PDM, FS is the most commonly used type of precedence relationship. The SF relationship is very rarely used, but it is included here to present a complete list of the PDM relationship types.

Two activities can have two logical relationships at the same time (for example, SS and FF). Multiple relationships between the same activities are not recommended, so a decision has to be made to select the relationship with the highest impact. Closed loops are also not recommended in logical relationships.

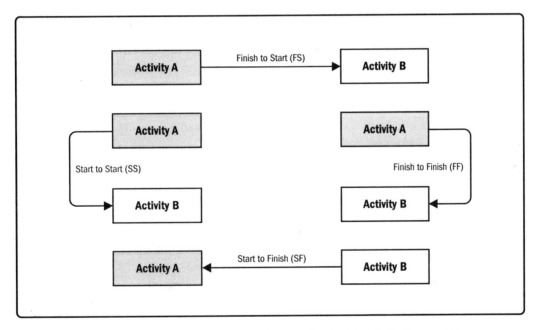

Figure 10-15. Precedence Diagramming Method (PDM) Relationship Types

Presentations. A presentation is the formal delivery of information and/or documentation. Clear and effective presentations of project information to relevant stakeholders can include but are not limited to:

- ▶ Progress reports and information updates to stakeholders;

- ▶ Background information to support decision making;

- ▶ General information about the project and its objectives, for the purposes of raising the profile of the work of the project and the team; and

- ▶ Specific information aimed at increasing understanding and support of the work and objectives of the project.

Presentations will be successful when the content and delivery take the following into account:

- ▶ Expectations and needs of the audience; and

- ▶ Needs and objectives of the project and project team.

Prioritization/ranking. Stakeholder requirements need to be prioritized and ranked, as do the stakeholders themselves. Stakeholders with the most interest and the highest influence are often prioritized at the top of the list.

Probability and impact matrix. A probability and impact matrix is a grid for mapping the probability of each risk occurrence and its impact on project objectives if that risk occurs. This matrix specifies combinations of probability and impact that allow individual project risks to be divided into priority groups (see Figure 10-16). Risks can be prioritized for further analysis and planning of risk responses based on their probability and impacts. The probability of occurrence for each individual project risk is assessed as well as its impact on one or more project objectives if it does occur, using definitions of probability and impact for the project as specified in the risk management plan. Individual project risks are assigned to a priority level based on the combination of their assessed probability and impact, using a probability and impact matrix.

An organization can assess a risk separately for each objective (e.g., cost, time, and scope) by having a separate probability and impact matrix for each. Alternatively, it may develop ways to determine one overall priority level for each risk, either by combining assessments for different objectives, or by taking the highest priority level regardless of which objective is affected.

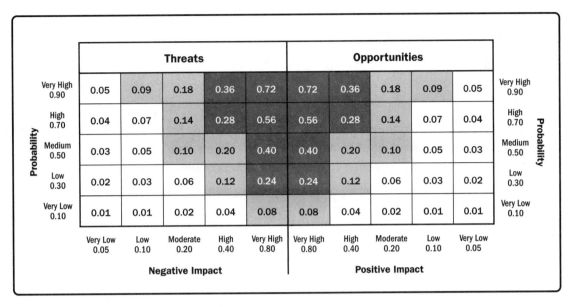

Figure 10-16. Example of Probability and Impact Matrix with Scoring Schemes

Problem solving. Problem solving entails finding solutions for issues or challenges. It can include gathering additional information; critical thinking; and creative, quantitative, and/or logical approaches. Effective and systematic problem solving is a fundamental element in quality assurance and quality improvement. Problems can arise as a result of the Control Quality process or from quality audits and can be associated with a process or deliverable. Using a structured problem-solving method will help eliminate the problem and develop a long-lasting solution. Problem-solving methods generally include the following actions:

▶ Define the problem,

▶ Identify the root cause,

▶ Generate possible solutions,

▶ Choose the best solution,

▶ Implement the solution, and

▶ Verify solution effectiveness.

Tools and Techniques

287

Process analysis. Process analysis identifies opportunities for process improvements. This analysis also examines problems, constraints, and non-value-added activities that occur during a process.

Product analysis. Product analysis can be used to define products and services. It includes asking questions about a product or service and forming answers to describe the use, characteristics, and other relevant aspects of what is going to be manufactured or delivered.

Each application area has one or more generally accepted methods for translating high-level product or service descriptions into meaningful deliverables. Requirements are captured at a high level and decomposed to the level of detail needed to design the final product. Examples of product analysis techniques include but are not limited to:

- ▶ Product breakdown,
- ▶ Requirements analysis,
- ▶ Systems analysis,
- ▶ Systems engineering,
- ▶ Value analysis, and
- ▶ Value engineering.

Project management information system (PMIS). An information system consisting of the tools and techniques used to gather, integrate, and disseminate the outputs of project management processes. A PMIS provides access to information technology software tools, such as scheduling software tools, work authorization systems, configuration management systems, information collection and distribution systems, as well as interfaces to other online automated systems such as organizational knowledge repositories. Automated gathering and reporting on key performance indicators (KPIs) can be part of this system.

Project reporting. Project reporting is the act of collecting and distributing project information. Project information is distributed to many groups of stakeholders and should be adapted to provide information at an appropriate level, format, and detail for each type of stakeholder. The format may range from a simple communication to more elaborate custom reports and presentations. Information may be prepared regularly or on an exception basis. While work performance reports are the output of the Monitor and Control Project Work process, the Manage Communications process develops ad hoc reports, project presentations, blogs, and other types of communication about the project.

Prompt lists. A prompt list is a predetermined list of risk categories that might give rise to individual project risks and that could also act as sources of overall project risk. The prompt list can be used as a framework to aid the project team in idea generation when using risk identification techniques. The risk categories in the lowest level of the risk breakdown structure can be used as a prompt list for individual project risks. Some common strategic frameworks are more suitable for identifying sources of overall project risk, for example PESTLE (political, economic, social, technological, legal, environmental), TECOP (technical, environmental, commercial, operational, political), or VUCA (volatility, uncertainty, complexity, ambiguity).

Proposal evaluation. Proposals are evaluated to ensure they are complete and respond in full to the bid documents, procurement statement of work, source selection criteria, and any other documents that went out in the bid package.

Prototypes. A method of obtaining early feedback on requirements by providing a working model of the expected product before building it. Examples of prototypes are small-scale products, computer-generated 2D and 3D models, mock-ups, or simulations. Prototypes allow stakeholders to experiment with a model of the final product rather than being limited to discussing abstract representations of their requirements. Prototypes support the concept of progressive elaboration in iterative cycles of mock-up creation, user experimentation, feedback generation, and prototype revision. When enough feedback cycles have been performed, the requirements obtained from the prototype are sufficiently complete to move to a design or build phase.

Storyboarding is a prototyping technique showing sequence or navigation through a series of images or illustrations. Storyboards are used on a variety of projects in a variety of industries, such as film, advertising, instructional design, and on agile and other software development projects. In software development, storyboards use mock-ups to show navigation paths through web pages, screens, or other user interfaces.

Quality improvement methods. Quality improvements can occur based on findings and recommendations from quality control processes, the findings of the quality audits, or problem solving in the Manage Quality process. Plan-do-check-act and Six Sigma are two of the most common quality improvement tools used to analyze and evaluate opportunities for improvement.

Questionnaires and surveys. Questionnaires and surveys are written sets of questions designed to quickly accumulate information from a large number of respondents. Questionnaires and/or surveys are most appropriate with varied audiences, when a quick turnaround is needed, when respondents are geographically dispersed, and where statistical analysis could be appropriate.

Recognition and rewards. Part of the team development process involves recognizing and rewarding desirable behavior. The original plan for rewarding people is developed during the Plan Resource Management process. Rewards will be effective only if they satisfy a need that is valued by that individual. Reward decisions are made, formally or informally, during the process of managing the project team. Cultural differences should be considered when determining recognition and rewards.

People are motivated when they feel they are valued in the organization and this value is demonstrated by the rewards given to them. Generally, money is viewed as a tangible aspect of any reward system, but intangible rewards could be equally or even more effective. Most project team members are motivated by an opportunity to grow, accomplish, be appreciated, and apply their professional skills to meet new challenges. A good strategy for project managers is to give the team recognition throughout the life cycle of the project rather than waiting until the project is completed.

Regression analysis. Regression analysis is an analytical technique where a series of input variables are examined in relation to their corresponding output results in order to develop a mathematical or statistical relationship. This technique analyzes the interrelationships between different project variables that contributed to project outcomes in order to improve performance on future projects.

Representations of uncertainty. Quantitative risk analysis requires inputs to a quantitative risk analysis model that reflect individual project risks and other sources of uncertainty.

Where the duration, cost, or resource requirement for a planned activity is uncertain, the range of possible values can be represented in the model as a probability distribution. The most commonly used forms are triangular, normal, lognormal, beta, uniform, or discrete distributions. Care should be taken when selecting an appropriate probability distribution to reflect the range of possible values for the planned activity.

Individual project risks may be covered by probability distributions. Alternatively, risks may be included in the model as probabilistic branches, where optional activities are added to the model to represent the time and/or cost impact of the risk should it occur, and the chance that these activities actually occur in a particular simulation run matches the risk's probability. Branches are most useful for risks that might occur independently of any planned activity. Where risks are related, for example, with a common cause or a logical dependency, correlation is used in the model to indicate this relationship.

Other sources of uncertainty may be represented using branches to describe alternative paths through the project.

Reserve analysis. Reserve analysis is an analytical technique to determine the essential features and relationships of components in the project management plan in order to establish a reserve for the schedule duration, budget, estimated cost, or funds for a project.

Cost estimates may include contingency reserves (sometimes called contingency allowances) to account for cost uncertainty. Contingency reserves are the budget within the cost baseline that is allocated for identified risks. Contingency reserves are often viewed as the part of the budget intended to address the known-unknowns that can affect a project. For example, rework for some project deliverables could be anticipated, while the amount of this rework is unknown. Contingency reserves may be estimated to account for this unknown amount of rework. Contingency reserves can be provided at any level from the specific activity to the entire project. The contingency reserve may be a percentage of the estimated cost, a fixed number, or may be developed by using quantitative analysis methods.

As more precise information about the project becomes available, the contingency reserve may be used, reduced, or eliminated. Contingency should be clearly identified in the cost documentation. Contingency reserves are part of the cost baseline and the overall funding requirements for the project.

Resource optimization. Resource optimization is used to adjust the start and finish dates of activities to adjust planned resource use to be equal to or less than resource availability. Examples of resource optimization techniques that can be used to adjust the schedule model due to demand and supply of resources include but are not limited to:

▶ **Resource leveling.** A technique in which start and finish dates are adjusted based on resource constraints with the goal of balancing the demand for resources with the available supply. Resource leveling can be used when shared or critically required resources are available only at certain times or in limited quantities, or are overallocated, such as when a resource has been assigned to two or more activities during the same time period (as shown in Figure 10-17), or there is a need to keep resource usage at a constant level. Resource leveling can often cause the original critical path to change. Available float is used for leveling resources. Consequently, the critical path through the project schedule may change.

▶ **Resource smoothing.** A technique that adjusts the activities of a schedule model such that the requirements for resources on the project do not exceed certain predefined resource limits. In resource smoothing, as opposed to resource leveling, the project's critical path is not changed, and the completion date may not be delayed. In other words, activities may only be delayed within their free and total float. Resource smoothing may not be able to optimize all resources.

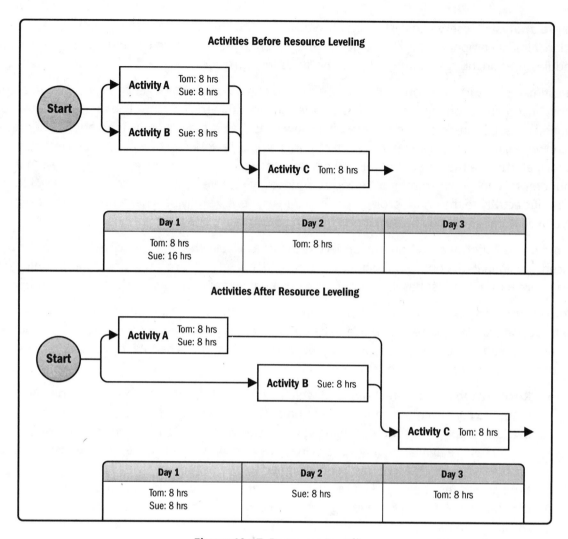

Figure 10-17. Resource Leveling

Responsibility assignment matrix (RAM). A grid that shows the project resources assigned to each work package. A RAM shows the project resources assigned to each work package. It is used to illustrate the connections between work packages, or activities, and project team members. On larger projects, RAMs can be developed at various levels. For example, a high-level RAM can define the responsibilities of a project team, group, or unit within each component of the WBS. Lower-level RAMs are used within the group to designate roles, responsibilities, and levels of authority for specific activities. The matrix format shows all activities associated with one person and all people associated with one activity. This also ensures that there is only one person accountable for any one task to avoid confusion about who is ultimately in charge or has authority for the work. One example of a RAM is a RACI (responsible, accountable, consulted, and informed) chart, shown in Figure 10-18. The sample chart shows the work to be done in the left column as activities. The assigned resources can be shown as individuals or groups. The project manager can select other options, such as "lead" and "resource" designations, as appropriate for the project. A RACI chart is a useful tool to ensure the clear assignment of roles and responsibilities when the team consists of internal and external resources.

RACI Chart	Person				
Activity	Ann	Ben	Carlos	Dina	Ed
Create charter	A	R	I	I	I
Collect requirements	I	A	R	C	C
Submit change request	I	A	R	R	C
Develop test plan	A	C	I	I	R

R = Responsible   A = Accountable   C = Consulted   I = Informed

Figure 10-18. Sample RACI Chart

Risk categorization. Risks to the project can be categorized by sources of risk (e.g., using the risk breakdown structure [RBS]); the area of the project affected (e.g., using the work breakdown structure [WBS]); or other useful categories (e.g., project phase, project budget, and roles and responsibilities) to determine the areas of the project most exposed to the effects of uncertainty. Risks can also be categorized by common root causes. Risk categories that may be used for the project are defined in the risk management plan.

Grouping risks into categories can lead to the development of more effective risk responses by focusing attention and effort on the areas of highest risk exposure, or by developing generic risk responses to address groups of related risks.

Risk data quality assessment. Risk data quality assessment evaluates the degree to which the data about individual project risks is accurate and reliable as a basis for qualitative risk analysis. The use of low-quality risk data may lead to a qualitative risk analysis that is of little use to the project. If data quality is unacceptable, it may be necessary to gather better data. Risk data quality may be assessed via a questionnaire measuring the project's stakeholder perceptions of various characteristics, which may include completeness, objectivity, relevancy, and timeliness. A weighted average of selected data quality characteristics can then be generated to give an overall quality score.

Risk probability and impact assessment. Risk probability assessment considers the likelihood that a specific risk will occur. Risk impact assessment considers the potential effect on one or more project objectives such as schedule, cost, quality, or performance. Impacts will be negative for threats and positive for opportunities. Probability and impact are assessed for each identified individual project risk. Risks can be assessed in interviews or meetings with participants selected for their familiarity with the types of risk recorded in the risk register. Project team members and knowledgeable persons external to the project are included. The level of probability for each risk and its impact on each objective are evaluated during the interview or meeting. Differences in the levels of probability and impact perceived by stakeholders are to be expected, and such differences should be explored. Explanatory detail, including assumptions justifying the levels assigned, are also recorded. Risk probabilities and impacts are assessed using the definitions given in the risk management plan. Risks with low probability and impact may be included within the risk register as part of a watch list for future monitoring. Refer to Table 9-2 for an example of definitions of probability and impacts.

Rolling wave planning. Rolling wave planning is an iterative planning technique in which the work to be accomplished in the near term is planned in detail, while work further in the future is planned at a higher level. It is a form of progressive elaboration applicable to work packages, planning packages, and release planning when using an agile or waterfall approach. Therefore, work can exist at various levels of detail depending on where it is in the project life cycle. During early strategic planning when information is less defined, work packages may be decomposed to the known level of detail. As more is known about the upcoming events in the near term, work packages can be decomposed into activities.

Root cause analysis. Root cause analysis is an analytical technique used to determine the basic underlying reason that causes a variance, defect, or risk. A root cause may underlie more than one variance, defect, or risk. It may also be used as a technique for identifying root causes of a problem and solving them. When all root causes for a problem are removed, the problem does not recur.

Scatter diagrams. A scatter diagram is a graph that shows the relationship between two variables. Scatter diagrams can demonstrate a relationship between any element of a process, environment, or activity on one axis and a quality defect on the other axis.

Schedule compression. Schedule compression techniques are used to shorten or accelerate the schedule duration without reducing the project scope in order to meet schedule constraints, imposed dates, or other schedule objectives. A helpful technique is the negative float analysis. The critical path is the one with the least float. Due to violating a constraint or imposed date, the total float can become negative. Schedule compression techniques are compared in Figure 10-19 and include:

▶ **Crashing.** A technique used to shorten the schedule duration for the least incremental cost by adding resources. Examples of crashing include approving overtime, bringing in additional resources, or paying to expedite delivery to activities on the critical path. Crashing works only for activities on the critical path where additional resources will shorten the activity's duration. Crashing does not always produce a viable alternative and may result in increased risk and/or cost.

▶ **Fast tracking.** A schedule compression technique in which activities or phases normally done in sequence are performed in parallel for at least a portion of their duration. An example is constructing the foundation for a building before completing all of the architectural drawings. Fast tracking may result in rework and increased risk. Fast tracking only works when activities can be overlapped to shorten the project duration on the critical path. Using leads in case of schedule acceleration usually increases coordination efforts between the activities concerned and increases quality risk. Fast tracking may also increase project costs.

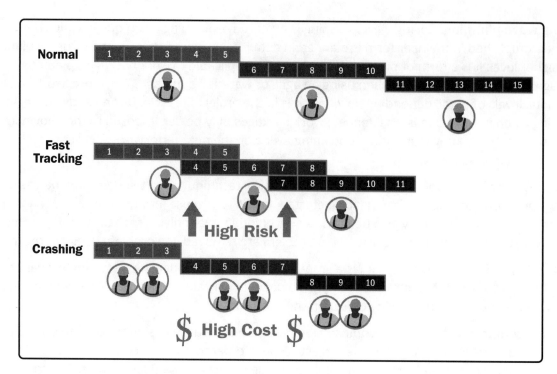

Figure 10-19. Schedule Compression Comparison

Schedule network analysis. Schedule network analysis is a technique to identify early and late start dates, including early and late finish dates, for the uncompleted portions of project activities. Schedule network analysis is the overarching technique used to generate the project schedule model. It employs several other techniques such as critical path method, resource optimization techniques, and modeling techniques. Additional analysis includes but is not limited to:

▶ Assessing the need to aggregate schedule reserves to reduce the probability of a schedule slip when multiple paths converge at a single point in time, or when multiple paths diverge from a single point in time, to reduce the probability of a schedule slip.

▶ Reviewing the network to see if the critical path has high-risk activities or long-lead items that would necessitate use of schedule reserves or the implementation of risk responses to reduce the risk on the critical path.

Schedule network analysis is an iterative process that is employed until a viable schedule model is developed.

Sensitivity analysis. An analysis technique to determine which individual project risks or other sources of uncertainty have the most potential impact on project outcomes, by correlating variations in project outcomes with variations in elements of a quantitative risk analysis model.

Sensitivity analysis helps to determine which individual project risks or other sources of uncertainty have the most potential impact on project outcomes. It correlates variations in project outcomes with variations in elements of the quantitative risk analysis model.

One typical display of sensitivity analysis is the tornado diagram, which presents the calculated correlation coefficient for each element of the quantitative risk analysis model that can influence the project outcome. This can include individual project risks, project activities with high degrees of variability, or specific sources of ambiguity. Items are ordered by descending strength of correlation, giving the typical tornado appearance. An example tornado diagram is shown in Figure 10-20.

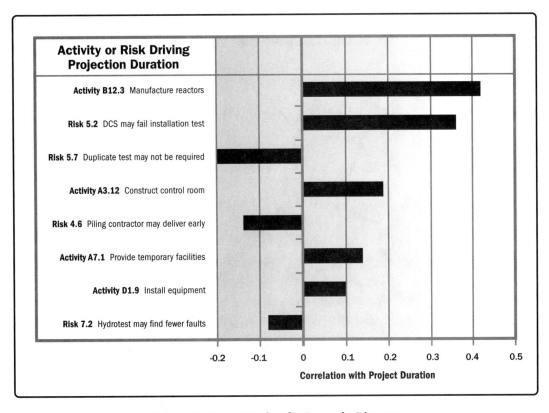

Figure 10-20. Example of a Tornado Diagram

Simulation. Simulation models the combined effects of individual project risks and other sources of uncertainty to evaluate their potential impact on achieving project objectives. The most common simulation technique is Monte Carlo analysis, in which risks and other sources of uncertainty are used to calculate possible schedule outcomes for the total project. Simulation involves calculating multiple work package durations with different sets of activity assumptions, constraints, risks, issues, or scenarios using probability distributions and other representations of uncertainty. Figure 10-21 shows a probability distribution for a project with the probability of achieving a certain target date (i.e., project finish date). In this example, there is a 10% probability that the project will finish on or before the target date of 13 May 2022, while there is a 90% probability of completing the project by 28 May 2022.

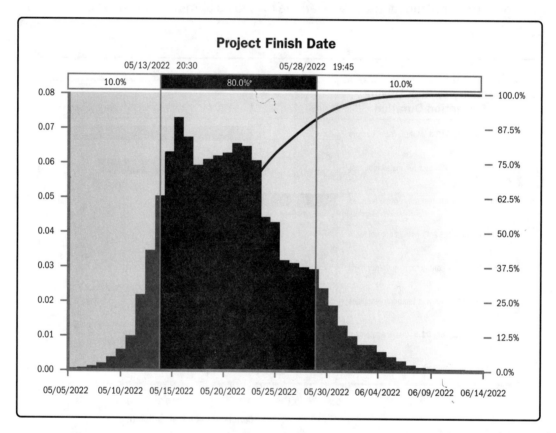

Figure 10-21. Example of a Probability Distribution of a Target Milestone

For more information on how Monte Carlo simulation is used for schedule models, see the *Practice Standard for Scheduling* [8].

Process Groups: A Practice Guide

Source selection analysis. It is necessary to review the prioritization of the competing demands for the project before deciding on the selection method. Since competitive selection methods may require sellers to invest a large amount of time and resources up front, it is a good practice to include the evaluation method in the bid documents so bidders know how they will be evaluated. Commonly used selection methods include the following:

- **Least cost.** The least cost method may be appropriate for procurements of a standard or routine nature where well-established practices and standards exist and from which a specific and well-defined outcome is expected, which can be executed at different costs.

- **Qualifications only.** The qualifications only selection method applies when the time and cost of a full selection process would not make sense because the value of the procurement is relatively small. The buyer establishes a short list and selects the bidder with the best credibility, qualifications, experience, expertise, areas of specialization, and references.

- **Quality-based/highest technical proposal score.** The selected firm is asked to submit a proposal with both technical and cost details and is then invited to negotiate the contract if the technical proposal proves acceptable. Using this method, technical proposals are first evaluated based on the quality of the technical solution offered. The seller who submitted the highest-ranked technical proposal is selected if their financial proposal can be negotiated and accepted.

- **Quality- and cost-based.** The quality- and cost-based method allows cost to be included as a factor in the seller selection process. In general, when risk and/or uncertainty are greater for the project, quality should be a key element when compared to cost.

- **Sole source.** The buyer asks a specific seller to prepare technical and financial proposals, which are then negotiated. Since there is no competition, this method is acceptable only when properly justified and should be viewed as an exception.

- **Fixed budget.** The fixed-budget method requires disclosing the available budget to invited sellers in the request for proposal (RFP) and selecting the highest-ranking technical proposal within the budget. Because sellers are subject to a cost constraint, they will adapt the scope and quality of their offer to that budget. The buyer should therefore ensure that the budget is compatible with the statement of work (SOW) and that the seller will be able to perform the tasks within the budget. This method is appropriate only when the SOW is precisely defined, no changes are anticipated, and the budget is fixed and cannot be exceeded.

Stakeholder analysis. Stakeholder analysis results in a list of stakeholders and relevant information such as their positions in the organization, roles on the project, "stakes," expectations, attitudes (their levels of support for the project), and their interest in information about the project. Stakeholders' stakes can include but are not limited to a combination of:

▶ **Interest.** A person or group can be affected by a decision related to the project or its outcomes.

▶ **Rights (legal or moral rights).** Legal rights, such as occupational health and safety, may be defined in the legislation framework of a country. Moral rights may involve concepts of protection of historical sites or environmental sustainability.

▶ **Ownership.** A person or group has a legal title to an asset or a property.

▶ **Knowledge.** Specialist knowledge, which can benefit the project through more effective delivery of project objectives, organizational outcomes, or knowledge of the power structures of the organization.

▶ **Contribution.** Provision of funds or other resources, including human resources, or providing support for the project in more intangible ways, such as advocacy in the form of promoting the objectives of the project or acting as a buffer between the project and the power structures of the organization and its politics.

Stakeholder engagement assessment matrix. A stakeholder engagement assessment matrix supports comparison between the current engagement levels of stakeholders and the desired engagement levels required for successful project delivery. One way to classify the engagement level of stakeholders is shown in Figure 10-22. The engagement level of stakeholders can be classified as follows:

▶ **Unaware.** Unaware of the project and potential impacts.

▶ **Resistant.** Aware of the project and potential impacts but resistant to any changes that may occur as a result of the work or outcomes of the project. These stakeholders will be unsupportive of the work or outcomes of the project.

▶ **Neutral.** Aware of the project, but neither supportive nor unsupportive.

▶ **Supportive.** Aware of the project and potential impacts and supportive of the work and its outcomes.

▶ **Leading.** Aware of the project and potential impacts and actively engaged in ensuring that the project is a success.

In Figure 10-22, C represents the current engagement level of each stakeholder and D indicates the level that the project team has assessed as essential to ensure project success (desired). The gap between current and desired for each stakeholder will direct the level of communications necessary to effectively engage the stakeholder. The closing of this gap between current and desired is an essential element of monitoring stakeholder engagement.

Stakeholder	Unaware	Resistant	Neutral	Supportive	Leading
Stakeholder 1	C			D	
Stakeholder 2			C	D	
Stakeholder 3				D C	

Figure 10-22. Stakeholder Engagement Assessment Matrix

Stakeholder mapping/representation. Stakeholder mapping and representation is a method of categorizing stakeholders using various methods. Categorizing stakeholders assists the team in building relationships with the identified project stakeholders. Common methods include:

▶ **Power/interest grid, power/influence grid, or impact/influence grid.** Each of these techniques supports a grouping of stakeholders according to their level of authority (power), level of concern about the project's outcomes (interest), ability to influence the outcomes of the project (influence), or ability to cause changes to the project's planning or execution. These classification models are useful for small projects or for projects with simple relationships between stakeholders and the project, or within the stakeholder community itself.

▶ **Stakeholder cube.** This is a refinement of the grid models previously mentioned. This model combines the grid elements into a three-dimensional model that can be useful to project managers and teams in identifying and engaging their stakeholder community. It provides a model with multiple dimensions that improves the depiction of the stakeholder community as a multidimensional entity and assists with the development of communication strategies.

Tools and Techniques

▶ **Salience model.** The salience model describes classes of stakeholders based on assessments of their power (level of authority or ability to influence the outcomes of the project), urgency (need for immediate attention, either time-constrained or relating to the stakeholders' high stakes in the outcome), and legitimacy (their involvement is appropriate). There is an adaptation of the salience model that substitutes proximity for legitimacy (applying to the team and measuring their level of involvement with the work of the project). The salience model is useful for large, complex communities of stakeholders or where there are complex networks of relationships within the community. It is also useful in determining the relative importance of the identified stakeholders.

▶ **Directions of influence.** This technique classifies stakeholders according to their influence on the work of the project or the project team itself. Stakeholders can be classified in the following ways:

  ▷ *Upward* (senior management of the performing organization or customer organization, sponsor, and steering committee),

  ▷ *Downward* (the team or specialists contributing knowledge or skills in a temporary capacity),

  ▷ *Outward* (stakeholder groups and their representatives outside the project team, such as suppliers, government departments, the public, end users, and regulators), or

  ▷ *Sideward* (the peers of the project manager, such as other project managers or middle managers who are in competition for scarce project resources or who collaborate with the project manager in sharing resources or information).

▶ **Prioritization.** Prioritizing stakeholders may be necessary for projects with a large number of stakeholders, where the membership of the stakeholder community is changing frequently, or when the relationships between stakeholders and the project team or within the stakeholder community are complex.

Statistical sampling. Statistical sampling involves choosing part of a population of interest for inspection (for example, selecting 10 engineering drawings at random from a list of 75). The sample is taken to measure controls and verify quality. Sample frequency and sizes should be determined during the Plan Quality Management process.

Strategies for overall project risk. Risk responses should be planned and implemented not only for individual project risks but also to address overall project risk. The same risk response strategies that are used to deal with individual project risks can also be applied to overall project risk:

▶ **Avoid.** Where the level of overall project risk is significantly negative and outside the agreed-upon risk thresholds for the project, an avoid strategy may be adopted. This involves taking focused action to reduce the negative effect of uncertainty on the project as a whole and bring the project back within the thresholds. An example of avoidance at the overall project level would include removal of high-risk elements of scope from the project. Where it is not possible to bring the project back within the thresholds, the project may be canceled. This represents the most extreme degree of risk avoidance and it should be used only if the overall level of threat is, and will remain, unacceptable.

▶ **Exploit.** Where the level of overall project risk is significantly positive and outside the agreed-upon risk thresholds for the project, an exploit strategy may be adopted. This involves taking focused action to capture the positive effect of uncertainty on the project as a whole. An example of exploiting at the overall project level would include addition of high-benefit elements of scope to the project to add value or benefits to stakeholders. Alternatively the risk thresholds for the project may be modified with the agreement of key stakeholders in order to embrace the opportunity.

▶ **Transfer/share.** If the level of overall project risk is high but the organization is unable to address it effectively, a third party may be involved to manage the risk on behalf of the organization. Where overall project risk is negative, a transfer strategy is required, which may involve payment of a risk premium. In the case of high positive overall project risk, ownership may be shared in order to reap the associated benefits. Examples of both transfer and share strategies for overall project risk include but are not limited to setting up a collaborative business structure in which the buyer and the seller share the overall project risk, launching a joint venture or special-purpose company, or subcontracting key elements of the project.

▶ **Mitigate/enhance.** These strategies involve changing the level of overall project risk to optimize the chances of achieving the project's objectives. The mitigation strategy is used where overall project risk is negative, and enhancement applies when it is positive. Examples of mitigation or enhancement strategies include replanning the project, changing the scope and boundaries of the project, modifying project priority, changing resource allocations, adjusting delivery times, etc.

> ▶ **Accept.** Where no proactive risk response strategy is possible to address overall project risk, the organization may choose to continue with the project as currently defined, even if overall project risk is outside the agreed-upon thresholds. Acceptance can be either active or passive. The most common active acceptance strategy is to establish an overall contingency reserve for the project, including amounts of time, money, or resources to be used if the project exceeds its thresholds. Passive acceptance involves no proactive action apart from periodic review of the level of overall project risk to ensure that it does not change significantly.

Strategies for threats. There are five alternative strategies that may be considered for dealing with threats, as follows:

> ▶ **Escalate.** Escalation is appropriate when the project team or the project sponsor agrees that a threat is outside the scope of the project or that the proposed response would exceed the project manager's authority. Escalated risks are managed at the program level, portfolio level, or other relevant part of the organization, but not on the project level. The project manager determines who should be notified about the threat and communicates the details to that person or part of the organization. It is important that the ownership of escalated threats is accepted by the relevant party in the organization. Threats are usually escalated to the level that matches the objectives that would be affected if the threat occurred. Escalated threats are not monitored further by the project team after escalation, although they may be recorded in the risk register for information.

> ▶ **Avoid.** Risk avoidance is when the project team acts to eliminate the threat or protect the project from its impact. Avoidance may be appropriate for high-priority threats with a high probability of occurrence and a large negative impact. Avoidance may involve changing some aspect of the project management plan or changing the objective that is in jeopardy in order to eliminate the threat entirely, reducing its probability of occurrence to zero. The risk owner may also take action to isolate the project objectives from the risk's impact if it were to occur. Examples of avoidance actions may include removing the cause of a threat, extending the schedule, changing the project strategy, or reducing scope. Some risks can be avoided by clarifying requirements, obtaining information, improving communication, or acquiring expertise.

- ▶ **Transfer.** Transfer involves shifting ownership of a threat to a third party to manage the risk and to bear the impact if the threat occurs. Risk transfer often involves the payment of a risk premium to the party taking on the threat. The risk transfer can be achieved by a range of actions, which include but are not limited to the use of insurance, performance bonds, warranties, guarantees, etc. Agreements may be used to transfer ownership and liability for specified risks to another party.

- ▶ **Mitigate.** In risk mitigation, action is taken to reduce the probability of occurrence and/or impact of a threat. Early mitigation action is often more effective than trying to repair the damage after the threat has occurred. Adopting less complex processes, conducting more tests, or choosing a more stable seller are examples of mitigation actions. Mitigation may involve prototype development to reduce the risk of scaling up from a bench-scale model of a process or product. Where it is not possible to reduce probability, a mitigation response might reduce the impact by targeting the factors that drive the severity. For example, designing redundancy into a system may reduce the impact from a failure of the original component.

- ▶ **Accept.** Risk acceptance acknowledges the existence of a threat, but no proactive action is taken. This strategy may be appropriate for low-priority threats, and it may also be adopted where it is not possible or cost-effective to address a threat in any other way. Acceptance can be either active or passive. The most common active acceptance strategy is to establish a contingency reserve, including amounts of time, money, or resources to handle the threat if it occurs. Passive acceptance involves no proactive action apart from periodic review of the threat to ensure that it does not change significantly.

Strategies for opportunities. There are five alternative strategies that may be considered for dealing with opportunities, as follows:

- ▶ **Escalate.** This risk response strategy is appropriate when the project team or the project sponsor agrees that an opportunity is outside the scope of the project or that the proposed response would exceed the project manager's authority. Escalated opportunities are managed at the program level, portfolio level, or other relevant part of the organization, and not on the project level. The project manager determines who should be notified about the opportunity and communicates the details to that person or part of the organization. It is important that ownership of escalated opportunities is accepted by the relevant party in the organization. Opportunities are usually escalated to the level that matches the objectives that would be affected if the opportunity occurred. Escalated opportunities are not monitored further by the project team after escalation, although they may be recorded in the risk register for information.

▶ **Exploit.** The exploit strategy may be selected for high-priority opportunities where the organization wants to ensure that the opportunity is realized. This strategy seeks to capture the benefit associated with a particular opportunity by ensuring that it definitely happens, increasing the probability of occurrence to 100%. Examples of exploiting responses may include assigning an organization's most talented resources to the project to reduce the time to completion or using new technologies or technology upgrades to reduce cost and duration.

▶ **Share.** Sharing involves transferring ownership of an opportunity to a third party so that it shares some of the benefit if the opportunity occurs. It is important to select the new owner of a shared opportunity carefully, so they are best able to capture the opportunity for the benefit of the project. Risk sharing often involves payment of a risk premium to the party taking on the opportunity. Examples of sharing actions include forming risk-sharing partnerships, teams, special-purpose companies, or joint ventures.

▶ **Enhance.** The enhance strategy is used to increase the probability and/or impact of an opportunity. Early enhancement action is often more effective than trying to improve the benefit after the opportunity has occurred. The probability of occurrence of an opportunity may be increased by focusing attention on its causes. Where it is not possible to increase probability, an enhancement response might increase the impact by targeting factors that drive the size of the potential benefit. Examples of enhancing opportunities include adding more resources to an activity to finish early.

▶ **Accept.** Accepting an opportunity acknowledges its existence but no proactive action is taken. This strategy may be appropriate for low-priority opportunities, and it may also be adopted where it is not possible or cost-effective to address an opportunity in any other way. Acceptance can be either active or passive. The most common active acceptance strategy is to establish a contingency reserve, including amounts of time, money, or resources to take advantage of the opportunity if it occurs. Passive acceptance involves no proactive action apart from periodic review of the opportunity to ensure that it does not change significantly.

SWOT analysis. The analysis of strengths, weaknesses, opportunities, and threats of an organization, project, or option. This technique examines a project from each of the strengths, weaknesses, opportunities, and threats (SWOT) perspectives. For risk identification, it is used to increase the breadth of identified risks by including internally generated risks. The technique starts with the identification of strengths and weaknesses of the organization, focusing on either the project, organization, or the business area in general. SWOT analysis then identifies any opportunities for the project that may arise from strengths, and any threats resulting from weaknesses. The analysis also examines the degree to which organizational strengths may offset threats and determines if weaknesses might hinder opportunities.

Team building. Team building is conducting activities that enhance the team's social relations and build a collaborative and cooperative working environment. Team-building activities can vary from a 5-minute agenda item in a status review meeting to an off-site, professionally facilitated event designed to improve interpersonal relationships. The objective of team-building activities is to help individual team members work together effectively. Team-building strategies are particularly valuable when team members operate from remote locations without the benefit of face-to-face contact. Informal communication and activities can help in building trust and establishing good working relationships. While team building is essential during the initial stages of a project, it should be a continuous process. Changes in a project environment are inevitable, and to manage them effectively, a continuous or renewed team-building effort may be applied. The project manager should continually monitor team functionality and performance to determine if any actions are needed to prevent or correct various team problems.

Technical performance analysis. Technical performance analysis compares technical accomplishments during project execution to the schedule of technical achievement. It requires the definition of objective, quantifiable measures of technical performance, which can be used to compare actual results against targets. Such technical performance measures may include weight, transaction times, number of delivered defects, storage capacity, etc. Deviation can indicate the potential impact of threats or opportunities.

Test and inspection planning. During the planning phase, the project manager and the project team determine how to test or inspect the product, deliverable, or service to meet the stakeholders' needs and expectations, as well as how to meet the goal for the product's performance and reliability. The tests and inspections are industry dependent and can include, for example, alpha and beta tests in software projects, strength tests in construction projects, inspection in manufacturing, and field tests and nondestructive tests in engineering.

Testing/product evaluations. Testing is an organized and constructed investigation conducted to provide objective information about the quality of the product or service under test in accordance with the project requirements. The intent of testing is to find errors, defects, bugs, or other nonconformance problems in the product or service. The type, amount, and extent of tests needed to evaluate each requirement are part of the project quality plan and depend on the nature of the project, time, budget, and other constraints. Tests can be performed throughout the project, as different components of the project become available, and at the end of the project on the final deliverables. Early testing helps identify nonconformance problems and helps reduce the cost of fixing the nonconforming components.

Different application areas require different tests. For example, software testing may include unit testing, integration testing, black-box, white-box, interface testing, regression testing, alpha testing, etc. In construction projects, testing may include cement strength, concrete workability tests, non-destructive tests at construction sites for testing the quality of hardened concrete structures, and soil tests. In hardware development, testing may include environmental stress screening, burn-in tests, system testing, and more.

Text-oriented formats. Team member responsibilities that require detailed descriptions can be specified in text-oriented formats. Usually in outline form, these documents provide information such as responsibilities, authority, competencies, and qualifications. The documents are known by various names including position descriptions and role-responsibility-authority forms. These documents can be used as templates for future projects, especially when the information is updated throughout the current project by applying lessons learned.

Three-point estimating. The accuracy of single-point duration estimates may be improved by considering estimation uncertainty and risk. Using three-point estimates helps define an approximate range for an activity's duration:

▶ **Most likely (*tM*).** This estimate is based on the duration of the activity, given the resources likely to be assigned, their productivity, realistic expectations of availability for the activity, dependencies on other participants, and interruptions.

▶ **Optimistic (*tO*).** The activity duration based on analysis of the best-case scenario for the activity.

▶ **Pessimistic (*tP*).** The duration based on analysis of the worst-case scenario for the activity.

Depending on the assumed distribution of values within the range of the three estimates, the expected duration, tE, can be calculated. One commonly used formula is triangular distribution:

$$tE = (tO + tM + tP) / 3.$$

Triangular distribution is used when there is insufficient historical data or when using judgmental data. Duration estimates based on three points with an assumed distribution provide an expected duration and clarify the range of uncertainty around the expected duration.

To-complete performance index (TCPI). The to-complete performance index (TCPI) is a measure of the cost performance that is required to be achieved with the remaining resources in order to meet a specified management goal, expressed as the ratio of the cost to finish the outstanding work to the remaining budget. TCPI is the calculated cost performance index that is achieved on the remaining work to meet a specified management goal, such as the budget at completion (BAC) or estimate at completion (EAC). If it becomes obvious that the BAC is no longer viable, the project manager should consider the forecasted EAC. Once approved, the EAC may replace the BAC in the TCPI calculation. The equation for TCPI is: (BAC − EV) / (BAC − AC) where: BAC = budget at completion, EV = earned value, and AC = actual cost.

The TCPI is conceptually displayed in Figure 10-23. The equation for the TCPI is shown in the lower left as the work remaining (defined as the BAC minus the EV) divided by the funds remaining (which can be either the BAC minus the AC, or the EAC minus the AC).

If the cumulative CPI falls below the baseline (as shown in Figure 10-23), all future work of the project will need to be performed immediately in the range of the TCPI (BAC) (as reflected in the top line of Figure 10-23) to stay within the authorized BAC. Whether this level of performance is achievable is a judgment call based on several considerations, including risk, time remaining in the project, and technical performance. This level of performance is displayed as the TCPI (EAC) line. The equation for the TCPI is based on the EAC: (BAC − EV) / (EAC − AC). The EVM formulas are provided in Table 10-1.

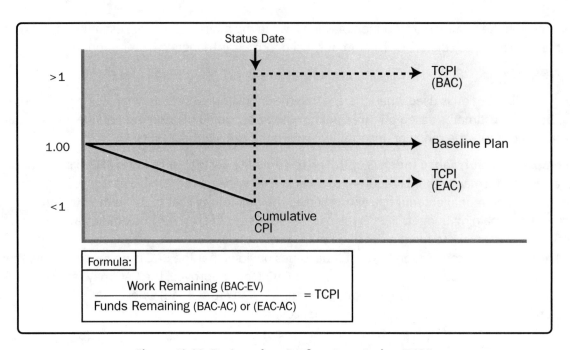

Figure 10-23. To-Complete Performance Index (TCPI)

Table 10-1. Earned Value Calculations Summary Table

			Earned Value Analysis		
Abbreviation	**Name**	**Lexicon Definition**	**How Used**	**Equation**	**Interpretation of Result**
PV	Planned Value	The authorized budget assigned to scheduled work.	The value of the work planned to be completed to a point in time, usually the data date, or project completion.		
EV	Earned Value	The measure of work performed expressed in terms of the budget authorized for that work.	The planned value of all the work completed (earned) to a point in time, usually the data date, without reference to actual costs.	EV = sum of the planned value of completed work	
AC	Actual Cost	The realized cost incurred for the work performed on an activity during a specific time period.	The actual cost of all the work completed to a point in time, usually the data date.		
BAC	Budget at Completion	The sum of all budgets established for the work to be performed.	The value of total planned work, the project cost baseline.		
CV	Cost Variance	The amount of budget deficit or surplus at a given point in time, expressed as the difference between the earned value and the actual cost.	The difference between the value of work completed to a point in time, usually the data date, and the actual costs to the same point in time.	CV = EV − AC	Positive = Under planned cost Neutral = On planned cost Negative = Over planned cost
SV	Schedule Variance	The amount by which the project is ahead or behind the planned delivery date, at a given point in time, expressed as the difference between the earned value and the planned value.	The difference between the work completed to a point in time, usually the data date, and the work planned to be completed to the same point in time.	SV = EV − PV	Positive = Ahead of Schedule Neutral = On schedule Negative = Behind Schedule
VAC	Variance at Completion	A projection of the amount of budget deficit or surplus, expressed as the difference between the budget at completion and the estimate at completion.	The estimated difference in cost at the completion of the project.	VAC = BAC − EAC	Positive = Under planned cost Neutral = On planned cost Negative = Over planned cost
CPI	Cost Performance Index	A measure of the cost efficiency of budgeted resources expressed as the ratio of earned value to actual cost.	A CPI of 1.0 means the project is exactly on budget, that the work actually done so far is exactly the same as the cost so far. Other values show the percentage of how much costs are over or under the budgeted amount for work accomplished.	CPI = EV/AC	Greater than 1.0 = Under planned cost Exactly 1.0 = On planned cost Less than 1.0 = Over planned cost
SPI	Schedule Performance Index	A measure of schedule efficiency expressed as the ratio of earned value to planned value.	An SPI of 1.0 means that the project is exactly on schedule, that the work actually done so far is exactly the same as the work planned to be done so far. Other values show the percentage of how much costs are over or under the budgeted amount for work planned.	SPI = EV/PV	Greater than 1.0 = Ahead of schedule Exactly 1.0 = On schedule Less than 1.0 = Behind schedule
EAC	Estimate At Completion	The expected total cost of completing all work expressed as the sum of the actual cost to date and the estimate to complete.	If the CPI is expected to be the same for the remainder of the project, EAC can be calculated using: If future work will be accomplished at the planned rate, use: If the initial plan is no longer valid, use: If both the CPI and SPI influence the remaining work, use:	EAC = BAC/CPI EAC = AC + BAC − EV EAC = AC + Bottom-up ETC EAC = AC + [(BAC − EV)/(CPI x SPI)]	
ETC	Estimate to Complete	The expected cost to finish all the remaining project work.	Assuming work is proceeding on plan, the cost of completing the remaining authorized work can be calculated using: Reestimate the remaining work from the bottom up.	ETC = EAC − AC ETC = Reestimate	
TCPI	To Complete Performance Index	A measure of the cost performance that must be achieved with the remaining resources in order to meet a specified management goal, expressed as the ratio of the cost to finish the outstanding work to the budget available.	The efficiency that must be maintained in order to complete on plan. The efficiency that must be maintained in order to complete the current EAC.	TCPI = (BAC−EV)/(BAC−AC) TCPI = (BAC − EV)/(EAC − AC)	Greater than 1.0 = Harder to complete Exactly 1.0 = Same to complete Less than 1.0 = Easier to complete Greater than 1.0 = Harder to complete Exactly 1.0 = Same to complete Less than 1.0 = Easier to complete

Training. Training includes all activities designed to enhance the competencies of the project team members. Training can be formal or informal. Examples of training methods include classroom, online, computer-based, on-the-job training from another project team member, mentoring, and coaching. If project team members lack the necessary management or technical skills, such skills can be developed as part of the project work.

Scheduled training takes place as stated in the resource management plan. Unplanned training takes place as a result of observation, conversation, and project performance appraisals conducted during management of the project team. Training costs could be included in the project budget or supported by the performing organization if the added skills may be useful for future projects. It may be performed by in-house or by external trainers.

Trend analysis. An analytical technique that uses mathematical models to forecast future outcomes based on historical results. It looks ahead in the project for expected slippages and warns the project manager ahead of time that there may be problems later in the schedule if established trends persist. This information is made available early enough in the project time line to give the project team time to analyze and correct any anomalies. The results of trend analysis can be used to recommend preventive actions if necessary.

Variance analysis. An analytical technique that uses mathematical models to forecast future outcomes based on historical results. Variance analysis reviews the differences (or variances) between planned and actual performance. This can include duration estimates, cost estimates, resources utilization, resources rates, technical performance, and other metrics.

Variance analysis reviews the variances from an integrated perspective considering cost, time, technical, and resource variances in relation to each other to get an overall view of variance on the project. This allows for the appropriate preventive or corrective actions to be initiated.

Voting. Voting is a collective decision-making technique and an assessment process having multiple alternatives with an expected outcome in the form of future actions. These techniques can be used to generate, classify, and prioritize product requirements. Examples of voting techniques include:

▶ **Unanimity.** A decision that is reached whereby everyone agrees on a single course of action.

▶ **Majority.** A decision that is reached with support obtained from more than 50% of the members of the group. Having a group size with an uneven number of participants can ensure that a decision will be reached rather than resulting in a tie.

▶ **Plurality.** A decision that is reached whereby the largest block in a group decides, even if a majority is not achieved. This method is generally used when the number of options nominated is more than two.

What-if scenario analysis. What-if scenario analysis is the process of evaluating scenarios in order to predict their effect, positive or negative, on project objectives. This is an analysis of the question, "What if the situation represented by scenario X happens?" A schedule network analysis is performed using the schedule to compute the different scenarios, such as delaying a major component delivery, extending specific engineering durations, or introducing external factors, such as a strike or a change in the permit process. The outcome of the what-if scenario analysis can be used to assess the feasibility of the project schedule under different conditions, and in preparing schedule reserves and response plans to address the impact of unexpected situations.

References

[1] Project Management Institute. 2021. *A Guide to the Project Management Body of Knowledge (PMBOK® Guide) – Seventh Edition*. Newtown Square, PA: Author.

[2] Project Management Institute. 2017. *The Standard for Organizational Project Management.* Newtown Square, PA: Author.

[3] Project Management Institute. 2015. *Business Analysis for Practitioners: A Practice Guide.* Newtown Square, PA: Author.

[4] Project Management Institute. 2017. *The Standard for Program Management* – Fourth Edition. Newtown Square, PA: Author.

[5] Project Management Institute. 2017. *The Standard for Portfolio Management* – Fourth Edition. Newtown Square, PA: Author.

[6] Project Management Institute. 2017. *Project Manager Competency Development Framework* – Third Edition. Newtown Square, PA: Author.

[7] Project Management Institute. 2014. *Navigating Complexity: A Practice Guide.* Newtown Square, PA: Author.

[8] Project Management Institute. 2019. *Practice Standard for Scheduling* – Third Edition. Newtown Square, PA: Author.

[9] Project Management Institute. 2019. *The Standard for Earned Value Management.* Newtown Square, PA: Author.

[10] Project Management Institute. 2019. *Practice Standard for Work Breakdown Structures* – Second Edition.

Appendix X1
Contributors and Reviewers of
Process Groups: A Practice Guide

The Project Management Institute is grateful to all of the contributors for their support and acknowledges their outstanding contributions to the project management profession.

X1.1 REVIEWERS

The following list of contributors participated in reviewing the content of this practice guide. Inclusion of an individual's name in the list does not represent his or her approval or endorsement of the final content in all its parts.

Panos Chatzipanos, PhD, Dr Eur Ing
Christopher Edwards, PMI-PBA, PMI-RPM, PMP
Mike Griffiths, PMI-ACP, PMP

Hagit Landman, MBA, PMI-SP, PMP
Maricarmen Suarez, MBA, PMI-ACP, PMP, PgMP
Vivian Taslakian, BSEE, MS, MBA, PMP

X1.2 PMI STAFF

Special mention is due to the following employees of PMI:

Fleur Connors, Product Coordinator, MA
Mike Griffiths, Agile Thought Leader
Leah Huf, Product Manager, Standards
Christie McDevitt, Product Specialist, APR
Joshua Parrott, Product Specialist, MBI

Danielle Ritter, Product Manager, MLIS, CSPO
Kim Shinners, Product Specialist
Roberta Storer, Product Specialist
Barbara Walsh, Product Manager,
  Publications, CSPO

Glossary

1. INCLUSIONS AND EXCLUSIONS

This glossary includes terms that are:

▶ Unique or nearly unique to project management (e.g., project scope statement, work package, work breakdown structure, critical path method).

▶ Not unique to project management, but used differently or with a narrower meaning in project management than in general everyday usage (e.g., early start date).

This glossary generally does not include:

▶ Application area-specific terms.

▶ Terms used in project management that do not differ in any material way from everyday use (e.g., calendar day, delay).

▶ Compound terms whose meaning is clear from the meanings of the component parts.

▶ Variants when the meaning of the variant is clear from the base term.

▶ Terms that are used only once and are not critical to understanding the point of the sentence. This can include a list of examples that would not have each term defined in the Glossary.

2. COMMON ACRONYMS

AC	actual cost
BA	business analyst
BAC	budget at completion
CCB	change control board
COQ	cost of quality
CPAF	cost plus award fee
CPFF	cost plus fixed fee
CPI	cost performance index
CPIF	cost plus incentive fee
CPM	critical path method
CV	cost variance
EAC	estimate at completion
EF	early finish date
ES	early start date
ETC	estimate to complete
EV	earned value
EVM	earned value management
FF	finish-to-finish
FFP	firm fixed price
FPEPA	fixed price with economic price adjustment
FPIF	fixed price incentive fee
FS	finish to start
IFB	invitation for bid
LF	late finish date
LOE	level of effort
LS	late start date
OBS	organizational breakdown structure
PDM	precedence diagramming method
PV	planned value
QFD	quality function deployment

RACI	responsible, accountable, consult, and inform
RAM	responsibility assignment matrix
RBS	risk breakdown structure
RFI	request for information
RFP	request for proposal
RFQ	request for quotation
SF	start-to-finish
SOW	statement of work
SPI	schedule performance index
SS	start-to-start
SV	schedule variance
SWOT	strengths, weaknesses, opportunities, and threats
T&M	time and material contract
WBS	work breakdown structure

3. DEFINITIONS

Many of the words defined here have broader, and in some cases different, dictionary definitions. In some cases, a single glossary term consists of multiple words (e.g., root cause analysis).

Acceptance Criteria. A set of conditions that is required to be met before deliverables are accepted.

Accepted Deliverables. Products, results, or capabilities produced by a project and validated by the project customer or sponsors as meeting their specified acceptance criteria.

Accuracy. Within the quality management system, accuracy is an assessment of correctness.

Acquire Resources. The process of obtaining team members, facilities, equipment, materials, supplies, and other resources necessary to complete project work.

Acquisition. Obtaining human and material resources necessary to perform project activities. Acquisition implies a cost of resources and is not necessarily financial.

Activity. A distinct, scheduled portion of work performed during the course of a project.

Activity Attributes. Multiple attributes associated with each schedule activity that can be included within the activity list. Activity attributes include activity codes, predecessor activities, successor activities, logical relationships, leads and lags, resource requirements, imposed dates, constraints, and assumptions.

Activity Duration. The time in calendar units between the start and finish of a schedule activity. See also *duration*.

Activity Duration Estimates. The quantitative assessments of the likely number of time periods that are required to complete an activity.

Activity List. A documented tabulation of schedule activities that shows the activity description, activity identifier, and a sufficiently detailed scope of work description so project team members understand what work is to be performed.

Activity-on-Node (AON). See *precedence diagramming method (PDM)*.

Actual Cost (AC). The realized cost incurred for the work performed on an activity during a specific time period.

Actual Duration. The time in calendar units between the actual start date of the schedule activity and either the data date of the project schedule if the schedule activity is in progress or the actual finish date if the schedule activity is complete.

Adaptive Life Cycle. A project life cycle that is iterative or incremental.

Affinity Diagrams. A technique that allows large numbers of ideas to be classified into groups for review and analysis.

Agile Life Cycle. See *adaptive life cycle*.

Agreements. Any document or communication that defines the initial intentions of a project. This can take the form of a contract, memorandum of understanding (MOU), letters of agreement, verbal agreements, email, etc.

Alternatives Analysis. A technique used to evaluate identified options in order to select the options or approaches to use to execute and perform the work of the project.

Analogous Estimating. A technique for estimating the duration or cost of an activity or a project using historical data from a similar activity or project.

Assumption. A factor in the planning process that is considered to be true, real, or certain, without proof or demonstration.

Assumption Log. A project document used to record all assumptions and constraints throughout the project life cycle.

Authority. The right to apply project resources, expend funds, make decisions, or give approvals.

Backlog. An ordered list of user-centric requirements that a team maintains for a product.

Backward Pass. A critical path method technique for calculating the late start and late finish dates by working backward through the schedule model from the project end date.

Bar Chart. A graphic display of schedule-related information. In the typical bar chart, schedule activities or work breakdown structure components are listed down the left side of the chart, dates are shown across the top, and activity durations are shown as date-placed horizontal bars.

Baseline. The approved version of a work product that can be changed only through formal change control procedures and is used as a basis for comparison to actual results.

Basis of Estimates. Supporting documentation outlining the details used in establishing project estimates such as assumptions, constraints, level of detail, ranges, and confidence levels.

Benchmarking. The comparison of actual or planned products, processes, and practices to those of comparable organizations to identify best practices, generate ideas for improvement, and provide a basis for measuring performance.

Benefits Management Plan. The documented explanation defining the processes for creating, maximizing, and sustaining the benefits provided by a project or program.

Bid Documents. All documents used to solicit information, quotations, or proposals from prospective sellers.

Bidder Conference. The meeting with prospective sellers prior to the preparation of a bid or proposal to ensure all prospective vendors have a clear and common understanding of the procurement. Also known as contractor conference, vendor conference, or pre-bid conference.

Bottom-Up Estimating. A method of estimating project duration or cost by aggregating the estimates of the lower-level components of the work breakdown structure (WBS).

Budget. The approved estimate for the project or any work breakdown structure component or any schedule activity.

Budget at Completion (BAC). The sum of all budgets established for the work to be performed.

Buffer. See *reserve*.

Business Analysis. The set of activities performed to support delivery of solutions that align to business objectives and provide continuous value to the organization.

Business Analyst (BA). Any resource who is doing the work of business analysis.

Business Case. A documented economic feasibility study used to establish validity of the benefits of a selected component lacking sufficient definition and that is used as a basis for the authorization of further project management activities.

Business Value. The net quantifiable benefit derived from a business endeavor. The benefit may be tangible, intangible, or both.

Cause and Effect Diagram. A decomposition technique that helps trace an undesirable effect back to its root cause.

Change. A modification to any formally controlled deliverable, project management plan component, or project document.

Change Control. A process whereby modifications to documents, deliverables, or baselines associated with the project are identified, documented, approved, or rejected.

Change Control Board (CCB). A formally chartered group responsible for reviewing, evaluating, approving, delaying, or rejecting changes to the project, and for recording and communicating such decisions.

Change Control System. A set of procedures that describes how modifications to the project deliverables and documentation are managed and controlled.

Change Control Tools. Manual or automated tools to assist with change and/or configuration management. At a minimum, the tools should support the activities of the CCB.

Change Log. A comprehensive list of changes submitted during the project and their current status.

Change Management Plan. A component of the project management plan that establishes the change control board, documents the extent of its authority, and describes how the change control system will be implemented.

Change Request. A formal proposal to modify a document, deliverable, or baseline.

Charter. See *project charter*.

Check Sheet. A tally sheet that can be used as a checklist when gathering data.

Checklist Analysis. A technique for systematically reviewing materials using a list for accuracy and completeness.

Claim. A request, demand, or assertion of rights by a seller against a buyer, or vice versa, for consideration, compensation, or payment under the terms of a legally binding contract, such as for a disputed change.

Claims Administration. The process of processing, adjudicating, and communicating contract claims.

Close Project or Phase. The process of finalizing all activities for the project, phase, or contract.

Closing Process Group. The process(es) performed to formally complete or close a project, phase, or contract.

Code of Accounts. A numbering system used to uniquely identify each component of the work breakdown structure (WBS).

Process Groups: A Practice Guide

Collect Requirements. The process of determining, documenting, and managing stakeholder needs and requirements to meet project objectives.

Colocation. An organizational placement strategy where the project team members are physically located close to one another in order to improve communication, working relationships, and productivity.

Communication Methods. A systematic procedure, technique, or process used to transfer information among project stakeholders.

Communication Models. A description, analogy, or schematic used to represent how the communication process will be performed for the project.

Communication Requirements Analysis. An analytical technique to determine the information needs of the project stakeholders through interviews, workshops, study of lessons learned from previous projects, etc.

Communications Management Plan. A component of the project, program, or portfolio management plan that describes how, when, and by whom information about the project will be administered and disseminated.

Communication Styles Assessment. A technique to identify the preferred communication method, format, and content for stakeholders for planned communication activities.

Communication Technology. Specific tools, systems, computer programs, etc., used to transfer information among project stakeholders.

Conduct Procurements. The process of obtaining seller responses, selecting a seller, and awarding a contract.

Configuration Management Plan. A component of the project management plan that describes how to identify and account for project artifacts under configuration control, and how to record and report changes to them.

Configuration Management System. A collection of procedures used to track project artifacts and monitor and control changes to these artifacts.

Conformance. Within the quality management system, conformance is a general concept of delivering results that fall within the limits that define acceptable variation for a quality requirement.

Constraint. A limiting factor that affects the execution of a project, program, portfolio, or process.

Context Diagrams. A visual depiction of the product scope showing a business system (process, equipment, computer system, etc.), and how people and other systems (actors) interact with it.

Contingency. An event or occurrence that could affect the execution of the project that may be accounted for with a reserve.

Contingency Reserve. Time or money allocated in the schedule or cost baseline for known risks with active response strategies.

Contingent Response Strategies. Responses provided which may be used in the event that a specific trigger occurs.

Contract. A contract is a mutually binding agreement that obligates the seller to provide the specified product or service or result and obligates the buyer to pay for it.

Control. Comparing actual performance with planned performance, analyzing variances, assessing trends to effect process improvements, evaluating possible alternatives, and recommending appropriate corrective action as needed.

Control Account. A management control point where scope, budget, actual cost, and schedule are integrated and compared to earned value for performance measurement.

Control Chart. A graphic display of process data over time and against established control limits, which has a centerline that assists in detecting a trend of plotted values toward either control limit.

Control Costs. The process of monitoring the status of the project to update the project costs and manage changes to the cost baseline.

Control Limits. The area composed of three standard deviations on either side of the centerline or mean of a normal distribution of data plotted on a control chart, which reflects the expected variation in the data. See also *specification limits*.

Control Procurements. The process of managing procurement relationships, monitoring contract performance, making changes and corrections as appropriate, and closing out contracts.

Control Quality. The process of monitoring and recording results of the quality management activities to assess performance and ensure the project outputs are complete, correct, and meet customer expectations.

Control Resources. The process of ensuring that the physical resources assigned and allocated to the project are available as planned, as well as monitoring the planned versus actual utilization of resources and performing corrective action as necessary.

Control Schedule. The process of monitoring the status of the project to update the project schedule and manage changes to the schedule baseline.

Control Scope. The process of monitoring the status of the project and product scope and managing changes to the scope baseline.

Corrective Action. An intentional activity that realigns the performance of the project work with the project management plan.

Cost Aggregation. Summing the lower-level cost estimates associated with the various work packages for a given level within the project's WBS or for a given cost control account.

Cost Baseline. The approved version of the time-phased project budget, excluding any management reserves, which can be changed only through formal change control procedures and is used as a basis for comparison to actual results.

Cost-Benefit Analysis. A financial analysis tool used to determine the benefits provided by a project against its costs.

Cost Management Plan. A component of a project or program management plan that describes how costs will be planned, structured, and controlled.

Cost of Quality (CoQ). All costs incurred over the life of the product by investment in preventing nonconformance to requirements, appraisal of the product or service for conformance to requirements, and failure to meet requirements.

Cost Performance Index (CPI). A measure of the cost efficiency of budgeted resources expressed as the ratio of earned value to actual cost.

Cost Plus Award Fee Contract (CPAF). A category of contract that involves payments to the seller for all legitimate actual costs incurred for completed work, plus an award fee representing seller profit.

Cost Plus Fixed Fee Contract (CPFF). A type of cost-reimbursable contract where the buyer reimburses the seller for the seller's allowable costs (allowable costs are defined by the contract) plus a fixed amount of profit (fee).

Cost Plus Incentive Fee Contract (CPIF). A type of cost-reimbursable contract where the buyer reimburses the seller for the seller's allowable costs (allowable costs are defined by the contract), and the seller earns its profit if it meets defined performance criteria.

Cost-Reimbursable Contract. A type of contract involving payment to the seller for the seller's actual costs, plus a fee typically representing the seller's profit.

Cost Variance (CV). The amount of budget deficit or surplus at a given point in time, expressed as the difference between the earned value and the actual cost.

Crashing. A technique used to shorten the schedule duration for the least incremental cost by adding resources.

Create WBS. The process of subdividing project deliverables and project work into smaller, more manageable components.

Criteria. Standards, rules, or tests on which a judgment or decision can be based or by which a product, service, result, or process can be evaluated.

Critical Path. The sequence of activities that represents the longest path through a project, which determines the shortest possible duration.

Critical Path Activity. Any activity on the critical path in a project schedule.

Critical Path Method (CPM). A method used to estimate the minimum project duration and determine the amount of schedule flexibility on the logical network paths within the schedule model.

Data. Discrete, unorganized, unprocessed measurements or raw observations.

Data Analysis Techniques. Techniques used to organize, assess, and evaluate data and information.

Data Date. A point in time when the status of the project is recorded.

Data Gathering Techniques. Techniques used to collect data and information from a variety of sources.

Data Representation Techniques. Graphic representations or other methods used to convey data and information.

Decision-Making Techniques. Techniques used to select a course of action from different alternatives.

Decision Tree Analysis. A diagramming and calculation technique for evaluating the implications of a chain of multiple options in the presence of uncertainty.

Decomposition. A technique used for dividing and subdividing the project scope and project deliverables into smaller, more manageable parts.

Defect. An imperfection or deficiency in a project component where that component does not meet its requirements or specifications and needs to be either repaired or replaced.

Defect Repair. An intentional activity to modify a nonconforming product or product component.

Define Activities. The process of identifying and documenting the specific actions to be performed to produce the project deliverables.

Define Scope. The process of developing a detailed description of the project and product.

Deliverable. Any unique and verifiable product, result, or capability to perform a service that is required to be produced to complete a process, phase, or project.

Dependency. See *logical relationship*.

Determine Budget. The process of aggregating the estimated costs of individual activities or work packages to establish an authorized cost baseline.

Develop Project Charter. The process of developing a document that formally authorizes the existence of a project and provides the project manager with the authority to apply organizational resources to project activities.

Develop Project Management Plan. The process of defining, preparing, and coordinating all plan components and consolidating them into an integrated project management plan.

Develop Schedule. The process of analyzing activity sequences, durations, resource requirements, and schedule constraints to create the project schedule model for project execution and monitoring and controlling.

Develop Team. The process of improving competences, team member interaction, and overall team environment to enhance project performance.

Development Approach. The method used to create and evolve the product, service, or result during the project life cycle, such as predictive, iterative, incremental, agile, or a hybrid method.

Direct and Manage Project Work. The process of leading and performing the work defined in the project management plan and implementing approved changes to achieve the project's objectives.

Duration. The total number of work periods required to complete an activity or work breakdown structure component, expressed in hours, days, or weeks. Contrast with *effort*.

Early Finish Date (EF). In the critical path method, the earliest possible point in time when the uncompleted portions of a schedule activity can finish based on the schedule network logic, the data date, and any schedule constraints.

Early Start Date (ES). In the critical path method, the earliest possible point in time when the uncompleted portions of a schedule activity can start based on the schedule network logic, the data date, and any schedule constraints.

Earned Value (EV). The measure of work performed expressed in terms of the budget authorized for that work.

Earned Value Management. A methodology that combines scope, schedule, and resource measurements to assess project performance and progress.

Effort. The number of labor units required to complete a schedule activity or work breakdown structure component, often expressed in hours, days, or weeks. Contrast with *duration*.

Emotional Intelligence. The ability to identify, assess, and manage the personal emotions of oneself and other people, as well as the collective emotions of groups of people.

Enterprise Environmental Factors. Conditions, not under the immediate control of the team, that influence, constrain, or direct the project, program, or portfolio.

Estimate. A quantitative assessment of the likely amount or outcome of a variable, such as project costs, resources, effort, or durations.

Estimate Activity Durations. The process of estimating the number of work periods needed to complete individual activities with the estimated resources.

Estimate Activity Resources. The process of estimating team resources and the type and quantities of material, equipment, and supplies necessary to perform project work.

Estimate at Completion (EAC). The expected total cost of completing all work expressed as the sum of the actual cost to date and the estimate to complete.

Estimate Costs. The process of developing an approximation of the monetary resources needed to complete project work.

Estimate to Complete (ETC). The expected cost to finish all the remaining project work.

Execute. Directing, managing, performing, and accomplishing the project work; providing the deliverables; and providing work performance information.

Executing Process Group. Those processes performed to complete the work defined in the project management plan to satisfy the project requirements.

Expert Judgment. Judgment provided based upon expertise in an application area, discipline, industry, etc., as appropriate for the activity being performed. Such expertise may be provided by any group or person with specialized education, knowledge, skill, experience, or training.

Explicit Knowledge. Knowledge that can be codified using symbols such as words, numbers, and pictures.

Fallback Plan. An alternative set of actions and tasks available in the event that the primary plan needs to be abandoned because of issues, risks, or other causes.

Fast Tracking. A schedule compression technique in which activities or phases normally done in sequence are performed in parallel for at least a portion of their duration.

Fee. Represents profit as a component of compensation to a seller.

Finish Date. A point in time associated with a schedule activity's completion. Usually qualified by one of the following: actual, planned, estimated, scheduled, early, late, baseline, target, or current.

Finish-to-Finish (FF). A logical relationship in which a successor activity cannot finish until a predecessor activity has finished.

Finish-to-Start (FS). A logical relationship in which a successor activity cannot start until a predecessor activity has finished.

Firm Fixed Price Contract (FFP). A type of fixed price contract where the buyer pays the seller a set amount (as defined by the contract), regardless of the seller's costs.

Fishbone diagram. See *cause and effect diagram*.

Fixed-Price Contract. An agreement that sets the fee that will be paid for a defined scope of work regardless of the cost or effort to deliver it.

Fixed Price Incentive Fee Contract (FPIF). A type of contract where the buyer pays the seller a set amount (as defined by the contract), and the seller can earn an additional amount if the seller meets defined performance criteria.

Fixed Price with Economic Price Adjustment Contract (FPEPA). A fixed-price contract, but with a special provision allowing for predefined final adjustments to the contract price due to changed conditions, such as inflation changes, or cost increases (or decreases) for specific commodities.

Float. Also called slack. See *total float* and *free float*.

Flowchart. The depiction in a diagram format of the inputs, process actions, and outputs of one or more processes within a system.

Focus Groups. An elicitation technique that brings together prequalified stakeholders and subject matter experts to learn about their expectations and attitudes about a proposed product, service, or result.

Forecast. An estimate or prediction of conditions and events in the project's future based on information and knowledge available at the time of the forecast.

Forward Pass. A critical path method technique for calculating the early start and early finish dates by working forward through the schedule model from the project start date or a given point in time.

Free Float. The amount of time that a schedule activity can be delayed without delaying the early start date of any successor or violating a schedule constraint.

Funding Limit Reconciliation. The process of comparing the planned expenditure of project funds against any limits on the commitment of funds for the project to identify any variances between the funding limits and the planned expenditures.

Grade. A category or rank used to distinguish items that have the same functional use but do not share the same requirements for quality.

Ground Rules. Expectations regarding acceptable behavior by project team members.

Histogram. A bar chart that shows the graphical representation of numerical data.

Historical Information. Documents and data on prior projects including project files, records, correspondence, closed contracts, and closed projects.

Identify Risks. The process of identifying individual risks as well as sources of overall risk and documenting their characteristics.

Identify Stakeholders. The process of identifying project stakeholders regularly and analyzing and documenting relevant information regarding their interests, involvement, interdependencies, influence, and potential impact on project success.

Implement Risk Responses. The process of implementing agreed-upon risk response plans.

Imposed Date. A fixed date imposed on a schedule activity or schedule milestone, usually in the form of a "start no earlier than" and "finish no later than" date.

Incentive Fee. A set of financial incentives related to cost, schedule, or technical performance of the seller.

Increment. A functional, tested, and accepted deliverable that is a subset of the overall project outcome.

Incremental Life Cycle. An adaptive project life cycle in which the deliverable is produced through a series of iterations that successively add functionality within a predetermined time frame. The deliverable contains the necessary and sufficient capability to be considered complete only after the final iteration.

Independent Estimates. A process of using a third party to obtain and analyze information to support prediction of cost, schedule, or other items.

Influence Diagram. A graphical representation of situations showing causal influences, time ordering of events, and other relationships among variables and outcomes.

Information. Organized or structured data, processed for a specific purpose to make it meaningful, valuable, and useful in specific contexts.

Initiating Process Group. Those processes performed to define a new project or a new phase of an existing project by obtaining authorization to start the project or phase.

Input. Any item, whether internal or external to the project, which is required by a process before that process proceeds. May be an output from a predecessor process.

Inspection. Examination of a work product to determine whether it conforms to documented standards.

Interpersonal and Team Skills. Skills used to effectively lead and interact with team members and other stakeholders.

Interpersonal Skills. Skills used to establish and maintain relationships with other people.

Interviews. A formal or informal approach to elicit information from stakeholders by talking to them directly.

Invitation for Bid (IFB). Generally, this term is equivalent to request for proposal. However, in some application areas, it may have a narrower or more specific meaning.

Issue. A current condition or situation that may have an impact on the project objectives.

Issue Log. A project document where information about issues is recorded and monitored.

Iteration. A timeboxed cycle of development on a product or deliverable in which all of the work that is needed to deliver value is performed.

Iterative Life Cycle. A project life cycle where the project scope is generally determined early in the project life cycle, but time and cost estimates are routinely modified as the project team's understanding of the product increases. Iterations develop the product through a series of repeated cycles, while increments successively add to the functionality of the product.

Knowledge. A mixture of experience, values and beliefs, contextual information, intuition, and insight that people use to make sense of new experiences and information.

Lag. The amount of time whereby a successor activity will be delayed with respect to a predecessor activity.

Late Finish Date (LF). In the critical path method, the latest possible point in time when the uncompleted portions of a schedule activity can finish based on the schedule network, the project completion date, and any schedule constraints.

Late Start Date (LS). In the critical path method, the latest possible point in time when the uncompleted portions of a schedule activity can start based on the schedule network logic, the project completion date, and any schedule constraints.

Lead. The amount of time whereby a successor activity can be advanced with respect to a predecessor activity.

Lessons Learned. The knowledge gained during a project which shows how project events were addressed or should be addressed in the future for the purpose of improving future performance.

Lessons Learned Register. A project document used to record knowledge gained during a project so that it can be used in the current project and entered into the lessons learned repository.

Lessons Learned Repository. A store of historical information about lessons learned in projects.

Level of Effort (LOE). An activity that does not produce definitive end products and is measured by the passage of time.

Life Cycle. See *project life cycle*.

Log. A document used to record and describe or denote selected items identified during execution of a process or activity. Usually used with a modifier, such as issue, change, or assumption.

Logical Relationship. A dependency between two activities, or between an activity and a milestone.

Make-or-Buy Analysis. The process of gathering and organizing data about product requirements and analyzing them against available alternatives including the purchase or internal manufacture of the product.

Make-or-Buy Decisions. Decisions made regarding the external purchase or internal manufacture of a product.

Manage Communications. The process of ensuring timely and appropriate collection, creation, distribution, storage, retrieval, management, monitoring, and the ultimate disposition of project information.

Manage Project Knowledge. The process of using existing knowledge and creating new knowledge to achieve the project's objectives and contribute to organizational learning.

Manage Quality. The process of translating the quality management plan into executable quality activities that incorporate the organization's quality policies into the project.

Manage Stakeholder Engagement. The process of communicating and working with stakeholders to meet their needs and expectations, address issues, and foster appropriate stakeholder involvement.

Manage Team. The process of tracking team member performance, providing feedback, resolving issues, and managing team changes to optimize project performance.

Management Reserve. An amount of the project budget or project schedule held outside of the performance measurement baseline (PMB) for management control purposes, that is reserved for unforeseen work that is within scope of the project.

Mandatory Dependency. A relationship that is contractually required or inherent in the nature of the work.

Matrix Diagrams. A quality management and control tool used to perform data analysis within the organizational structure created in the matrix. The matrix diagram seeks to show the strength of relationships between factors, causes, and objectives that exist between the rows and columns that form the matrix.

Methodology. A system of practices, techniques, procedures, and rules used by those who work in a discipline.

Milestone. A significant point or event in a project, program, or portfolio.

Mind Mapping. A technique used to consolidate ideas created through individual brainstorming sessions into a single map to reflect commonality and differences in understanding and to generate new ideas.

Monitor. Collect project performance data, produce performance measures, and report and disseminate performance information.

Monitor and Control Project Work. The process of tracking, reviewing, and reporting overall progress to meet the performance objectives defined in the project management plan.

Monitor Communications. The process of ensuring that the information needs of the project and its stakeholders are met.

Monitor Risks. The process of monitoring the implementation of agreed-upon risk response plans, tracking identified risks, identifying and analyzing new risks, and evaluating risk process effectiveness throughout the project.

Monitor Stakeholder Engagement. The process of monitoring project stakeholder relationships, and tailoring strategies for engaging stakeholders through the modification of engagement strategies and plans.

Monitoring and Controlling Process Group. Those processes required to track, review, and regulate the progress and performance of the project; identify any areas in which changes to the plan are required; and initiate the corresponding changes.

Monte Carlo Simulation. An analysis technique where a computer model is iterated many times, with the input values chosen at random for each iteration driven by the input data, including probability distributions and probabilistic branches. Outputs are generated to represent the range of possible outcomes for the project.

Multicriteria Decision Analysis. This technique utilizes a decision matrix to provide a systematic analytical approach for establishing criteria, such as risk levels, uncertainty, and valuation, to evaluate and rank many ideas.

Network. See *project schedule network diagram*.

Network Logic. All activity dependencies in a project schedule network diagram.

Network Path. A sequence of activities connected by logical relationships in a project schedule network diagram.

Networking. Establishing connections and relationships with other people from the same or other organizations.

Node. A point at which dependency lines connect on a schedule network diagram.

Nominal Group Technique. A technique that enhances brainstorming with a voting process used to rank the most useful ideas for further brainstorming or for prioritization.

Objective. Something toward which work is to be directed, a strategic position to be attained, a purpose to be achieved, a result to be obtained, a product to be produced, or a service to be performed.

Opportunity. A risk that would have a positive effect on one or more project objectives.

Organizational Breakdown Structure (OBS). A hierarchical representation of the project organization, which illustrates the relationship between project activities and the organizational units that will perform those activities.

Organizational Learning. A discipline concerned with the way individuals, groups, and organizations develop knowledge.

Organizational Process Assets. Plans, processes, documents, and knowledge repositories that are specific to and used by the performing organization.

Output. A product, result, or service generated by a process. May be an input to a successor process.

Overall Project Risk. The effect of uncertainty on the project as a whole, arising from all sources of uncertainty including individual risks, representing the exposure of stakeholders to the implications of variations in project outcome, both positive and negative.

Parametric Estimating. An estimating technique in which an algorithm is used to calculate cost or duration based on historical data and project parameters.

Path Convergence. A relationship in which a schedule activity has more than one predecessor.

Path Divergence. A relationship in which a schedule activity has more than one successor.

Percent Complete. An estimate expressed as a percent of the amount of work that has been completed on an activity or a work breakdown structure component.

Perform Integrated Change Control. The process of reviewing all change requests; approving changes and managing changes to deliverables, organizational process assets, project documents, and the project management plan; and communicating the decisions.

Perform Qualitative Risk Analysis. The process of prioritizing individual project risks for further analysis or action by assessing their probability of occurrence and impact as well as other characteristics.

Perform Quantitative Risk Analysis. The process of numerically analyzing the combined effect of identified individual project risks and other sources of uncertainty on overall project objectives.

Performance Measurement Baseline (PMB). Integrated scope, schedule, and cost baselines used for comparison to manage, measure, and control project execution.

Performance Reviews. A technique that is used to measure, compare, and analyze actual performance of work in progress on the project against the baseline.

Phase. See *project phase*.

Phase Gate. A review at the end of a phase in which a decision is made to continue to the next phase, to continue with modification, or to end a project or program.

Plan Communications Management. The process of developing an appropriate approach and plan for project communication activities based on the information needs of each stakeholder or group, available organizational assets, and the needs of the project.

Plan Cost Management. The process of defining how the project costs will be estimated, budgeted, managed, monitored, and controlled.

Plan Procurement Management. The process of documenting project procurement decisions, specifying the approach, and identifying potential sellers.

Plan Quality Management. The process of identifying quality requirements and/or standards for the project and its deliverables, and documenting how the project will demonstrate compliance with quality requirements and/or standards.

Plan Resource Management. The process of defining how to estimate, acquire, manage, and utilize physical and team resources.

Plan Risk Management. The process of defining how to conduct risk management activities for a project.

Plan Risk Responses. The process of developing options, selecting strategies, and agreeing on actions to address overall project risk exposure, as well as to treat individual project risks.

Plan Schedule Management. The process of establishing the policies, procedures, and documentation for planning, developing, managing, executing, and controlling the project schedule.

Plan Scope Management. The process of creating a scope management plan that documents how the project and product scope will be defined, validated, and controlled.

Plan Stakeholder Engagement. The process of developing approaches to involve project stakeholders, based on their needs, expectations, interests, and potential impact on the project.

Planned Value (PV). The authorized budget assigned to scheduled work.

Planning Package. A work breakdown structure component below the control account with known work content but without detailed schedule activities. See also *control account*.

Planning Process Group. Those processes required to establish the scope of the project, refine the objectives, and define the course of action required to attain the objectives that the project was undertaken to achieve.

Plurality. Decisions made by the largest block in a group, even if a majority is not achieved.

Policy. A structured pattern of actions adopted by an organization such that the organization's policy can be explained as a set of basic principles that govern the organization's conduct.

Portfolio. Projects, programs, subsidiary portfolios, and operations managed as a group to achieve strategic objectives.

Portfolio Management. The centralized management of one or more portfolios to achieve strategic objectives.

Practice. A specific type of professional or management activity that contributes to the execution of a process and that may employ one or more techniques and tools.

Precedence Diagramming Method (PDM). A technique used for constructing a schedule model in which activities are represented by nodes and are graphically linked by one or more logical relationships to show the sequence in which the activities are to be performed.

Precedence Relationship. A logical dependency used in the precedence diagramming method.

Predecessor Activity. An activity that logically comes before a dependent activity in a schedule.

Predictive Life Cycle. A form of project life cycle in which the project scope, time, and cost are determined in the early phases of the life cycle.

Preventive Action. An intentional activity that ensures the future performance of the project work is aligned with the project management plan.

Probability and Impact Matrix. A grid for mapping the probability of occurrence of each risk and its impact on project objectives if that risk occurs.

Procedure. An established method of accomplishing a consistent performance or result, a procedure typically can be described as the sequence of steps that will be used to execute a process.

Process. A systematic series of activities directed toward causing an end result such that one or more inputs will be acted upon to create one or more outputs.

Procurement Audits. The review of contracts and contracting processes for completeness, accuracy, and effectiveness.

Procurement Documentation. All documents used in signing, executing, and closing an agreement. Procurement documentation may include documents predating the project.

Procurement Management Plan. A component of the project or program management plan that describes how a project team will acquire goods and services from outside of the performing organization.

Procurement Statement of Work. Describes the procurement item in sufficient detail to allow prospective sellers to determine if they are capable of providing the products, services, or results.

Procurement Strategy. The approach by the buyer to determine the project delivery method and the type of legally binding agreement(s) that should be used to deliver the desired results.

Product. An artifact that is produced, is quantifiable, and can be either an end item in itself or a component item. Additional words for products are material and goods. See also *deliverable*.

Product Analysis. For projects that have a product as a deliverable, it is a tool to define scope that generally means asking questions about a product and forming answers to describe the use, characteristics, and other relevant aspects of what is going to be manufactured.

Product Life Cycle. The series of phases that represent the evolution of a product, from concept through delivery, growth, maturity, and to retirement.

Product Scope. The features and functions that characterize a product, service, or result.

Product Scope Description. The documented narrative description of the product scope.

Program. Related projects, subsidiary programs, and program activities that are managed in a coordinated manner to obtain benefits not available from managing them individually.

Program Management. The application of knowledge, skills, and principles to a program to achieve the program objectives and obtain benefits and control not available by managing program components individually.

Progressive Elaboration. The iterative process of increasing the level of detail in a project management plan as greater amounts of information and more accurate estimates become available.

Project. A temporary endeavor undertaken to create a unique product, service, or result.

Project Calendar. A calendar that identifies working days and shifts that are available for scheduled activities.

Project Charter. A document issued by the project initiator or sponsor that formally authorizes the existence of a project and provides the project manager with the authority to apply organizational resources to project activities.

Project Funding Requirements. Forecast project costs to be paid that are derived from the cost baseline for total or periodic requirements, including projected expenditures plus anticipated liabilities.

Project Governance. The framework, functions, and processes that guide project management activities in order to create a unique product, service, or result to meet organizational, strategic, and operational goals.

Project Initiation. Launching a process that can result in the authorization of a new project.

Project Life Cycle. The series of phases that a project passes through from its start to its completion.

Project Management. The application of knowledge, skills, tools, and techniques to project activities to meet the project requirements.

Project Management Information System. An information system consisting of the tools and techniques used to gather, integrate, and disseminate the outputs of project management processes.

Project Management Office (PMO). A management structure that standardizes the project-related governance processes and facilitates the sharing of resources, methodologies, tools, and techniques.

Project Management Plan. The document that describes how the project will be executed, monitored and controlled, and closed.

Project Management Process Group. A logical grouping of project management inputs, tools and techniques, and outputs. The Project Management Process Groups include initiating processes, planning processes, executing processes, monitoring and controlling processes, and closing processes. Project Management Process Groups are not project phases.

Project Management Team. The members of the project team who are directly involved in project management activities. See also *project team*.

Project Manager. The person assigned by the performing organization to lead the team that is responsible for achieving the project objectives.

Project Organization Chart. A document that graphically depicts the project team members and their interrelationships for a specific project.

Project Phase. A collection of logically related project activities that culminates in the completion of one or more deliverables.

Project Schedule. An output of a schedule model that presents linked activities with planned dates, durations, milestones, and resources.

Project Schedule Network Diagram. A graphical representation of the logical relationships among the project schedule activities.

Project Scope. The work performed to deliver a product, service, or result with the specified features and functions.

Project Scope Statement. The description of the project scope, major deliverables, and exclusions.

Project Team. A set of individuals who support the project manager in performing the work of the project to achieve its objectives. See also *project management team*.

Project Team Directory. A documented list of project team members, their project roles, and communication information.

Prototypes. A method of obtaining early feedback on requirements by providing a working model of the expected product before actually building it.

Quality. The degree to which a set of inherent characteristics fulfills requirements.

Quality Audits. A quality audit is a structured, independent process to determine if project activities comply with organizational and project policies, processes, and procedures.

Quality Control Measurements. The documented results of control quality activities.

Quality Management Plan. A component of the project or program management plan that describes how applicable policies, procedures, and guidelines will be implemented to achieve the quality objectives.

Quality Management System. The organizational framework whose structure provides the policies, processes, procedures, and resources required to implement the quality management plan. The typical project quality management plan should be compatible to the organization's quality management system.

Quality Metrics. A description of a project or product attribute and how to measure it.

Quality Policy. A policy that establishes the basic principles that should govern the organization's actions as it implements its system for quality management.

Quality Report. A project document that includes quality management issues, recommendations for corrective actions, and a summary of findings from quality control activities and may include recommendations for process, project, and product improvements.

Quality Requirement. A condition or capability that will be used to assess conformance by validating the acceptability of an attribute for the quality of a result.

Questionnaires. Written sets of questions designed to quickly accumulate information from a large number of respondents.

RACI Chart. A common type of responsibility assignment matrix that uses responsible, accountable, consult, and inform statuses to define the involvement of stakeholders in project activities.

Regression Analysis. An analytical technique where a series of input variables are examined in relation to their corresponding output results in order to develop a mathematical or statistical relationship.

Regulations. Requirements imposed by a governmental body. These requirements can establish product, process, or service characteristics, including applicable administrative provisions that have government-mandated compliance.

Request for Information (RFI). A type of procurement document whereby the buyer requests a potential seller to provide various pieces of information related to a product or service or seller capability.

Request for Proposal (RFP). A type of procurement document used to request proposals from prospective sellers of products or services. In some application areas, it may have a narrower or more specific meaning.

Request for Quotation (RFQ). A type of procurement document used to request price quotations from prospective sellers of common or standard products or services. Sometimes used in place of request for proposal and, in some application areas, it may have a narrower or more specific meaning.

Requirement. A condition or capability that is necessary to be present in a product, service, or result to satisfy a business need.

Requirements Documentation. A description of how individual requirements meet the business need for the project.

Requirements Management Plan. A component of the project or program management plan that describes how requirements will be analyzed, documented, and managed.

Requirements Traceability Matrix. A grid that links product requirements from their origin to the deliverables that satisfy them.

Reserve. A provision in the project management plan to mitigate cost and/or schedule risk. Often used with a modifier (e.g., management reserve, contingency reserve) to provide further detail on what types of risk are meant to be mitigated.

Reserve Analysis. An analytical technique to determine the essential features and relationships of components in the project management plan to establish a reserve for the schedule duration, budget, estimated cost, or funds for a project.

Resource. A team member or any physical item needed to complete the project.

Resource Breakdown Structure. A hierarchical representation of resources by category and type.

Resource Calendar. A calendar that identifies the working days and shifts upon which each specific resource is available.

Resource Histogram. A bar chart showing the amount of time that a resource is scheduled to work over a series of time periods.

Resource Leveling. A resource optimization technique in which adjustments are made to the project schedule to optimize the allocation of resources and which may affect critical path. See also *resource optimization technique* and *resource smoothing*.

Resource Management Plan. A component of the project management plan that describes how project resources are acquired, allocated, monitored, and controlled.

Resource Manager. An individual with management authority over one or more resources.

Resource Optimization Technique. A technique in which activity start and finish dates are adjusted to balance demand for resources with the available supply. See also *resource leveling* and *resource smoothing*.

Resource Requirements. The types and quantities of resources required for each activity in a work package.

Resource Smoothing. A resource optimization technique in which free and total float are used without affecting the critical path. See also *resource leveling* and *resource optimization technique*.

Responsibility. An assignment that can be delegated within a project management plan such that the assigned resource incurs a duty to perform the requirements of the assignment.

Responsibility Assignment Matrix (RAM). A grid that shows the project resources assigned to each work package.

Result. An output from performing project management processes and activities. Results include outcomes (e.g., integrated systems, revised process, restructured organization, tests, trained personnel, etc.) and documents (e.g., policies, plans, studies, procedures, specifications, reports, etc.). See also *deliverable*.

Rework. Action taken to bring a defective or nonconforming component into compliance with requirements or specifications.

Risk. An uncertain event or condition that, if it occurs, has a positive or negative effect on one or more project objectives.

Risk Acceptance. A risk response strategy whereby the project team decides to acknowledge the risk and not take any action unless the risk occurs.

Risk Appetite. The degree of uncertainty an organization or individual is willing to accept in anticipation of a reward.

Risk Audit. A type of audit used to consider the effectiveness of the risk management process.

Risk Avoidance. A risk response strategy whereby the project team acts to eliminate the threat or protect the project from its impact.

Process Groups: A Practice Guide

Risk Breakdown Structure (RBS). A hierarchical representation of potential sources of risks.

Risk Categorization. Organization by sources of risk (e.g., using the RBS), the area of the project affected (e.g., using the WBS), or other useful category (e.g., project phase) to determine the areas of the project most exposed to the effects of uncertainty.

Risk Category. A group of potential causes of risk.

Risk Data Quality Assessment. Technique to evaluate the degree to which the data about risks are useful for risk management.

Risk Enhancement. A risk response strategy whereby the project team acts to increase the probability of occurrence or impact of an opportunity.

Risk Escalation. A risk response strategy whereby the team acknowledges that a risk is outside of its sphere of influence and shifts the ownership of the risk to a higher level of the organization where it is more effectively managed.

Risk Exploiting. A risk response strategy whereby the project team acts to ensure that an opportunity occurs.

Risk Exposure. An aggregate measure of the potential impact of all risks at any given point in time in a project, program, or portfolio.

Risk Management Plan. A component of the project, program, or portfolio management plan that describes how risk management activities will be structured and performed.

Risk Mitigation. A risk response strategy whereby the project team acts to decrease the probability of occurrence or impact of a threat.

Risk Owner. The person responsible for monitoring the risks and for selecting and implementing an appropriate risk response strategy.

Risk Register. A repository in which outputs of risk management processes are recorded.

Risk Report. A project document developed progressively throughout the risk management processes, which summarizes information on individual project risks and the level of overall project risk.

Risk Review. A meeting to examine and document the effectiveness of risk responses in dealing with overall project risk and with identified individual project risks.

Risk Sharing. A risk response strategy whereby the project team allocates ownership of an opportunity to a third party who is best able to capture the benefit of that opportunity.

Risk Threshold. The measure of acceptable variation around an objective that reflects the risk appetite of the organization and stakeholders. See also *risk appetite*.

Risk Transference. A risk response strategy whereby the project team shifts the impact of a threat to a third party, together with ownership of the response.

Role. A defined function to be performed by a project team member, such as testing, filing, inspecting, or coding.

Rolling Wave Planning. An iterative planning technique in which the work to be accomplished in the near term is planned in detail, while the work in the future is planned at a higher level.

Root Cause Analysis. An analytical technique used to determine the basic underlying reason that causes a variance or a defect or a risk. A root cause may underlie more than one variance or defect or risk.

Schedule. See *project schedule* and *schedule model*.

Schedule Baseline. The approved version of a schedule model that can be changed only through formal change control procedures and is used as the basis for comparison to actual results.

Schedule Compression. A technique used to shorten the schedule duration without reducing the project scope.

Schedule Data. The collection of information for describing and controlling the schedule.

Schedule Forecasts. Estimates or predictions of conditions and events in the project's future based on information and knowledge available at the time the schedule is calculated.

Schedule Management Plan. A component of the project or program management plan that establishes the criteria and the activities for developing, monitoring, and controlling the schedule.

Schedule Model. A representation of the plan for executing the project's activities, including durations, dependencies, and other planning information, used to produce a project schedule along with other scheduling artifacts.

Schedule Network Analysis. A technique to identify early and late start dates, as well as early and late finish dates, for the uncompleted portions of project activities.

Schedule Performance Index (SPI). A measure of schedule efficiency expressed as the ratio of earned value to planned value.

Schedule Variance (SV). A measure of schedule performance expressed as the difference between the earned value and the planned value.

Scheduling Tool. A tool that provides schedule component names, definitions, structural relationships, and formats that support the application of a scheduling method.

Scope. The sum of the products, services, and results to be provided as a project. See also *project scope* and *product scope*.

Scope Baseline. The approved version of a scope statement, work breakdown structure (WBS), and its associated WBS dictionary, that can be changed using formal change control procedures and is used as a basis for comparison to actual results.

Scope Creep. The uncontrolled expansion to product or project scope without adjustments to time, cost, and resources.

Scope Management Plan. A component of the project or program management plan that describes how the scope will be defined, developed, monitored, controlled, and validated.

Secondary Risk. A risk that arises as a direct result of implementing a risk response.

Seller. A provider or supplier of products, services, or results to an organization.

Seller Proposals. Formal responses from sellers to a request for proposal or other procurement document specifying the price, commercial terms of sale, and technical specifications or capabilities the seller will do for the requesting organization that, if accepted, would bind the seller to perform the resulting agreement.

Sensitivity Analysis. An analysis technique to determine which individual project risks or other sources of uncertainty have the most potential impact on project outcomes, by correlating variations in project outcomes with variations in elements of a quantitative risk analysis model.

Sequence Activities. The process of identifying and documenting relationships among the project activities.

Simulation. An analytical technique that models the combined effect of uncertainties to evaluate their potential impact on objectives.

Source Selection Criteria. A set of attributes desired by the buyer which a seller is required to meet or exceed to be selected for a contract.

Specification. A precise statement of the needs to be satisfied and the essential characteristics that are required.

Specification Limits. The area, on either side of the centerline, or mean, of data plotted on a control chart that meets the customer's requirements for a product or service. This area may be greater than or less than the area defined by the control limits. See also *control limits*.

Sponsor. A person or group who provides resources and support for the project, program, or portfolio and is accountable for enabling success.

Sponsoring Organization. The entity responsible for providing the project's sponsor and a conduit for project funding or other project resources.

Stakeholder. An individual, group, or organization that may affect, be affected by, or perceive itself to be affected by a decision, activity, or outcome of a project, program, or portfolio.

Stakeholder Analysis. A technique of systematically gathering and analyzing quantitative and qualitative information to determine whose interests should be taken into account throughout the project.

Stakeholder Engagement Assessment Matrix. A matrix that compares current and desired stakeholder engagement levels.

Stakeholder Engagement Plan. A component of the project management plan that identifies the strategies and actions required to promote productive involvement of stakeholders in project or program decision making and execution.

Stakeholder Register. A project document including the identification, assessment, and classification of project stakeholders.

Standard. A document established by an authority, custom, or general consent as a model or example.

Start Date. A point in time associated with a schedule activity's start, usually qualified by one of the following: actual, planned, estimated, scheduled, early, late, target, baseline, or current.

Start-to-Finish (SF). A logical relationship in which a predecessor activity cannot finish until a successor activity has started.

Start-to-Start (SS). A logical relationship in which a successor activity cannot start until a predecessor activity has started.

Statement of Work (SOW). A narrative description of products, services, or results to be delivered by the project.

Statistical Sampling. Choosing part of a population of interest for inspection.

Successor Activity. A dependent activity that logically comes after another activity in a schedule.

SWOT Analysis. Analysis of strengths, weaknesses, opportunities, and threats of an organization, project, or option.

Tacit Knowledge. Personal knowledge that can be difficult to articulate and share such as beliefs, experiences, and insights.

Tailoring. Determining the appropriate combination of processes, inputs, tools, techniques, outputs, and life cycle phases to manage a project.

Team Charter. A document that records the team values, agreements, and operating guidelines, as well as establishing clear expectations regarding acceptable behavior by project team members.

Team Management Plan. A component of the resource management plan that describes when and how team members will be acquired and how long they will be needed.

Technique. A defined systematic procedure employed by a human resource to perform an activity to produce a product or result or deliver a service, and that may employ one or more tools.

Templates. A partially complete document in a predefined format that provides a defined structure for collecting, organizing, and presenting information and data.

Test and Evaluation Documents. Project documents that describe the activities used to determine if the product meets the quality objectives stated in the quality management plan.

Threat. A risk that would have a negative effect on one or more project objectives.

Three-Point Estimating. A technique used to estimate cost or duration by applying an average or weighted average of optimistic, pessimistic, and most likely estimates when there is uncertainty with the individual activity estimates.

Threshold. A predetermined value of a measurable project variable that represents a limit that requires action to be taken if it is reached.

Time and Material Contract (T&M). A type of contract that is a hybrid contractual arrangement containing aspects of both cost-reimbursable and fixed-price contracts.

To-Complete Performance Index (TCPI). A measure of the cost performance that is required to be achieved with the remaining resources in order to meet a specified management goal, expressed as the ratio of the cost to finish the outstanding work to the remaining budget.

Tolerance. The quantified description of acceptable variation for a quality requirement.

Tool. Something tangible, such as a template or software program, used in performing an activity to produce a product or result.

Tornado Diagram. A special type of bar chart used in sensitivity analysis for comparing the relative importance of the variables.

Total Float. The amount of time that a schedule activity can be delayed or extended from its early start date without delaying the project finish date or violating a schedule constraint.

Trend Analysis. An analytical technique that uses mathematical models to forecast future outcomes based on historical results.

Trigger Condition. An event or situation that indicates a risk is about to occur.

Unanimity. Agreement by everyone in the group on a single course of action.

Update. A modification to any deliverable, project management plan component, or project document that is not under formal change control.

Validate Scope. The process of formalizing acceptance of the completed project deliverables.

Validation. The assurance that a product, service, or result meets the needs of the customer and other identified stakeholders. Contrast with *verification*.

Variance. A quantifiable deviation, departure, or divergence away from a known baseline or expected value.

Variance Analysis. A technique for determining the cause and degree of difference between the baseline and actual performance.

Variation. An actual condition that is different from the expected condition that is contained in the baseline plan.

Verification. The evaluation of whether or not a product, service, or result complies with a regulation, requirement, specification, or imposed condition. Contrast with *validation*.

Verified Deliverables. Completed project deliverables that have been checked and confirmed for correctness through the Control Quality process.

Virtual Teams. Groups of people with a shared goal who fulfill their roles with little or no time spent meeting face to face.

WBS Dictionary. A document that provides detailed deliverable, activity, and scheduling information about each component in the work breakdown structure.

What-If Scenario Analysis. The process of evaluating scenarios in order to predict their effect on project objectives.

Work Breakdown Structure (WBS). A hierarchical decomposition of the total scope of work to be carried out by the project team to accomplish the project objectives and create the required deliverables.

Work Breakdown Structure Component. An entry in the work breakdown structure that can be at any level.

Work Package. The work defined at the lowest level of the work breakdown structure for which cost and duration are estimated and managed.

Work Performance Data. The raw observations and measurements identified during activities being performed to carry out the project work.

Work Performance Information. The performance data collected from controlling processes, analyzed in comparison with project management plan components, project documents, and other work performance information.

Work Performance Reports. The physical or electronic representation of work performance information compiled in project documents, intended to generate decisions, actions, or awareness.

Index

procurement, 248, 336
quality, 248, 287, 289, 338
risk, 249, 340
Authority, 228, 323
Autocratic decision making, 249, 264
Avoid strategy, 259, 303, 304
Awards, 218

B

BA (business analyst), 324
BAC. *See* Budget at completion
Backlog, 323
Backward pass, 262–263, 323
Bar chart, 323. *See also specific types*
Baselines, 32, 78, 80. *See also specific baselines*
  comparisons of, 78
  controlling changes to, 171–178
  definition of, 323
Basis of estimates, 202, 323
BCA. *See* Benefit-cost analysis
BCR. *See* Benefit-cost ratio
Benchmarking, 249, 323
Benefit(s)
  target, 28, 203
  time frame for realizing, 28, 203
Benefit-cost analysis, 261, 281, 326
Benefit-cost ratio (BCR), 34
Benefits management, 27–30
Benefits management plan, 28–30, 70, 203,
    205, 323
Benefits owner, 28, 203
Best practices
  benchmarking and, 249, 323
  discretionary dependencies and, 269
  project management office and, 48, 49
  quality audits and, 248
Bidder conferences, 249, 323
Bid documents, 128, 204, 323
Bid invitation, 331
Bottom-up estimating, 249, 323
Brainstorming, 249
  mind mapping and, 282, 333
  nominal group technique and, 283
Breakdown structure. *See* Organizational

breakdown structure; Resource breakdown
  structure;
  Risk breakdown structure; Work breakdown
  structure
Budget
  definition of, 323
  determining, 103–104, 328
  fixed, 299
  updating, 178
Budget at completion (BAC), 219, 309–311, 323
Burndown chart, 243, 277
Business acumen, 58–59
Business analysis, 6, 51, 56, 323
Business analyst (BA), 117, 228, 324
Business case, 27–30, 69–70, 205
  and benefits management plan, 28–30, 203–
  204, 205
  definition of, 205, 324
Business documents, 29–30, 69–70, 205
Business value
  creation of, 6–7
  definition of, 6, 324

C

CA. *See* Control account
Calendars
  project, 218, 337
  resource, 95–96, 99, 228, 340
Cause-and-effect diagrams, 250, 324
CCB. *See* Change control board
Change
  definition of, 324
  project-driven, 5–6
Change control
  definition of, 324
  integrated process for, 66, 80, 165–168, 172,
  335
Change control board (CCB), 80, 168, 205, 250
Change control tools, 250–251, 324
Change-driven life cycle. *See* Adaptive life cycle
Change log, 205, 324
Change management plan, 32, 205, 324
Change requests, 206
  approved, 202

Feedback/response, 255–256
FF. *See* Finish-to-finish
FFP. *See* Firm fixed price contract
Final product, service, or result transition, 211
Final report, 211–212
Financing, 272
Finish date
    definition of, 329
      early, 262–263, 296, 328
      late, 262–263, 296, 332
Finish-to-finish (FF), 285, 329
Finish-to-start (FS), 284–285, 330
Firm fixed price contract (FFP), 217–218, 330
Fishbone diagrams, 250
Fixed-budget method, 299
Fixed-price contract, 217–218, 330
Fixed price incentive fee contract (FPIF), 330
Fixed price with economic price adjustment contract (FPEPA), 330
Float, 262–263, 270, 291, 295 *See also* Free float and Total float
    definition of, 330
Flowcharts, 273, 330
Focus groups, 274, 278, 330
Forecast
    cost, 208
    definition of, 330
    schedule, 235, 342
Forward pass, 262–263, 330
FPEPA. *See* Fixed price with economic price adjustment contract
FPIF. *See* Fixed price incentive fee contract
Free float, 262–263, 291, 295, 330
FS. *See* Finish-to-start
Functional organization, 46
Funding limit reconciliation, 274, 330
Funding requirements, 219, 337

G

Governance, 42–44
    organizational, 42–43
    project, 42–44, 337
    and project environment, 37–38
    tailoring of, 25–26

Grade, definition of, 330
Ground rules, 274, 330

H

Hierarchical charts, 274
Histograms, 274
    definition of, 330
    resource, 235, 340
Historical information, 330
Historical information review, 275
Hybrid life cycle, 14–15
Hybrid organizations, 46

I

Identification of resources, 228
Identify Risks process, 115–117, 230, 234
    data flow diagram for, 116
    definition of, 115, 330
    inputs for, 115–116
    key benefit of, 115
    outputs of, 115–116
    participants in, 117
    tools and techniques for, 115
Identify Stakeholders process, 73–76
    data flow diagram for, 75
    definition of, 73, 331
    inputs for, 73–75
    key benefit of, 73
    outputs of, 73–75
    tools and techniques for, 74
IFB. *See* Invitation for bid
Impact/influence grid, 301
Implement Risk Responses process, 154–156, 229, 234
    data flow diagram for, 155
    definition of, 154, 331
    inputs for, 154–155
    key benefit of, 154
    outputs of, 154–155
    tools and techniques for, 155
Imposed date, 235, 274, 295, 331
Incentive(s), 217–218

S

power, 58–59
relationship, 55, 60
soft, 54–55
Slack. *See* Float
Small group communication, 253
SMEs. *See* Subject matter experts
Smoothing, resource, 291, 340
Social computing communication, 253, 278
Social media, 207, 241, 252, 256, 257, 258
Soft logic, 269–270
Soft skills, 54–55, 59
Software
    critical path, 263
    knowledge repositories, 42
    project management, 93, 207, 220, 288
    risk, 122
    work breakdown structure, 267
Sole source, 299
Source selection analysis, 299
Source selection criteria, 238–239, 343
Specification, 251, 343
Specification limits, 261, 343
Sphere of influence, project manager's, 52–57
SPI. *See* Schedule performance index
Sponsor
    definition of, 343
    project, 69–70, 73
Sponsoring organization, 203, 343
SS. *See* Start-to-start
Stakeholder(s), 57
    assessment of, 239, 300–301, 343
    classification of, 239
    communication with, 54
    definition of, 57, 343
    Manage Stakeholder Engagement, process,
    159–160
    external, 57
    Identify Stakeholders, process, 73–76, 331
    internal, 57
    involving, 71
    Monitor Stakeholder Engagement, process,
    192–194
    Plan Stakeholder Engagement, process,
    129–131
    register, 239
Stakeholder analysis, 300, 343

Stakeholder cube, 301
Stakeholder engagement
    Manage Stakeholder Engagement, process,
    159–160, 333
    Monitor Stakeholder Engagement, process,
    192–194, 333
    Plan Stakeholder Engagement, process,
    129-131, 335
Stakeholder engagement assessment matrix,
    300–301, 343
Stakeholder engagement plan, 31, 239
    definition of, 343
    developing, 129–131, 335
    as output, 129–130
    updates to, situations requiring, 131
Stakeholder mapping/representation, 301–302
Stakeholder register, 239, 343
Stakeholder risk appetite, 233
Stand-alone project, 4, 9
Standard(s), definition of, 343
Start date
    definition of, 343
    early, 262–263, 296, 328
    late, 262–263, 296, 332
Start-to-finish (SF), 285, 343
Start-to-start (SS), 285, 344
Statement of work (SOW), 128, 204, 212, 299
    definition of, 344
    procurement, 216–217, 336
Statistical sampling, 302, 344
Stories, user, 246, 268
Storyboarding, 289
Strategic alignment, 28, 49, 203
Strategies. *See also specific strategies*
    for conflict, 259
    for opportunities, 305–306
    for risk, 303–304
    for threats, 304–305
Strengths, analysis of, 307
Student Syndrome, 96
Subject matter experts (SMEs), 117, 249, 274,
    276, 277
Subsidiary management plans, 31
Success measures, 34–35
Successor activity, 93, 201, 220, 279, 284–285, 344
Summary activities, 220

Work performance reports, 23, 243, 288, 346
Work shadowing, 278
Writing style, 154

X

X, Design for (DfX), 270